Survey of Accounting

James D. Stice, PhD

Brigham Young University

Earl K. Stice, PhD

Brigham Young University

W. Steve Albrecht, PhD, CPA, CIA, CFE

Brigham Young University

K. Fred Skousen, PhD, CPA

Brigham Young University

South-Western College Publishing

an International Thomson Publishing company I(T)P®

Cincinnati • Albany • Boston • Detroit • Johannesburg • London • Madrid • Melbourne • Mexico City
New York • Pacific Grove • San Francisco • Scottsdale • Singapore • Tokyo • Toronto

Accounting Team Director: Richard Lindgren
Acquisitions Editor: Sharon Oblinger
Developmental Editor: Leslie Kauffman
Marketing Manager: Matt Filimonov
Media Production Editor: Lora Craver
Production Editor: Mike Busam

I(T)P®

International Thomson Publishing
South-Western College Publishing is an ITP Company.
The ITP trademark is used under license.

2 3 4 5 6 GP 3 2 1 0 9

ISBN: 0-538-87324-8

Printed in the United States of America

Contents

To the Student

The study of accounting involves four major elements:

1. Understanding the role of accounting in business.
2. Learning the terms associated with accounting.
3. Understanding the concepts, procedures, and financial statements that are used to record and summarize economic events.
4. Being able, on the basis of that understanding, to record and summarize economic transactions in accordance with generally accepted accounting principles.

Accounting is considered by most students to be a challenging course, partly because there is a lot to learn, and partly because accounting knowledge is cumulative—that is, concepts and procedures in later chapters are built upon what has been learned in earlier chapters. This makes it impractical to cram for an accounting exam; you must learn as you go, each day building on what you learned yesterday and last week and last month.

The challenge, therefore, is to keep up with the work, not to fall behind in doing the assigned reading and the problems, even though this course will probably require more of your time than most others. This Study Guide should help you to understand the material and to retain what you have learned by providing opportunities to review the subject matter in several different ways. Through it, you will be able to test your understanding of the concepts and your ability to perform the corresponding procedures.

The authors of the textbook are also the authors of this Study Guide; we wrote it to facilitate and reinforce your understanding of the text in every way possible. While we initially had in mind those students who have difficulty with the course, we have found the guide also useful to those who learn accounting fairly readily.

Each Study Guide chapter should be reviewed after you have read the corresponding text chapter. We recommend that you use the Study Guide chapters in the following way:

1. Read the *learning objectives* to pinpoint the areas where study is needed.
2. Read the concise, point-by-point *chapter review* carefully. It will help you decide which areas you understand well and which require more study. These reviews also will be useful when preparing for exams.
3. If you are having problems with certain topics, read *common errors* for suggestions on ways to better understand the material.
4. Work through each of the four sets of questions to test your knowledge.
   a. *Match* the key terms with their definitions in order to test your mastery of the new words introduced in the chapter. Your understanding of, and ability to use, accounting terms is important to your success in this course. Accounting is the language of business, and if you don't understand the language, you'll find it difficult to understand the concepts and problems.
   b. Answer the *true-false* questions.
   c. Answer the *multiple-choice* questions. If your answer to a question is "none of the above," think about what the correct answer should be.

d. Complete each of the short *exercises*. These cover the major topics in the chapter and are similar to the exercises in the textbook. Each exercise should not take more than 15 to 20 minutes to complete.

e. Finally, check your answers against those that appear at the end of each Study Guide chapter.

By using the Study Guide conscientiously, you will be reviewing what you have learned in each text chapter in several different ways: with the point-by-point review, the matching definitions, the true-false questions, the multiple-choice questions, and the short exercises. At first, it may take you three to four hours to work through a chapter of the Study Guide. After you have finished four or five chapters, however, it will become apparent which sections are most helpful to you. You should then be able to complete the Study Guide chapters more quickly. You may also find that some topics will come easier to you than others. For those that are more difficult, extra time with the Study Guide may be needed.

The experiences of students who have used the Study Guide indicate that its regular use will improve your understanding of accounting and help you to achieve the best possible results in this course.

Good luck!

James D. Stice
Earl K. Stice
W. Steve Albrecht
K. Fred Skousen

Chapter 1
Accounting Information: Users and Uses

LEARNING OBJECTIVES

After studying this chapter, you should be able to:

1. Describe the purpose of accounting and explain its role in business and society.
2. Identify the primary users of accounting information.
3. Describe the environment of accounting, including the effects of generally accepted accounting principles, international business, ethical considerations, and technology.
4. Analyze the reasons for studying accounting.

CHAPTER REVIEW

What's the Purpose of Accounting?

1. Accounting is a system for providing quantitative, financial information about economic entities that is useful for making sound business decisions. Accounting is often called the "language of business" because it provides the means of recording and communicating business activities and the results of those activities.

The Relationship of Accounting to Business

2. Organizations acquire and exchange resources. Accounting is used to keep track of an entity's resources and to see how well it is accomplishing its objectives.

Who Uses Accounting Information?

3. The outputs of the accounting process are financial reports, including the general-purpose financial statements, income tax returns, special reports provided to various regulatory agencies such as the Securities and Exchange Commission, and managerial reports.
4. Financial accounting focuses on the information needs of external financial statement users. Lenders (creditors) and investors are the primary external users of accounting information.
5. Management accounting focuses on the accounting information used by management in making decisions.

1

6. Other users of accounting information include suppliers and customers, employees, competitors, government agencies, and the press.

What Kind of Environment Does Accounting Operate Within?

7. Accounting is a dynamic, service-oriented discipline continuously evolving to meet the needs of those it serves.

The Significance and Development of Accounting Standards

8. Generally accepted accounting principles (GAAP) are guidelines to accounting practice that have been accepted by the accounting profession through time-tested applications. Accounting reports that are based on consistently applied GAAP provide investors and creditors with more comparable data.

9. Accounting principles have evolved over time. In recent years they have been influenced largely by such organizations as the FASB, SEC, AICPA, IMA, and IRS.

International Business

10. Business activity is expanding rapidly on a worldwide basis. The environment of accounting is based on a global economy.

11. Accounting practices often must be modified to reflect international operations and transactions. Attempts are being made to establish comparable accounting practices worldwide through the International Accounting Standards Committee (IASC).

Ethics in Accounting

12. There is a growing concern about ethics in our society. This concern is especially relevant for CPAs and CMAs because of the public trust professional accountants have been given.

13. CPAs and CMAs have adopted standards of conduct to guide their actions and help them fulfill their responsibilities to the public, to their clients, and to their colleagues in the accounting profession.

Technology

14. Advances in technology are impacting business and accounting in significant ways. Technology allows companies to gather vast amounts of information and to process it quickly and accurately. Technology also allows user access to data in new and exciting ways. However, technology has not replaced the need for judgment and accounting expertise.

So, Why Should I Study Accounting?

15. Everyone is affected to some degree by accounting information. Those who recognize the value of accounting information and learn how to use it to make better decisions will have a competitive advantage over those who do not.

COMMON ERRORS

This first chapter does not contain problem material. Its purpose is to provide an overview and perspective of accounting. The major difficulty in this chapter is unfamiliar accounting or business terminology. This is a basic challenge of the first several chapters, since you are beginning to learn about accounting, the language of business. Throughout the text, new terms are defined in the margins and highlighted at the end of each chapter to assist you in learning this new language.

SELF-TEST

Matching

Instructions: Write the letter of each of the following terms in the space to the left of its appropriate definition.

a.	accounting	**f.**	accounting cycle
b.	business	**g.**	Securities and Exchange Commission
c.	generally accepted accounting principles	**h.**	nonprofit organization
d.	management accounting	**i.**	financial accounting
e.	Financial Accounting Standards Board		

_____ 1. The private organization responsible for establishing the standards for financial accounting and reporting in the United States.

_____ 2. The area of accounting concerned with reporting financial information to interested external parties.

_____ 3. The government body responsible for regulating the financial reporting practices of most publicly-owned corporations in connection with the buying and selling of stocks and bonds.

_____ 4. An organization operated with the objective of making a profit from the sale of goods or services.

_____ 5. A system for providing quantitative, financial information about economic entities for decision-making purposes.

_____ 6. The area of accounting concerned with providing internal financial reports to assist management in making decisions.

_____ 7. The sequence of events in which accounting data are analyzed, recorded, classified, summarized, and reported.

_____ 8. Authoritative guidelines that define accounting practice at a particular time.

_____ 9. An entity without a profit objective, oriented toward providing services efficiently and effectively.

True/False

Instructions: Place a check mark in the appropriate column to indicate whether each of the following statements is true or false.

	True	False
1. In a nonprofit organization, the primary goal is to earn income.	_____	_____
2. All organizations need accounting to keep track of their resources and activities and to measure how well they are accomplishing their objectives.	_____	_____
3. Accounting helps organizations determine how to best use their resources.	_____	_____
4. Accounting provides all information, financial and otherwise, needed for decision making.	_____	_____
5. The primary external user of accounting information is management.	_____	_____
6. The income statement, the balance sheet, and the corporate tax return are the three general-purpose financial statements.	_____	_____
7. Monetary resources are obtained through investments by owners, loans from creditors, and business earnings.	_____	_____
8. General-purpose financial statements are prepared primarily to meet the needs of investors and creditors.	_____	_____
9. Management accounting is the area of accounting concerned with reporting financial information to interested external parties.	_____	_____
10. Today's business environment is more national than international.	_____	_____
11. Generally accepted accounting principles (GAAP) are prescribed by law.	_____	_____
12. The IRS is currently the primary standard-setting body for accounting principles in the private sector.	_____	_____

Multiple Choice

Instructions: Circle the letter that best completes each of the following statements.

1. An example of a nonprofit organization is a

   a. grocery store.
   b. car dealership.
   c. hospital.
   d. machine shop.

2. Which of the following best describes accounting?

   a. A system for providing quantitative, financial information about entities for decision-making purposes
   b. A science used by management for determining future costs
   c. A form of mathematical economics
   d. A system of predicting future outcomes

3. The basic purpose of financial accounting is to

   a. provide financial information for use by decision makers.
   b. determine the amount of taxes to be paid.
   c. evaluate the worth of a company.
   d. determine the cash receipts and disbursements of corporations.

4. Which of the following groups is *not* considered an external user of accounting information?

   a. Creditors
   b. Investors
   c. Bankers
   d. Managers

5. Which of the following statements does *not* reflect the impact of technology on business and accounting?

   a. Technology allows organizations to gather vast amounts of transaction data.
   b. Technology allows for the processing of information in a quick and accurate manner.
   c. Technology eliminates the need for accountants.
   d. Technology is continuing to change, which suggests future changes in the way business is conducted.

6. The accounting cycle provides all of the following outputs except

   a. budgets.
   b. the income statement.
   c. the statement of cash flows.
   d. Each of the above is provided.

7. Which of the following organizations is the most directly involved in developing worldwide accounting standards?

   a. FASB
   b. IASC
   c. SEC
   d. AICPA

8. Currently, the primary standard-setting body for accounting principles in the private sector is the

   a. SEC.
   b. AICPA.
   c. FASB.
   d. IRS.

9. Why is there growing concern over ethics as an environmental factor affecting accounting?
   a. Ethical considerations affect all society, including accounting and business.
   b. Ethical problems result from too much focus on short-term results.
   c. Major incidents of improper acts are highlighted by reporting in the news media.
   d. All of the above cause a growing concern over ethics.

Exercises

Because of the conceptual nature of this chapter, there are no workout exercises.

ANSWERS

Matching

1.	e		4.	b		7.	f
2.	i		5.	a		8.	c
3.	g		6.	d		9.	h

True/False

1.	F		5.	F		9.	F
2.	T		6.	F		10.	F
3.	T		7.	T		11.	F
4.	F		8.	T		12.	F

Multiple Choice

1.	c		4.	d		7.	b
2.	a		5.	c		8.	c
3.	a		6.	a		9.	d

Chapter 2
Financial Statements: An Overview

LEARNING OBJECTIVES

After studying this chapter, you should be able to:

1. Understand the basic elements and formats of the three primary financial statements—balance sheet, income statement, and statement of cash flows.

2. Recognize the need for financial statement notes and identify the types of information included in the notes.

3. Describe the purpose of an audit report and the incentives the auditor has to perform a good audit.

4. Use financial ratios to identify a company's strengths and weaknesses and to forecast its future performance.

5. Explain the fundamental concepts and assumptions that underlie financial accounting.

CHAPTER REVIEW

The Financial Statements

1. Because many different groups use the financial statements of companies, they are sometimes referred to as "general-purpose" financial statements. The three primary financial statements are the balance sheet, the income statement, and the statement of cash flows.

The Balance Sheet

2. The balance sheet (or statement of financial position) provides a financial picture of a company's assets, liabilities, and owners' equity at a particular date. It helps external parties assess a company's liquidity and solvency.

3. Assets are economic resources that are owned or controlled by a company and are measurable in monetary terms.

4. Liabilities are the obligations of a company; they represent creditors' claims against the company's assets.

5. Owners' equity represents the remaining interest in the assets of an enterprise after the claims of creditors are satisfied.

6. Investments by owners, usually in the form of cash, increase owners' equity. If the business is a corporation, the amount invested by owners is often labeled stockholders' equity.

7. Owners' equity is decreased by distributions to owners. If the business is a corporation, distributions to owners (stockholders) are called dividends.

8. Owners' equity is also affected by the results of a company's operations—profits increase owners' equity, while losses decrease owners' eq-

uity. For a corporation, the amount of accumulated profits (or earnings) that have not been distributed to owners is called retained earnings, and this amount is added to capital stock to determine total owners' (stockholders') equity.

9. The balance sheet presents information based on the basic accounting equation—Assets = Liabilities + Owners' Equity.

10. Most companies prepare classified balance sheets, showing assets and liabilities subdivided into current and noncurrent categories. Also, balance sheets are usually presented on a comparative basis so that users can identify significant changes in a company's financial position from year to year.

11. The balance sheet has two primary limitations: (1) it does not reflect the current value of a business because items are reported at their historical costs, and (2) it reports only resources that can be measured in monetary terms.

The Income Statement

12. The income statement (or statement of earnings) shows the results of a company's operations over a period of time, usually a year. It summarizes a firm's revenues and expenses, thus helping investors and creditors assess an enterprise's profitability.

13. Revenues are increases in resources, primarily from the sale of goods or services.

14. Expenses are the costs incurred in normal business operations to generate revenues.

15. Net income (or net loss) is the overall measure of performance of a company's activities. It is equal to all revenues minus all expenses for the period. Net income increases owners' equity; net loss decreases owners' equity.

16. In addition to revenues, expenses, and the resulting net income or loss, a corporation's income statement reports the amount of earnings per share (EPS), computed by dividing the net income (or loss) for the period by the number of shares of stock outstanding.

17. A corporation's income statement is often accompanied by a statement of retained earnings that reports the changes in retained earnings during a period.

The Statement of Cash Flows

18. The statement of cash flows is one of the three primary financial statements. This statement shows the cash inflows (receipts) and outflows (payments) of a company for a period of time. Cash flows are classified according to operating, investing, and financing activities.

How the Financial Statements Tie Together

19. The notion of "articulation" means that financial statements tie together, with certain figures in an operating statement helping to explain figures in comparative balance sheets.

Notes to the Financial Statements

20. The notes to the financial statements are considered an integral part of the statements. They provide vital information that cannot be captured solely by the reported dollar amounts in the financial statements.

21. The notes to financial statements are of four general types:

- summary of significant accounting policies
- additional information about the summary totals
- disclosure of information not recognized
- supplementary information

The External Audit

22. The audit report is a statement issued by an independent certified public accountant expressing an opinion concerning a company's financial statements. The audit report adds assurance that management's representations are not misleading, but it does not *guarantee* the accuracy of the statements. CPA firms perform credible audits to preserve their reputations and to avoid lawsuits.

Financial Statement Analysis

23. Financial statements are analyzed to detect signs of existing deficiencies and to predict future performance. Financial statement analysis involves examination of key relationships among financial statement numbers (called financial ratios) and trends in those relationships. It is important to compare ratios against past years and to values for other companies in the same industry rather than to rely on absolute values.

Fundamental Concepts and Assumptions

24. Certain fundamental concepts and assumptions underlie the practice of accounting. They include the separate entity concept, the assumption of arm's-length transactions, the cost principle, the monetary measurement concept, and the going-concern assumption.

COMMON ERRORS

The three most common problems students have with this chapter are:

1. Dealing with the new terms and the elements of the financial statements, which may be somewhat overwhelming at first glance.

2. Understanding how the financial statements relate to one another, that is, how they articulate.

3. Understanding the nature of financial statement analysis.

1. New Terms

This chapter is an overview; the details will be explained carefully in subsequent chapters. Here you should concentrate on the general format and relationships of the primary financial statements: the balance sheet, the income statement, and the statement of cash flows.

2. Articulation of the Financial Statements

The relationship of the income statement to the balance sheet is sometimes confusing. Revenues less expenses equal net income, which is reported on the income statement. The amount of net income increases owners' equity. Net income therefore becomes a key element not only in the income statement, but also on the balance sheet, as part of the owners' equity section.

To illustrate this concept, assume that Simple Company has assets totaling $450,000; if its liabilities are $150,000, then owners' equity has to be $300,000. (Remember the basic accounting equation: Assets = Liabilities + Owners' Equity; therefore, $450,000 − $150,000 = $300,000.)

Recall that owners' equity has two main components: the amount contributed by owners and the amount earned and retained by the business (called retained earnings for a corporation). Thus, in the example, the $300,000 might consist of $100,000 contributed by the owners and $200,000 of retained earnings (the amount of earnings since the business began operations

less any amounts paid back to owners in the form of dividends).

Continuing the illustration, assume that Simple Company has revenues of $750,000 and expenses of $525,000 during the next accounting period. Assets at the end of that period are $575,000 and liabilities remain at $150,000. During the period, the company distributes $100,000 to its stockholders in the form of a cash dividend. There is no change in the $100,000 of capital contributed by owners. What is the amount of retained earnings at the end of the accounting period? To determine the ending retained earnings, first compute net income ($750,000 revenues − $525,000 expenses = $225,000). The beginning retained earnings of $200,000 is increased by net income and decreased by the dividends. Therefore, the ending retained earnings balance is $325,000 ($200,000 + $225,000 − $100,000). We can see also that the accounting equation is still in balance at the end of the accounting period:

Assets = Liabilities + Owners' Equity

$575,000 = $150,000 + $425,000

$100,000 + $325,000

3. Financial Statement Analysis

Financial statement analysis involves examination of key relationships among the numbers reported on the financial statements. These relationships are referred to as financial ratios. Don't try to memorize the formulas for computing the ratios, but, instead, try to see the logic of the relationship and what the ratio is trying to explain. For example, the current ratio shows the relationship of current assets to current liabilities. It helps explain the liquidity position of a company. That is, how many current assets (cash and other assets that can be converted easily to cash) are available to pay the current obligations of the company.

Again, this is an introductory chapter. These relationships will become much more familiar to you as you study the rest of the chapters in the text.

SELF-TEST

Matching

Instructions: Write the letter of each of the following terms in the space to the left of its appropriate definition.

a. net income
b. liabilities
c. statement of cash flows
d. expenses
e. comparative financial statements
f. balance sheet
g. financial ratios
h. primary financial statements

i. income statement
j. retained earnings
k. owners' equity
l. assets
m. revenues
n. dividends
o. current ratio
p. going concern

_____ 1. Relationships among financial statement amounts.

_____ 2. Costs incurred in the normal course of business to generate revenues.

_____ 3. Financial statements prepared for two or more years.

_____ 4. The financial statement that shows the financial resources and claims against them, therefore showing the relationships of assets, liabilities, and owners' equity.

_____ 5. Economic resources that are owned or controlled by an enterprise.

_____ 6. A measure of the overall performance of a company, equal to all revenues minus all expenses for the period.

_____ 7. Obligations of an enterprise that represent creditors' claims against assets.

_____ 8. The accumulated portion of stockholders' equity that has been earned from profitable operations and has not been paid out in dividends.

_____ 9. Resource increases from the sale of goods or services during the normal operations of a business.

_____ 10. The financial statement that summarizes the revenues generated and the expenses incurred during a period.

_____ 11. The periodic distribution of earnings, usually in the form of cash, to the owners of the corporation.

_____ 12. The balance sheet, income statement, and statement of cash flows.

_____ 13. The ownership interest in an enterprise's assets; equals net assets (total assets minus total liabilities).

_____ 14. The financial statement showing cash inflows and outflows during a period.

_____ 15. The relationship of current assets to current liabilities.

_____ 16. The assumption that a business will continue to operate for the foreseeable future

True/False

Instructions: Place a check mark in the appropriate column to indicate whether each of the following statements is true or false.

	True	False
1. Financial statement analysis helps identify deficiencies and future potential for company performance.	_____	_____
2. Some financial statements are called general-purpose statements because they are used by many groups of people for differing purposes.	_____	_____
3. Transactions are always reported at current market values, even after the transaction date.	_____	_____
4. Liquidity is a measure of long-term, debt-paying ability.	_____	_____

	True	False
5. Profitability is directly related to an enterprise's ability to generate revenues in excess of expenses.	_____	_____
6. Assets are economic resources owned or controlled by a company.	_____	_____
7. For accounting purposes, an entity is the organizational unit for which accounting records are maintained.	_____	_____
8. The PE ratio is computed by dividing the current price per share by earnings per share.	_____	_____
9. Owners' equity fluctuates solely in relation to an entity's profitability.	_____	_____
10. The basic accounting equation can be written as A – L = OE.	_____	_____
11. The concept of net income encompasses revenues and expenses.	_____	_____
12. The statement of cash flows is *not* one of the three primary financial statements.	_____	_____
13. Revenues and expenses are listed on the balance sheet.	_____	_____
14. The income statement is for a period of time, rather than for a particular date.	_____	_____
15. Notes to financial statements are not needed to provide adequate disclosure of financial information.	_____	_____
16. An independent CPA's audit report guarantees the accuracy of the financial statements.	_____	_____

Multiple Choice

Instructions: Circle the letter that best completes each of the following statements.

1. Which of the following is *not* one of the primary financial statements?
   a. The balance sheet
   b. The income statement
   c. The current year's budget
   d. The statement of cash flows

2. Which of the following is *not* a basic element of a balance sheet?
   a. Revenues
   b. Owners' equity
   c. Assets
   d. Liabilities

3. A balance sheet
   a. shows the relationships among assets, liabilities, and owners' equity.
   b. shows the relationships between revenues and expenses.
   c. is for a period of time.
   d. shows the current value of a business.

4. Which of the following would be classified as an asset?
   a. Notes payable
   b. Dividends
   c. Retained earnings
   d. Notes receivable

5. Which of the following would be classified as a liability?

   a. Accounts payable
   b. Inventory
   c. Cash
   d. Accounts receivable

6. Which of the following statements is *not* correct?

   a. Owners' equity represents a claim against assets.
   b. Owners' equity equals assets plus liabilities.
   c. Owners' equity represents the net assets of an entity.
   d. Owners' equity is a residual amount.

7. Owners' equity is decreased by

   a. operating profits.
   b. investments by owners.
   c. distributions to owners.
   d. sale of stock to investors.

8. Which of the following ratios relates most closely to the concept of leverage?

   a. Current ratio
   b. Debt ratio
   c. PE ratio
   d. Asset turnover

9. The income statement

   a. shows the results of an enterprise's operations.
   b. lists revenues and expenses.
   c. measures profitability for a period of time.
   d. All of the above

10. Liquidity deals primarily with

    a. current assets and current liabilities.
    b. revenues and expenses.
    c. owners' equity.
    d. long-term debt.

11. Which of the following is *not* one of the three categories of cash flows reported on the statement of cash flows?

    a. Selling activities
    b. Investing activities
    c. Operating activities
    d. Financing activities

12. The concept of articulation means

    a. the financial statements are usually prepared on a comparative basis.
    b. accounting is considered more an art than a science.
    c. the statement of cash flows is based on the same data as the income statement and the balance sheet.
    d. the financial statements tie together, with operating statement items explaining or reconciling changes in major balance sheet categories.

E2-2 Balance Sheet Preparation

IBC Company
Balance Sheet
December 31, 2000

Assets		Liabilities and Owners' Equity		
Cash	$ 2,000	Liabilities:		
Accounts receivable	4,500	Accounts payable	$ 3,000	
Inventory	10,000	Notes payable	12,500	
Plant and equipment	25,000	Total liabilities		$15,500
		Owners' equity		26,000*
Total assets	$41,500	Total liabilities and owners' equity		$41,500

$$* \text{Assets} = \text{Liabilities} + \text{Owners' Equity}$$
$$\$41,500 = \$15,500 + X$$
$$X = \$26,000$$

E2-3 Income Statement Preparation

Office Supplies, Inc.
Income Statement
For the Year Ended December 31, 2000

Sales revenue		$175,000
Expenses:		
Cost of goods sold	$100,000	
Advertising expense	2,500	
Salaries expense	20,000	
Other expenses	15,000	137,500
Income before taxes		$ 37,500
Income taxes		18,000
Net income		$ 19,500
EPS ($19,500/1,000).......................................		$19.50

E2-4 Owners' Equity Computations

1. Beginning owners' equity	$64,500
Plus net income	12,750
	$77,250
Less cash dividends paid	4,000
Ending owners' equity	$73,250
2. Revenues	$45,000
Less expenses	32,250*
Net income	$12,750

$$*\$45,000 - X = \$12,750$$
$$X = \$32,250$$

E2-5   Comparative Balance Sheet Relationships

1. $32,000 + X (long-term debt) + $81,000 = $187,000
   X = $74,000

2. $81,000 + X (net income) - $9,000 = $107,000
   X = $35,000

3. X (revenues) - $29,000 = $35,000
   X = $64,000

4. Current ratio $= \dfrac{\text{Current assets}}{\text{Current liabilities}} = \dfrac{\$91,000}{\$25,000} = 3.64$

5. Debt ratio $= \dfrac{\text{Total liabilities}}{\text{Total assets}} = \dfrac{\$89,000}{\$196,000} = .45$

6. Return on equity $= \dfrac{\text{Net income}}{\text{Owners' equity}} = \dfrac{\$35,000}{\$107,000} = .33$

Chapter 3
The Mechanics of Accounting

LEARNING OBJECTIVES

After studying this chapter, you should be able to:

1. Understand the process of transforming transaction data into useful accounting information.

2. Analyze transactions and determine how those transactions affect the accounting equation (Step One of the Accounting Cycle).

3. Record the effects of transactions using journal entries (Step Two of the Accounting Cycle).

4. Summarize the resulting journal entries through posting and prepare a trial balance (Step Three of the Accounting Cycle).

5. Understand the need for adjusting entries, how financial statements are prepared, and how the books are closed (step four of the accounting cycle).

CHAPTER REVIEW

How Can We Collect All This Information?

1. Business transactions must be analyzed to determine how well an enterprise is managing its financial resources.

2. Business documents—such as invoices, check stubs, and other records—verify that transactions have occurred and provide objective evidence of the amounts involved

3. By recording and summarizing transactions, the accounting cycle enables statement users to analyze the efficiency of business entities. This process transforms financial data into useful information.

4. The outputs of the accounting cycle are accounting reports based on the transactions of business entities.

How Do Transactions Affect The Accounting Equation?

5. The basic accounting equation (Assets = Liabilities + Owners' Equity) shows that a firm's resources are equal to the claims of creditors and owners against those resources.

6. The accounting equation must always remain in balance. An increase on one side of the equation must be exactly offset by a corresponding increase on the other side, or by a decrease on the same side.

7. Accounts provide an efficient way of categorizing transactions. Each account has two sides: debits are shown on the left side, and credits are shown on the right side.

8. A T-account is a simplified form of an account.

9. Debits and credits also refer to the increases and decreases in account balances that result from each transaction. As shown below, debits increase asset account balances and decrease liability and owners' equity account balances; the opposite is true for credits. You should memorize these important relationships.

	Assets		=	Liabilities		+	Owner's Equity	
	DR	CR		DR	CR		DR	CR
	(+)	(−)		(−)	(+)		(−)	(+)

10. A major characteristic of the double-entry accounting system is that debits must always equal credits for each transaction.

11. Revenues increase owners' equity by increasing retained earnings, while expenses decrease owners' equity. Dividends, or other distributions to owners, also decrease owners' equity. The expanded accounting equation is shown in Exhibit 3-2 on page 86 of the textbook.

How Do We Record the Effects of Transactions?

12. Results of transactions are recorded first in chronological order in books of original entry called journals. Smaller companies use only a General Journal; larger companies may use special journals.

13. With a manual accounting system, the following format is used for journalizing transactions in a company's General Journal:

Date   Debit Entry................. xxx

             Credit Entry...........   xxx
             Explanation.

14. A company's transactions can be analyzed by examining the common elements of business activity, which include acquiring cash and other assets, using assets to produce products and services, collecting cash, and paying obligations and dividends.

15. For a corporation, dividends represent a return to stockholders of part of a company's earnings. The payment of dividends reduces retained earnings.

Posting Journal Entries and Preparing a Trial Balance

16. Results of transactions are classified by posting journal entries to accounts in the General Ledger. Each account has a title and a number that is specified in the company's chart of accounts.

17. At the end of a period, accounts are reviewed to determine their balances. A trial balance then lists all ledger account balances and checks to see if the total debits (on the left side of accounts) equal the total credits (on the right side of accounts).

18. The accounting model assumes the need for periodic reporting and accrual accounting.

19. The time period concept states that an accounting entity's total life may be divided into distinct periods for reporting accounting information on a timely basis. Most companies use a 12-month reporting period.

20. Accrual-basis accounting recognizes revenues and expenses when they are earned or incurred regardless of when cash is received or paid. For measuring income for most business entities, accrual-basis accounting is more appropriate than cash-basis accounting.

21. Because the life of a business is divided into reporting periods, accountants must use estimates and judgments in assigning the revenues and expenses to different accounting periods and in measuring assets and liabilities.

22. In measuring income on an accrual basis, only those revenues that actually have been earned during a period are reported. This is called the *revenue recognition principle.*

23. Two criteria must be met in recognizing revenues: (a) the earnings process must be substantially complete, and (b) cash has either been collected, or collectibility is reasonably assured.

24. The *matching principle* states that all expenses incurred to generate revenues should be reported in the same accounting period as the revenues.

25. Under accrual-basis accounting, net income is determined by subtracting matched expenses from the revenues recognized during an accounting period.

26. Accrual-basis accounting is necessary not only for determining net income but also for reporting proper balance sheet amounts at year-end.

Adjusting Entries

27. Adjusting entries usually are required at the end of each accounting period to report all asset, liability, and owners' equity account balances

properly and to recognize all revenues and expenses for the period on an accrual basis.

28. The areas most commonly requiring analysis to see if adjusting entries are needed are: unrecorded revenues, unrecorded expenses, prepaid expenses, and unearned revenues.

29. Preparing adjusting entries involves two steps: (1) determine whether the amounts recorded for all assets, liabilities, and owners' equity accounts are correct (fix the balance sheet) and (2) determine whether revenues and expenses are reported correctly (fix the income statement).

Preparing Financial Statements

30. When all transactions have been analyzed, journalized, and posted to the ledger accounts, and when all adjusting entries have been made, the accounts can be summarized and presented in the form of financial statements.

31. The notes to the financial statements are an integral part of the statements. The notes describe the assumptions made and methods used in preparing the statements. They also provide additional detail about specific items.

32. An audit is generally conducted by independent accountants (CPAs) to add credibility and assurance that the financial statements have been prepared in conformity with generally accepted accounting principles.

Closing the Books

33. *Real accounts* are those that are not closed to a zero balance at the end of each accounting period. They are permanent accounts appearing on the balance sheet.

34. *Nominal accounts* are temporary in that they are reduced to a zero balance through the closing process at the end of each accounting period. They are used to accumulate and classify all revenue and expense items for the period.

35. Closing entries reduce all nominal accounts to a zero balance, making the accounting records ready for a new cycle of transactions. Without closing entries, revenue and expense balances would extend from period to period, which would make it difficult to separate the operating results of each accounting period.

36. Revenue accounts are closed by being debited; expense accounts are closed by being credited. For a corporation, the difference between total revenues and total expenses (net income or loss) is debited or credited to Retained Earnings.

37. In a corporation, the Dividends account is a temporary account and is closed directly to Retained Earnings by being credited.

38. The last step in the accounting cycle (an optional one) is to balance the accounts and to prepare a post-closing trial balance, which lists all real account balances. This step, which is performed prior to the start of a new cycle, provides some assurance that the previous steps in the cycle have been performed properly.

COMMON ERRORS

The five most important, and sometimes most difficult, concepts to master in this chapter are:

1. The debit/credit, increase/decrease relationships of the accounts in the expanded accounting equation.

2. How to journalize transactions, giving proper recognition to the impact that each transaction has on the accounting equation.

3. The process of posting to ledger accounts.

4. How and when to make adjusting entries, especially for prepaid expenses and unearned revenues.

5. The closing process.

1. Debits and Credits

The debit/credit, increase/decrease relationships often are difficult to learn, because most people tend to associate assets and revenues, the two "plus" categories—and liabilities, expenses, and dividends, the three "minus" categories. They think that because assets and revenues involve resources coming into a company, all such accounts would be treated the same way. In fact, they are treated in opposite ways. Assets are increased by debits and decreased by credits; revenues are increased by credits and decreased by debits. Similarly, liabilities are treated the opposite of expenses and dividends. Liabilities are increased by credits and decreased by debits; expenses and dividends are increased by debits and decreased by credits. Owners' equity, the remaining category, is increased by credits and decreased by debits; these accounts are treated in the same way as liabilities, since they are both on the same side of the accounting equation.

To help you understand the debit/credit, increase/decrease relationships of accounts, study the illustration of the expanded accounting equation on text page 86, which summarizes these important relationships. You should study these relationships until they become second nature to you. Remember, asset, expense, and dividend accounts are always increased by debits and decreased by credits; liability, owners' equity, and revenue accounts are always increased by credits and decreased by debits. The entire system of double-entry accounting is based on these relationships.

2. Journalizing Transactions

Once transactions are analyzed by looking at supporting business documents, they are journalized in books of original entry called journals. The format for making such entries is shown on page 87 of the text. In double-entry accounting, each recorded transaction must have equal debit and credit entries to the accounts, and the accounting equation must always stay in balance. You should review text pages 88-95 to see how various transactions are recorded and how they affect the accounting equation.

The three-step process for journal entries explained on page 95 should help you.

3. Posting to the General Ledger

Once journal entries are made, similar transactions are classified and summarized in the accounts through the posting process. The result of this process is that all transactions affecting cash are accumulated in the Cash account, and a balance for the total amount of cash available can be determined. The same is true for all other accounts. Exhibit 3-6 on text page 97 provides an illustration of this process and shows how the journal and the ledger are cross-referenced.

4. How and when to make adjusting entries, especially for prepaid expenses and unearned revenues.

The major difficulty with adjusting entries is in making the adjustments for prepaid expenses and unearned revenues. Unrecorded revenues and expenses are easier to see, since earned revenues that are not previously recorded obviously need to be recorded. Similarly, if expenses have been incurred but not yet recorded, they must be entered into the accounting records if the financial statements are to be reported accurately.

The problem with prepaid expenses and unearned revenues is that you must determine what entry was made originally in order to make the appropriate adjusting entry, so that the ending balances will be brought current. A related problem is knowing which accounts go together, that is, which are the proper "companion" accounts.

a. Prepaid Expenses

When cash is paid, the Cash account is credited to reduce it, but what is debited? A common practice is to debit a Prepaid Expense account (an asset), showing that cash was paid for an asset having future benefit to the company. If an asset account is debited initially, the year-end adjustment records the amount of service potential that has been used up from that asset, that is, the amount of expense. This is done by debiting the expense account and crediting the prepaid asset account.

To illustrate, if a company pays $3,600 for one year's rent in advance, it might debit Prepaid Rent and credit Cash. At year-end Prepaid Rent would be credited (reduced) and the companion account—Rent Expense—would be debited to show the amount of expense for that period.

b. Unearned Revenues

To illustrate adjusting entries for unearned revenues, assume that on July 1 a company received $2,400 cash in advance for services to be rendered over the next 12 months. At year-end (December 31), $1,200 must be recognized as revenue and $1,200 as a liability (for unearned revenue). First you must determine what original entry was made upon the receipt of the cash. Obviously, the Cash account was debited (increased), but what was credited? If Unearned Service Revenue (a liability) was credited originally, then the adjusting entry must debit the liability (to reduce it) and credit the companion or related account—Service Revenue—to increase it to the proper amount that has been earned by the end of the accounting period. Thus, the companion accounts are Unearned Service Revenue (a liability) and Service Revenue (a revenue). If the liability account is originally credited when the cash is received, at year-end it must be reduced and the revenue account increased.

5. Closing Process

To understand the closing process, you must first distinguish between real, or permanent, accounts and nominal, or temporary, accounts. All income statement accounts are nominal accounts. Dividends also is a temporary account.

All temporary accounts must be closed to a zero balance at the end of an accounting period, so that the amounts will not be carried over into the next period. Since the totals in these accounts reflect the results of operations *during* a period of time, it is important that only relevant amounts be counted in that period. If nominal accounts were cumulative, financial statement readers would have no way of judging the results of a company's operations during a period, or of comparing one period with the next.

All balance sheet accounts are real accounts and are not closed at the end of an accounting period. This is because they represent a company's cumulative financial status as of a point in time. If balance sheet accounts were closed, then long-term assets, for example, would be underrepresented. Land purchased for $50,000 in 1995, for example, would not be shown on the balance sheet, even though it still had future benefit to the company.

Thus revenue, expense, and dividend accounts are closed at the end of each accounting period, while asset, liability, and owners' equity accounts (including Retained Earnings) remain open. Since revenue accounts normally have credit balances, they are closed by being debited; expenses and dividends normally have debit balances, so they are closed by being credited. These accounts may be closed directly to Retained Earnings.

SELF-TEST

Matching

Instructions: Write the letter of each of the following terms in the space to the left of its appropriate definition.

a.	account	**n.**	trial balance
b.	credit	**o.**	fiscal year
c.	journal	**p.**	accrual-basis accounting
d.	chart of accounts	**q.**	time period concept
e.	basic accounting equation	**r.**	closing entries
f.	business documents	**s.**	unearned revenues
g.	dividends	**t.**	calendar year
h.	revenues	**u.**	real accounts
i.	T-account	**v.**	adjusting entries
j.	posting	**w.**	post-closing trial balance
k.	ledger	**x.**	nominal accounts
l.	debit	**y.**	cash-basis accounting
m.	accounting cycle	**z.**	prepaid expenses

_____ 1. The means of transforming accounting data into accounting reports that can be interpreted and used in decision making.

_____ 2. An entry on the right side of an account.

_____ 3. A book or grouping of accounts in which data from recorded transactions are posted and thereby summarized.

_____ 4. A systematic listing of all accounts used by a company.

_____ 5. A distribution to stockholders of part of the earnings of a company.

_____ 6. A listing of all account balances; provides a means of testing whether total debits equal total credits for all accounts.

_____ 7. Assets equal liabilities plus owners' equity (A = L + OE).

_____ 8. The accounting record in which transactions are first entered; provides a chronological record of all business activities.

_____ 9. Records of transactions used as the basis for recording accounting entries.

_____ 10. The process of classifying, grouping, and recording similar transactions in common accounts by transferring amounts from the journal to the ledger.

_____ 11. Increases in resources from the sale of goods or services during the normal operations of a business.

_____ 12. An accounting record for classifying and accumulating the results of similar transactions; shows increases, decreases, and a balance.

_____ 13. An entry on the left side of an account.

_____ 14. A simplified depiction of an account in the form of the letter T.

_____ 15. A system of accounting in which transactions are recorded, and revenues and expenses are recognized, only when cash is received or paid.

_____ 16. The idea that the life of a business is divided into distinct and relatively short time periods so that accounting information can be timely.

_____ 17. A listing of all real account balances after the closing process has been completed.

_____ 18. Amounts received in advance of the actual earnings process.

_____ 19. Entries that reduce all nominal, or temporary, accounts to a zero balance at the end of each accounting period, transferring their balances to a permanent balance sheet account.

_____ 20. Entries required in accrual-basis accounting at the end of each accounting period to recognize all revenues and expenses for the period and to report proper amounts for asset, liability, and owners' equity accounts.

_____ 21. An entity's reporting year, covering 12 months ending on December 31.

_____ 22. Permanent accounts that are not closed to a zero balance at the end of each accounting period.

_____ 23. Payments in advance for items normally charged to expense at a later date.

_____ 24. An entity's reporting year, covering a 12-month accounting period and ending at the end of a month other than December.

_____ 25. Temporary accounts that are closed to a zero balance at the end of each accounting period.

_____ 26. A system of accounting in which revenues and expenses are recorded as they are earned and incurred, not necessarily when cash is received or paid.

True/False

Instructions: Place a check mark in the appropriate column to indicate whether each of the following statements is true or false.

	True	False
1. The accounting cycle facilitates transaction analysis through the recording and summarizing functions.	_____	_____
2. Inputs to the accounting process are transaction data as evidenced by business documents.	_____	_____
3. Debits (entries on the left side of accounts) increase asset, expense, and dividend accounts.	_____	_____
4. Credits (entries on the right side of accounts) decrease liability and owners' equity accounts.	_____	_____
5. The expanded accounting equation is Assets = Liabilities + Owners' Equity + (Revenues - Expenses - Dividends).	_____	_____
6. In using double-entry accounting, debits must always equal credits for the accounting equation to balance.	_____	_____
7. Small businesses do not follow the same steps in their accounting cycles as large companies do.	_____	_____
8. Ledgers are books of original entry.	_____	_____
9. Entries are made in chronological order in the General Journal.	_____	_____
10. Posting occurs before journalizing.	_____	_____
11. The list of accounts used by a company is known as a chart of accounts.	_____	_____
12. If the trial balance balances (that is, if total debits equal total credits), there is complete assurance that the accounting records are correct.	_____	_____
13. The going concern assumption states that it is important to report accounting information on a timely basis.	_____	_____
14. The life of a business enterprise is divided into distinct accounting periods because users need timely information to make ongoing economic decisions.	_____	_____
15. A company that closes its books on December 31 of each year is said to report on a fiscal year.	_____	_____
16. Most corporations issue an annual report that includes the primary financial statements.	_____	_____
17. When the life of a business enterprise is divided into distinct accounting periods, estimates and judgments are required in measuring financial information.	_____	_____

	True	False
18. Accrual-basis accounting recognizes revenues only when the company collects cash.	_____	_____
19. Over the life of an enterprise, cash-basis accounting and accrual-basis accounting measure the same amount of net income.	_____	_____
20. An independent audit guarantees the accuracy of financial statements.	_____	_____
21. According to the matching principle, expenses are matched with revenues in the accounting period in which they are paid.	_____	_____
22. Net income, as measured by accrual accounting, is the difference between cash receipts and cash disbursements.	_____	_____
23. Source documents signal the need for adjusting entries to be made at the end of each accounting period.	_____	_____
24. Unrecorded revenues and unrecorded expenses generally do not require adjusting entries.	_____	_____
25. Adjusting entries must be journalized and posted just as other entries must be..........	_____	_____
26. At the end of every accounting period, liability accounts are closed by being debited.	_____	_____
27. Expense accounts are closed by being credited.	_____	_____
28. Dividends are closed directly to Retained Earnings.	_____	_____
29. A post-closing trial balance lists only real accounts.	_____	_____

Multiple Choice

Instructions: Circle the letter that best completes each of the following statements.

1. The basic inputs to the accounting process are

   a. economic indicators.
   b. transactions.
   c. managerial policies.
   d. computer tapes.

2. Outputs of the accounting process include

   a. general-purpose financial statements.
   b. government reports.
   c. managerial reports.
   d. All of the above

3. Which of the following functions is *not* a part of the accounting cycle?

   a. Auditing
   b. Analysis
   c. Reporting
   d. Summarizing

4. Which of the following is *not* a step in the accounting cycle?

   a. Analyzing transactions and business documents
   b. Journalizing and posting closing entries
   c. Preparing financial statements
   d. Selling goods or providing services

5. Which of the following is the correct sequence for the accounting cycle?

   a. Analyzing, journalizing, posting, adjusting entries, financial statements, closing entries
   b. Analyzing, posting, journalizing, financial statements, adjusting entries, closing entries
   c. Analyzing, journalizing, posting, financial statements, adjusting entries, closing entries
   d. None of the above

6. Which of the following items is least likely to be shown in a journal?

   a. The date of a transaction
   b. The accounts to be debited and credited
   c. The amounts to be debited and credited
   d. The source documents of a transaction

7. Which of the following statements is *not* true?

   a. Debits should always equal credits.
   b. Debits increase liability accounts.
   c. Debits increase asset accounts.
   d. Debits are always shown on the left side of an account.

8. If revenues exceed expenses during an accounting period and there are no distributions to owners

   a. total assets will be decreased.
   b. total owners' equity will be increased.
   c. total liabilities will be increased.
   d. None of the above

9. Expenses

   a. are increased by credits.
   b. are decreased by debits.
   c. increase owners' equity.
   d. decrease owners' equity.

10. When a company borrows money from a bank, the transaction

    a. increases assets and increases owners' equity.
    b. decreases assets and decreases liabilities.
    c. increases assets and increases liabilities.
    d. decreases assets and decreases owners' equity.

11. The issuance of stock by a company

    a. increases assets and increases liabilities.
    b. decreases assets and decreases liabilities.
    c. increases assets and increases owners' equity.
    d. decreases assets and increases owners' equity.

12. Revenue accounts

    a. have no effect on owners' equity.
    b. are increased by debits.
    c. usually have a debit balance.
    d. have the same debit/credit, increase/decrease relationship as owners' equity.

13. Which of the following is *not* true for expense accounts?

    a. They have the same debit/credit, increase/decrease relationship as assets.
    b. They are decreased by credits.
    c. They usually have a credit balance.
    d. They have the effect of decreasing owners' equity.

14. A trial balance
   a. is a formal statement presented to stockholders.
   b. lists all accounts with their appropriate balances.
   c. is an essential step in the accounting cycle.
   d. proves that all the journal entries have been made correctly.

15. Which of the following is *not* true for dividends?
   a. They are not liabilities until declared.
   b. They are net reductions in owners' equity.
   c. They are normal expenses of doing business.
   d. They reduce net assets.

16. Which of the following journal entries is probably *not* correct?

   a. Cash xxx
         Notes Payable   xxx
   b. Inventory xxx
         Cash...   xxx
   c. Cash... xxx
         Capital Stock   xxx
   d. Rent Expense.. xxx
         Interest Expense   xxx

17. Which of the following transactions would increase owners' equity?
   a. Purchased inventory
   b. Paid accounts payable
   c. Sold goods at a profit
   d. Sold goods at a loss

18. Which of the following is *not* a characteristic of the accounting model?
   a. The accounting entity is considered a separate and distinct economic unit
   b. Arm's-length transactions provide the basis for accounting entries
   c. The cash basis of accounting
   d. The necessity of periodic reporting

19. Which of the following accounts will *not* appear on a post-closing trial balance?
   a. Dividends
   b. Retained Earnings
   c. Dividends Payable
   d. Accounts Payable

20. A fiscal-year accounting period
   a. covers 12 months and usually ends on the last day of a month other than December 31.
   b. covers 12 months and always ends on December 31.
   c. is always the same as the calendar year.
   d. is set by a company's board of directors and usually lasts for more than a year.

21. Accrual-basis accounting
   a. recognizes revenues only when cash is received.
   b. recognizes revenues when they are earned.
   c. is used by all businesses.
   d. eliminates the need to divide the life of a business into reporting periods.

E3-8   Closing Entries

Instructions: Based on the following account balances, taken from the adjusted trial balance of Pitch & Hit Company, prepare the closing entry at the end of the accounting period.

Cash	$ 1,500
Accounts Receivable	2,200
Inventory	15,400
Land	28,000
Accounts Payable	700
Mortgage Payable	18,000
Capital Stock	20,000
Retained Earnings (Beginning)	8,400
Sales Revenue	49,000
Cost of Goods Sold	24,800
Selling Expenses	11,500
General and Administrative Expenses	5,600
Dividends	2,000

JOURNAL   **PAGE**

DATE	DESCRIPTION	POST. REF.	DEBIT	CREDIT

ANSWERS

Matching

1.	m	10.	j	19.	r	
2.	b	11.	h	20.	v	
3.	k	12.	a	21.	t	
4.	d	13.	l	22.	u	
5.	g	14.	i	23.	z	
6.	n	15.	y	24.	o	
7.	e	16.	q	25.	x	
8.	c	17.	w	26.	p	
9.	f	18.	s			

True/False

1.	T	11.	T	21.	F
2.	T	12.	F	22.	F
3.	T	13.	F	23.	F
4.	F	14.	T	24.	F
5.	T	15.	F	25.	T
6.	T	16.	T	26.	F
7.	F	17.	T	27.	T
8.	F	18.	F	28.	T
9.	T	19.	T	29.	T
10.	F	20.	F		

Multiple Choice

1.	b	13.	c	25.	b
2.	d	14.	b	26.	c
3.	a	15.	c	27.	a
4.	d	16.	d	28.	a
5.	a	17.	c	29.	a
6.	d	18.	c	30.	d
7.	b	19.	a	31.	d
8.	b	20.	a	32.	b
9.	d	21.	b	33.	d
10.	c	22.	b	34.	b
11.	c	23.	d	35.	c
12.	d	24.	b	36.	b

Exercises

E3-1   The Accounting Equation

1. Increases assets (Inventory) and increases liabilities (Accounts Payable).
2. Increases assets (Cash) and increases liabilities (Notes Payable).
3. Decreases assets (Inventory), increases assets (Accounts Receivable), increases expenses (Cost of Goods Sold), and increases revenues (Sales Revenue).
4. Increases assets (Cash) and decreases assets (Accounts Receivable).
5. Decreases assets (Cash) and decreases liabilities (Accounts Payable).
6. Increases assets (Cash) and increases owners' equity (Capital Stock).
7. Decreases assets (Cash) and increases Dividends, which reduces Retained Earnings and therefore decreases owners' equity.
8. Increases assets (Building) and increases liabilities (Mortgage Payable).
9. Decreases assets (Cash) and increases expenses (Utilities Expense), which reduces Retained Earnings and therefore decreases owners' equity.
10. Increases assets (Inventory) and decreases assets (Cash).

E3-2   Decreasing an Account

Account	Decreased by Debit or Credit	Normal Balance
1. Land	Credit	Debit
2. Accounts Payable	Debit	Credit
3. Capital Stock	Debit	Credit
4. Notes Payable	Debit	Credit
5. Accounts Receivable	Credit	Debit
6. Inventory	Credit	Debit
7. Retained Earnings	Debit	Credit
8. Dividends	Credit	Debit
9. Prepaid Insurance	Credit	Debit
10. Mortgage Payable	Debit	Credit

E3-3   Journalizing Transactions

Jan.	3	Cash	10,000	
		Capital Stock		10,000
		Issued 1,000 shares of stock for $10,000.		
	5	Equipment	3,500	
		Cash		500
		Notes Payable		3,000
		Purchased equipment costing $3,500 for $500 and a note of $3,000.		
	8	Inventory	6,000	
		Accounts Payable		6,000
		Purchased merchandise for $6,000 on account.		
	10	Salary Expense	1,500	
		Cash		1,500
		Paid employee salaries of $1,500.		
	15	Rent Expense	400	
		Cash		400
		Paid rent of $400.		
	18	Accounts Receivable	3,500	
		Cost of Goods Sold	2,000	
		Sales Revenue		3,500
		Inventory		2,000
		Sold merchandise costing $2,000 for $3,500 on credit.		
	24	Utilities Expense	150	
		Cash		150
		Paid utilities of $150.		
	29	Dividends	5,000	
		Cash		5,000
		Paid cash dividends of $5,000 to shareholders.		

E3-4   Describing Journal Entries

Jan.	1	Purchased inventory on credit for $3,000.
	3	Sold merchandise costing $3,000 for $5,000 on credit.
	10	Paid accounts payable of $3,000.
	12	Paid salary expense of $2,000.
	17	Collected accounts receivable of $5,000.
	19	Paid rent of $1,000.

E3-5   Preparing a Trial Balance

	Debits	Credits
Cash	$ 17,000	
Accounts Receivable	13,000	
Inventory	28,000	
Equipment	55,000	
Land	85,000	
Accounts Payable		$ 24,000
Mortgage Payable		32,000
Capital Stock		75,000
Retained Earnings		48,000*
Sales Revenue		114,000
Selling Expenses	60,000	
Administrative Expenses	35,000	
Totals	$293,000	$293,000

*$293,000 = $245,000 (total of other credits) + X (Retained Earnings)
X = $48,000

E3-6   Adjusting Entries

1. Salary Expense 2,000
        Salaries Payable 2,000

2. Insurance Expense 1,000
        Prepaid Insurance 1,000
   ($3,000 ÷ 3 = $1,000 per year)

3. Accounts Receivable 10,000
        Service Revenues 10,000

4. Interest Expense 12,000
        Interest Payable 12,000
   ($100,000 x 0.12 x 1 year = $12,000)

E3-7   Adjusting Entries

1. Rent Expense 2,500
        Prepaid Rent 2,500
   To recognize 10 months' rent expense at $250 per month and show 2 months' prepaid rent applicable to next period.

	Prepaid Rent		Cash		Rent Expense	
Original entry	3,000		3,000			
Adjusting entry		2,500			2,500	
Updated balance	500				2,500	
	To balance sheet (Asset)				To income statement (Expense)	

2. Unearned Service Revenues............   325
       Service Revenues   325
   *To adjust the liability for unearned
   service revenues received in advance and to recognize partial
   earning of service revenues.*

	Unearned Service Revenues		Cash		Service Revenues	
Original entry..............................		1,025	1,025			
Adjusting entry	325					325
Updated balance		700				325

To balance sheet (Liability)		To income statement (Revenue)

E3-8   Closing Entry

Sales Revenue...	49,000	
Cost of Goods Sold....................................		24,800
Selling Expenses..		11,500
General and Administrative Expenses......		5,600
Dividends..		2,000
Retained Earnings......................................		5,100

Chapter 4
Operating Activities—Inflows

LEARNING OBJECTIVES

After studying this chapter, you should be able to:

1. Understand the three basic types of business activities: operating, investing, and financing.

2. Use the two revenue recognition criteria to decide when the revenue from a sale or service should be recorded in the accounting records.

3. Properly account for the collection of cash and describe the business controls necessary to safeguard cash.

4. Record the losses resulting from credit customers who do not pay their bills.

5. Evaluate a company's management of its receivables by computing and analyzing appropriate financial ratios.

6. Match revenues and expenses by estimating and recording future warranty and service costs associated with a sale.

CHAPTER REVIEW

Major Activities of a Business

1. Activities of a business can be divided into three groups: (1) operating activities, (2) investing activities, and (3) financing activities.

2. Operating activities involve selling products and/or services, buying inventory for resale, and incurring and paying for necessary expenses associated with the primary activities of the business.

3. Investing activities involve purchasing assets for use in the business. Operating assets purchased include such items as property, plant, and equipment. Nonoperating assets purchased include such items as investments in stocks and bonds of other companies.

4. Financing activities involve raising money by means other than operations to finance a business. Financing activities include borrowing money and selling stock.

Recognizing Revenue

5. Revenues are increases in resources from the sale of goods or the performance of services. Revenues are usually recognized when (1) the work has been substantially completed, and (2) cash, or a valid promise of future payment, has been received.

6. In most cases, revenues are recognized when goods are shipped to customers.

7. When there is significant uncertainty about whether cash from a sale will be collected, revenue should probably be recognized when cash is collected.

8. When sales are made in advance, such as with airline tickets or athletic season tickets, revenues are usually recognized when the service is performed (flight is taken or game is attended).

Cash Collection

9. Sales discounts, or cash discounts, are reductions in the amount customers owe if payment is made within a specified time limit. A typical discount is 2/10, n/30, which means that customers receive a 2 percent discount if payment is made within 10 days of the date of purchase, and the total amount is due within 30 days.

10. Typical entries needed to account for sales, receivables, and sales discounts are shown below, when 1/10, n/30 sales terms are given on a $1,000 sale.

Transaction	Journal Entries		
Sale	Accounts Receivable	1,000	
	Sales Revenue		1,000
Payment (if made within the discount period)	Cash..........................	990	
	Sales Discounts	10	
	Accounts Receivable		1,000
Payment (if not made within the discount period)	Cash..........................	1,000	
	Accounts Receivable		1,000

11. When merchandise previously sold is returned, an account called Sales Returns and Allowances is debited and either Accounts Receivable or Cash is credited.

12. Both Sales Discounts and Sales Returns and Allowances are contra-revenue accounts that are deducted from gross sales revenue on the income statement.

13. Because cash is so liquid, companies usually develop elaborate internal control systems to protect it. Common internal controls for cash are:

   a. Separation of the duties in accounting for and handling of cash. (This helps prevent the practice of *lapping* by employees.)
   b. The daily depositing of all cash receipts in bank accounts.
   c. The use of prenumbered checks to make all cash disbursements.

Accounting for Credit Customers Who Don't Pay

14. Receivables are a company's claims for money, goods, or services. Receivables arise when merchandise is sold or services are performed on credit.

15. Accounts receivable are short-term liquid assets that arise from credit sales to customers. When companies sell goods or services on credit, the entry includes a debit to Accounts Receivable and a credit to Sales Revenue. When the receivable is collected, Cash is debited and Accounts Receivable is credited.

16. When customers do not pay the amount they owe, bad-debt losses occur.

17. There are two well-known methods of accounting for uncollectible receivables. The direct write-off method recognizes a loss from a receivable at the time it is deemed to be uncollectible. Since uncollectibility is often determined several months after a sale takes place, this method sometimes violates the matching principle, and thus is not allowed under generally accepted accounting principles. The allowance method satisfies the matching principle by requiring that estimates of uncollectible receivables be made in the same period that sales are recognized. The journal entry recording the estimate is usually made as an adjusting entry at the end of the accounting period.

18. The most common methods of estimating the amount of uncollectible accounts receivable when using the allowance method are (1) a straight percentage of credit sales, (2) a percentage of receivables, and (3) aging the accounts receivables.

19. When estimating bad debt expense as a percentage of credit sales, the existing balance in Allowance for Bad Debts, if there is one, is not considered in the adjusting entry.

20. "Aging" receivables refers to the process whereby receivables are classified according to age, such as current, 1-30 days past due, 31-60 days past due, and so on. Then an estimate is made of the amount of uncollectible receivables in each category.

Assessing How Well Companies Manage Their Receivables

21. Organizations use two ratios to evaluate how well they manage their resources: (1) accounts receivable turnover, and (2) average collection period. Accounts receivable turnover is calculated by dividing total sales for the period by accounts receivable. Average collection period is calculated by dividing 365 (days in a year) by the accounts receivable turnover ratio.

Recording Warranty and Service Costs Associated With a Sale

22. Organizations that provide warranties on the products or services they sell must recognize those customer service expenses in the period in which the sale takes place. A proper matching requires that an estimate be made of future warranty expenses related to the current period's sales.

23. When accounting for warranties, the entry to record the estimate of future expenditures includes a debit to Customer Service Expense and a credit to Estimated Liability for Service. When services are performed, Estimated Liability for Service is debited and Wages Payable and Supplies are credited.

COMMON ERRORS

The most common error made when studying this chapter is confusing the percentage of sales and percentage of receivables methods for estimating uncollectible accounts receivable.

Most students quickly understand why the allowance method of accounting for losses from uncollectible receivables is preferred over the direct write-off method. You can see that the direct write-off method often violates the important matching principle, especially for sales made near the end of an accounting period.

The same distinction can be made between the percentage of sales and the percentage of receivables estimation methods. The former enforces the matching principle, and the latter violates it. Sales are reported on the income statement, which includes transactions from only one period, since income statement accounts are closed every year. Accounts Receivable is a balance sheet account and, strictly speaking, the balance in receivables could come from any period. In the first case, where the estimate is a percentage of sales, the matching principle is enforced and any existing balance in the allowance account, which relates to prior periods, is ignored. With the percentage of receivables method, the existing balance in Allowance for Bad Debts must be considered because receivables could come from any period. To reinforce this idea, consider the following example.

Account Balance at 12/31/2000 (Before Adjustment)

Accounts Receivable	$100,000
Allowance for Bad Debts	350 (credit balance)
Sales Revenue	220,000

Under the percentage of sales method, the $350 is assumed to be left from the previous year. If 1 percent of sales are considered uncollectible in the current year, $2,200 (0.01 x $220,000) would be added to the Allowance account and the balance would be $2,550 ($2,200 + $350).

Under the percentage of receivables method, the $350 is assumed to be associated with the receivables (which could come from any period). If 2 percent of receivables are considered uncollectible, only $1,650 [(100,000 x 0.02) - $350] would be added to the account.

SELF-TEST

Matching

Instructions: Write the letter of each of the following terms in the space to the left of its appropriate definition.

a.	receivable	**g.**	accounts receivable turnover
b.	allowance method	**h.**	average collection period
c.	account receivable	**i.**	net realizable value
d.	sales discount	**j.**	revenue recognition
e.	allowance for bad debts	**k.**	investing activities
f.	direct write-off method		

_____ 1. A reduction in the sales price that is allowed if payment is received within a specified period; also called cash discount.

_____ 2. Claims for money, goods, or services.

_____ 3. The recording of estimated losses due to uncollectible accounts as expenses during the period in which the sales occurred.

_____ 4. Sales divided by accounts receivable.

_____ 5. A contra-account, deducted from Accounts Receivable, that shows the estimated losses from uncollectible accounts.

_____ 6. Money due from rendering services or selling merchandise on credit.

_____ 7. 365 divided by accounts receivable turnover.

_____ 8. The recording of actual losses from uncollectible accounts as expenses during the period in which accounts receivable are determined to be uncollectible.

_____ 9. The net amount of accounts receivable; equal to accounts receivable less allowance for bad debts.

_____ 10. Recording of a sale through a journal entry.

_____ 11. Purchasing assets for use in the business.

True/False

Instructions: Place a check mark in the appropriate column to indicate whether each of the following statements is true or false.

	True	False
1. The main criterion for deciding whether or not to recognize a revenue is usually cash collection.	_____	_____
2. Accounts receivable arise when merchandise is purchased from suppliers.	_____	_____
3. A 2/10, n/30 sales discount means that 10 percent interest will be charged if the account is not paid within 30 days.	_____	_____
4. When recording credit sales, Accounts Receivable is debited.	_____	_____
5. The Sales Discounts and Sales Returns and Allowances accounts are contra-revenue accounts.	_____	_____
6. Accounts receivable are usually not interest-bearing.	_____	_____
7. When collecting credit sales, Accounts Receivable is debited.	_____	_____
8. The direct write-off method of accounting for uncollectible receivables is required under generally accepted accounting principles.	_____	_____
9. The allowance method of accounting for uncollectible receivables is an estimation method.	_____	_____
10. An aging of accounts receivable identifies which customers are most delinquent in their payments.	_____	_____

	True	False
11. Warranty expenses are always recognized in the period when incurred or paid.	_____	_____
12. Accounts receivable turnover is calculated by dividing 365 by credit sales for the period.	_____	_____

Multiple Choice

Instructions: Circle the letter that best completes each of the following statements.

1. Buying inventory for resale is considered to be a(n)

    a. operating activity.
    b. investing activity.
    c. financing activity.
    d. operating asset.

2. Revenues are

    a. reported on the balance sheet.
    b. reported on the statement of cash flows.
    c. reported on the income statement.
    d. liabilities.

3. Net sales (in a merchandising firm) is equal to

    a. gross sales minus sales discounts plus sales returns and allowances.
    b. gross sales minus sales discounts minus sales returns and allowances.
    c. gross sales plus sales discounts plus sales returns and allowances.
    d. gross sales.

4. When merchandise is sold on credit

    a. Sales Revenue is debited.
    b. Cash is debited.
    c. Accounts Receivable is debited.
    d. Accounts Receivable is credited.

5. A sales discount of 2/10, n/30 means that

    a. a 2 percent discount will be allowed if payment is received within 30 days.
    b. the net amount must be paid within 10 days.
    c. interest of 10 percent will be charged after 30 days.
    d. a 2 percent discount will be allowed if payment is made within 10 days but the full amount must be paid in 30 days.

6. The Sales Returns and Allowances account is a(n)

    a. revenue account.
    b. contra-revenue account.
    c. liability account.
    d. asset account.

7. The direct write-off method of accounting for uncollectible receivables usually

    a. violates the matching principle.
    b. is an estimation method.
    c. is allowed under generally accepted accounting principles.
    d. violates the going concern assumption.

8. The allowance method of accounting for uncollectible receivables

   a. is an estimation method.
   b. violates the matching principle.
   c. Both *a* and *b*
   d. violates GAAP.

9. An aging of accounts receivable

   a. helps identify slow-paying customers.
   b. is a method of estimating uncollectible receivables.
   c. Both *a* and *b*
   d. None of the above

10. ABC Company has a credit balance of $200 in Allowance for Bad Debts. If it estimates that 2 percent of this year's total sales of $45,000 are uncollectible, Bad Debt Expense would be

    a. debited for $900.
    b. credited for $900.
    c. debited for $700.
    d. credited for $700.

11. The net realizable value of receivables is equal to

    a. total accounts receivable plus the allowance for bad debts.
    b. total accounts receivable less the allowance for bad debts.
    c. total accounts receivable only.
    d. total accounts receivable plus cash.

12. The denominator in the "average collection period" calculation is

    a. 365
    b. accounts receivable turnover.
    c. average receivables.
    d. credit sales.

13. Warranty (Customer Service) liabilities are recorded

    a. in the same period as the products are sold.
    b. in periods subsequent to the sale.
    c. in periods prior to the sale.
    d. only when cash is paid to provide customer service.

Exercises

E4-1   Sales Entries

Maxey Company is a wholesale clothing distributor that sells women's coats to clothing stores. During January the firm had the following transactions.

Jan. 3   Sold 8 coats that cost $120 each on account to Paris Clothing Store at $200 each (terms 2/10, n/30).
      5   Sold 5 coats that cost $100 each on account to Extravaganza Clothing Store at $200 each (terms 2/10, n/30).
     11   Received payment in full from Paris Clothing Store.
     19   Received payment in full from Extravaganza Clothing Store.

Instructions: Provide journal entries to account for these transactions.

		JOURNAL				PAGE	
DATE		DESCRIPTION	POST. REF.	DEBIT		CREDIT	

E4-2   Accounting for Accounts Receivable

During 2000, Johnson Manufacturing had sales of $2,000,000, 70 percent of which were on credit. Also during 2000, $20,000 of accounts receivable were written off as uncollectible. At December 31, 2000, the Accounts Receivable balance showed a total of $300,000, which was aged as follows:

Age	Amount
Current	$200,000
1-30 days past due	70,000
31-60 days past due	20,000
61-90 days past due	8,000
Over 90 days past due	2,000
Total	$300,000

Instructions: Prepare the journal entries required on December 31, 2000, to properly record the bad debt expense under each of the following methods. (Assume, where applicable, that the credit balance in Allowance for Bad Debts is $3,000 before any adjusting entries at December 31, 2000.)

1. The direct write-off method. (Assume that all accounts determined to be uncollectible are written off in a single year-end entry.)
2. Based on experience, uncollectible accounts for the year are estimated to be approximately 4 percent of the Accounts Receivable balance.
3. Based on experience, uncollectible accounts are estimated to be the sum of:
   0.5% of current accounts
   1.5% of accounts 1-30 days past due
   3.0% of accounts 31-60 days past due
   10.0% of accounts 61-90 days past due
   30.0% of accounts 90 days past due

JOURNAL   **PAGE**

DATE	DESCRIPTION	POST. REF.	DEBIT	CREDIT

E4-3   Accounting for Accounts Receivable

Assume the same data as in E4-2. Also assume that based on experience, uncollectible accounts are estimated to be approximately 1 percent of total credit sales for the year.

Instructions: Make the journal entry as of December 31, 2000, to record the bad debts expense.

	JOURNAL					PAGE	
DATE	DESCRIPTION	POST. REF.	DEBIT			CREDIT	

E4-4   Assessing How Well Companies Manage Their Receivables

Tanner Company has the following data related to its sales and receivables:

Total Credit Sales—1999	$2,000,000
Total Credit Sales—2000	2,500,000
Accounts Receivable Balances:	
January 1, 1999	180,000
December 31, 1999	300,000
December 31, 2000	500,000

Instructions: Based on these numbers, calculate the following:
1.   Accounts receivable turnover for 1999.
2.   Accounts receivable turnover for 2000.
3.   Average collection period for 1999.
4.   Average collection period for 2000.

E4-5   Accounting for Warranty Expense

RTV sells stereo systems with a 2-year warranty. Past experience indicates that 10 percent of all systems sold will require repairs during the first year and an additional 20 percent will need repairs during the second year. The average cost to repair a system is $50. The number of systems sold in 1999 and 2000 was 5,000 and 6,000, respectively. Actual repair costs were $12,500 in 1999 and $55,000 in 2000.

Instructions: Assume all repair costs involve cash expenditures and provide journal entries to account for the following:
1. 1999 actual customer service costs.
2. Estimated warranty expense at 12/31/99 to account for warranty work that will be done in the future related to 1999 sales.
3. 2000 actual customer service costs.
4. Estimated warranty expense at 12/31/2000 to account for warranty that will be done in the future related to 2000 sales.

JOURNAL   **PAGE**

DATE	DESCRIPTION	POST. REF.	DEBIT	CREDIT

ANSWERS

Matching

1.	d	5.	e	9.	i
2.	a	6.	c	10.	j
3.	b	7.	h	11.	k
4.	g	8.	f		

True/False

1.	F	5.	T	9.	T
2.	F	6.	T	10.	T
3.	F	7.	F	11.	F
4.	T	8.	F	12.	F

Multiple Choice

1.	a	6.	b	10.	a
2.	c	7.	a	11.	b
3.	b	8.	a	12.	b
4.	c	9.	c	13.	a
5.	d				

Exercises

E4-1   Sales Entries

Jan.	3	Accounts Receivable	1,600	
		Sales Revenue		1,600
		Cost of Goods Sold	960	
		Inventory		960
		Sold 8 coats to Paris Clothing Store.		
	5	Accounts Receivable	1,000	
		Sales Revenue		1,000
		Cost of Goods Sold	500	
		Inventory		500
		Sold 5 coats to Extravaganza Clothing Store.		
	11	Cash	1,568	
		Sales Discounts	32	
		Accounts Receivable		1,600
		Received full payment (within the discount period) from		
		Paris Clothing Store ($1,600 x 0.02 = $32 discount).		
	19	Cash	1,000	
		Accounts Receivable		1,000
		Received full payment (after the discount period) from		
		Extravaganza Clothing Store.		

E4-2   Accounting for Accounts Receivable

1.	Bad Debt Expense	20,000	
	Accounts Receivable		20,000
	To write off uncollectible accounts in 2000.		
2.	Bad Debt Expense	9,000	
	Allowance for Bad Debts		9,000
	To estimate uncollectible accounts as a percentage of the receivables		
	(0.04 x $300,000 = $12,000; $12,000 - $3,000 existing credit balance = $9,000).		

Note: When the estimate is based on receivables, the existing balance in Allowance for Bad Debts is considered because receivables relate to sales from all periods. No attempt to match expenses with revenues is made when the estimate is based on receivables.

3.   Bad Debt Expense.. 1,050
            Allowance for Bad Debts   1,050
            To estimate uncollectible accounts based on an aging of the receivables.

        Calculation:

0.005	x	$200,000	=	$1,000
0.015	x	70,000	=	1,050
0.030	x	20,000	=	600
0.100	x	8,000	=	800
0.300	x	2,000	=	600

                                                      $4,050
                                                      -3,000   Existing credit balance
                                                      $1,050

E4-3   Accounting for Accounts Receivable

Bad Debt Expense.. 14,000
    Allowance for Bad Debts..   14,000
To estimate uncollectible accounts as a percentage of credit sales ($2,000,000 x 0.70 x 0.01).

Note: When the estimate is based on sales, the existing balance in Allowance for Bad Debts is ignored. The existing balance is related to the previous period's sales and, under a strict interpretation of the matching rule, the 1 percent of uncollectible accounts from this year's sales should be added to it.

E4-4   Assessing How Well Companies Manage Their Receivables

		1999		2000	
1 & 2	Accounts Receivable Turnover	$\dfrac{\$2,000,000}{(\$180,000 + \$300,000) / 2}$ = 8.33 times		$\dfrac{\$2,500,000}{(\$300,000 + \$500,000) / 2}$ = 6.25 times	
3 & 4	Average Collection Period	$\dfrac{365}{8.33}$ = 43.82 days		$\dfrac{365}{6.25}$ = 58.40 days	

It appears that accounts receivable collection is getting worse.

E4-5   Accounting For Warranty Expense

1.   Estimated Liability for Service 12,500
            Cash...   12,500
            To record cost of actual repairs in 1999.
2.   Customer Service Expense.. 75,000
            Estimated Liability for Service..   75,000
            To record estimated warranty expense based on systems sold.
            (5,000 x 0.30 x $50 = $75,000)
3.   Estimated Liability for Service 55,000
            Cash...   55,000
            To record cost of actual repairs in 2000.
4.   Customer Service Expense.. 90,000
            Estimated Liability for Service..   90,000
            To record estimated warranty expense based on systems sold.
            (6,000 x 0.30 x $50 = $90,000)

Chapter 5
Operating Activities—Expenditures

LEARNING OBJECTIVES

After studying this chapter, you should be able to:

1. Identify what items and costs should be included in inventory and cost of goods sold.

2. Account for inventory purchases and sales using both a perpetual and a periodic inventory system, calculate cost of goods sold using the results of an inventory count, and understand the impact of errors in ending inventory on reported cost of goods sold.

3. Apply the four inventory cost flow alternatives: specific identification, FIFO, LIFO, and average cost.

4. Discuss and account for additional day-to-day activities related to the operating cycle.

5. Prepare an income statement summarizing operating activities as well as other revenues and expenses, extraordinary items, and earnings per share.

6. Analyze a company's inventory level and liquidity using various analysis techniques.

CHAPTER REVIEW

Inventory and Cost of Goods Sold

1. When inventory is purchased or manufactured, it is an asset; when it is sold, its cost becomes an expense (usually called *cost of goods sold*).

2. The cost of merchandise sold is usually referred to as "cost of goods sold," and is deducted from revenues on the income statement. The difference between revenues and cost of goods sold is the gross margin of a firm.

3. A manufacturing firm has three types of inventory: (1) raw materials, (2) work in process, and (3) finished goods.

4. Inventory purchased or manufactured during the period is added to beginning inventory and the total cost of this inventory is known as *cost of goods available for sale.*

Accounting for Inventory Purchases and Sales

5. There are two common methods of accounting for inventories: the perpetual method and the periodic method. Under the perpetual method, the inventory records are adjusted each time inventory is purchased or sold. Thus, at any time, the inventory records should accurately reflect how much inventory is on hand. With the periodic inventory method, adjustments to inventory accounts are made only when the inventory is physically counted (usually at the end of a period).

6. The entries to record inventory transactions under the perpetual and periodic methods are shown in Exhibit 5-1. (Assume beginning inventory was $2,000 and ending inventory is $3,000.)

Exhibit 5-1   Entries for Periodic and Perpetual Inventory Transactions

Transaction	Periodic Inventory Method	Perpetual Inventory Method

Sale of merchandise	Accounts Receivable (or Cash)... 1,000
	    Sales... 1,000
	Sold inventory costing $600 for $1,000.
		Accounts Receivable (or Cash)... 1,000
		    Sales... 1,000
		Cost of Goods Sold..................... 600
		    Inventory................................. 600

Sales return by customer	Sales Returns 50
	    Accounts Receivable (or Cash) 50
	Customer returned inventory that cost $30 and was sold for $50.
		Sales Returns 50
		    Accounts Receivable (or Cash) 50
		Inventory...................................... 30
		    Cost of Goods Sold 30

Purchase of merchandise	Purchases 700
	    Accounts Payable (or Cash).... 700
	Purchased merchandise costing $700.
		Inventory...................................... 700
		    Accounts Payable (or Cash).... 700

Purchase return to suppliers	Accounts Payable (or Cash)........ 40
	    Purchase Returns..................... 40
	Returned $40 of merchandise to suppliers.
		Accounts Payable (or Cash)........ 40
		    Inventory................................. 40

Closing entries following physical count of inventory	Inventory............................... 12,900
	Purchase Discounts 60
	Purchase Returns 40
	    Purchases 13,000
	Eliminated beginning inventory balance of $2,000 and entered ending balance of $3,000.
	
	Cost of Goods Sold..................... 11,900
	    Inventory................................. 11,900
	Adjustment of inventory account to appropriate ending balance.
		No Entry (unless there is shrinkage).

Counting Inventory and Calculating Cost of Goods Sold

7. Most companies physically count their inventories at year-end. With the perpetual method, the count is confirmation of the amount recorded and a way to reveal shortages. With the periodic method, the count is necessary to determine the amount of ending inventory, and subsequently cost of goods sold.

8. There are two parts to a physical inventory count: (1) quantity count and (2) inventory costing.

9. The calculations for an income statement (through gross margin) are:

> Net sales revenue (gross sales revenue – sales discounts – sales returns)
> – Cost of goods sold:
> Beginning inventory
> + Net purchases (gross purchases – purchase discounts – purchase returns + freight-in)
> = Cost of goods available for sale
> – Ending inventory
> = Cost of goods sold
> = Gross margin (net sales revenue – cost of goods sold)

10. An error in the reported ending inventory amount can have a significant effect on reported cost of goods sold, gross margin, and net income. For example, overstatement of ending inventory results in understatement of cost of goods sold and overstatement of net income.

Inventory Cost Flow Assumptions

11. There are four patterns in which inventories can flow through a firm.

 a. Specific identification: The units sold can be specifically identified as being purchased at a certain time.

 b. FIFO (first in, first out): The units sold are assumed to be the first inventory items purchased.

 c. LIFO (last in, first out): The units sold are assumed to be the last inventory items purchased.

 d. Average cost: The units sold are considered to be a mixture of all items purchased.

Just as inventory physically flows through a firm, costs of inventory must also flow through the accounting records in one of the four patterns described.

12. For accounting purposes, if inventory costs remained stable over time, it would not matter which of the above alternatives were used. However, if prices are changing (as they usually are because of inflation and other factors), the alternative used can dramatically affect the amounts a firm reports for cost of goods sold and net income. Specifically, under FIFO the oldest costs become the cost of goods sold; whereas with LIFO the most recent costs become the cost of goods sold.

13. Even though a firm has goods that flow on a FIFO basis, it can use any alternative to flow the costs of the inventory through the accounting records. Many firms have switched to LIFO inventory costing because, in an inflationary environment, it allows a firm to report lower profits, and hence to pay lower taxes.

Additional Business Events Related to the Operating Cycle

14. Accounting for payroll usually involves several different current liabilities. When salary expense is recorded, the following liabilities are recognized.

Payee	Nature of Liability
Individual employees	Take-home pay
State government	State income taxes withheld from employees' checks
Federal government	Federal income and FICA (Social Security) taxes withheld from employees' checks
Unions, charitable organizations, insurance companies, etc.	Other deductions (usually voluntary) from employees' checks

15. Besides the taxes withheld from employees' checks, employers must also pay unemployment taxes (to both the state and federal governments) and FICA taxes. These taxes—together with those withheld from employees' checks—are paid to the governments on a periodic basis.

16. In addition to current wages paid to employees, there are a number of other employee-related expenses and liabilities that must be recognized. The most common of these are: (1) compensated absences; (2) bonus-related liabilities such as stock options and bonuses; (3) post-employment benefits that are paid after an employee ceases to work for an organization but before the employee retires, such as severance packages; and (4) post-retirement benefits such as pensions, retirement medical insurance, and other benefits.

Summarizing Operations on an Income Statement

17. A firm prepares an income statement that shows revenues, cost of goods sold, gross margin, operating expenses, income from operations, other revenues and expenses, pretax income, income before extraordinary items, extraordinary items, net income, and earnings per share.

18. Extraordinary items (events that are unusual in nature, infrequent in occurrence, and material in amount) are separated from other revenues and expenses on the income statement because they are not part of normal operations.

19. If applicable, an income statement should provide three earnings-per-share (EPS) numbers: (1) EPS before extraordinary items, (2) EPS on extraordinary items, and (3) EPS on net income. EPS is calculated by dividing these income numbers by the number of shares of stock outstanding.

Operating Cycle Ratios and Analysis

20. One way to analyze financial statements is to convert them to percentages—to "common size" them. On an income statement, for example, net sales can be 100 percent and all the items on the income statement can be shown as a percentage of net sales. Common-size financial statements allow you to compare companies of different sizes.

21. Two ratios are commonly used to measure a company's liquidity. The current or working capital ratio is calculated by dividing total current assets by total current liabilities. The acid-test or quick ratio is calculated by dividing all current assets except inventory and prepaid expenses (cash, receivables, and short-term securities) by current liabilities.

22. Two inventory turnover ratios are used to evaluate how effectively a company manages its inventory. The inventory turnover ratio is calculated by dividing cost of goods sold by average inventory. The number of days' sales in inventory is calculated by dividing 365

(number of days in a year) by the inventory turnover ratio.

23. Number of days' sales in accounts payable, when combined with number of days' sales in inventory and number of days' sales in receivables, identifies how much of a company's operating cycle is being financed by a company's vendors and how much is being paid for by the company. These ratios measure a firm's liquidity and operating efficiency.

COMMON ERRORS

Two common inventory-related errors often made by students are:

1. confusing the journal entries for recording perpetual and periodic inventory transactions,

2. making errors when calculating inventory cost flow assumptions, and

A third error made in conjunction with the material in this chapter is the misclassification of income statement items.

1. **The Perpetual and Periodic Inventory Methods**

   The dictionary defines the word *perpetual* as "unceasing" or "constant." With the perpetual method, you "constantly" (with every sales or purchase transaction) adjust the Inventory account. If you adjust the inventory records for each transaction, then the records should always reflect the amount of inventory in the warehouse. Any shortage must be due to theft, loss, or accounting errors. On the other hand, the dictionary defines *periodic* as "occurring from time to time" or "intermittent." With the periodic method, the accounting records are adjusted "from time to time," namely, at the end of each accounting period so the records can be updated. If you understand the different meanings of *perpetual* and *periodic*, you really should not confuse the two methods. Just remember that, with the perpetual method, inventory must be debited every time inventory comes into the firm and credited every time it leaves the firm. With the periodic method, the inventory records are not adjusted during the period, so other accounts must be used to account for inventory purchase transactions. Those accounts are Purchases, Purchase Discounts, Purchase Returns, and Freight-In.

2. **Inventory Cost Flow Calculations**

   On examinations and quizzes, you will probably be asked to compute ending inventory or cost of goods sold using periodic LIFO, perpetual LIFO, or some other inventory costing method. Because of the similarity of these methods, it is easy to use the calculations for one method while working with another method. The best way to overcome this confusion is to remember the following.

   a. With the periodic method, you need not keep track of units on hand during the period. At the end of the period, you simply add total units available, then subtract total units sold to determine how many are left in inventory. If you are using FIFO, the costs assigned to the remaining inventory are those of the last units purchased. If you are using LIFO, the costs assigned to inventory are those of the first units purchased. And, if you are using average cost, an average cost of all goods available for sale is assigned to inventory. There is no need to know when goods were purchased or sold within a period when using the periodic method. In fact, you can assign costs of merchandise to cost of goods sold even though those units were not purchased at the time of the sale.

   b. With the perpetual method, you must keep track of purchases and sales within the period and you assign only the costs of inventory actually on hand to cost of goods sold. Using this method, you progressively work through the inventory records of the period, calculating inventory on hand after every purchase and sale.

   It will also help you understand the calculations if you realize that although periodic FIFO and perpetual FIFO methods result in the same numbers, the process of calculation is very different.

3. **Misclassifying Income Statement items**

   Probably the most common error is misclassifying accounts when preparing an income statement. When preparing a final income statement, it is important that items be placed in proper categories. For example, cost of goods sold comes before gross margin, selling and administrative expenses are subtracted from gross margin, interest and gains and losses go in other revenue and expenses, and extraordinary items have their own classification.

SELF-TEST

Matching

Instructions: Write the letter of each of the following terms in the space to the left of its appropriate definition.

a.	inventory	**n.**	periodic inventory system
b.	perpetual inventory system	**o.**	earnings per share
c.	cost of goods available for sale	**p.**	acid-test ratio
d.	cost of goods sold	**q.**	sales tax payable
e.	average cost	**r.**	compensated absences
f.	LIFO	**s.**	current ratio
g.	finished goods	**t.**	extraordinary items
h.	work in process	**u.**	income taxes expense
i.	FIFO	**v.**	post-employment benefits
j.	inventory turnover	**w.**	liquidity
k.	specific identification	**x.**	pensions
l.	net purchases	**y.**	other revenues and expenses
m.	raw materials	**z.**	prepaid expenses

_____ 1. A periodic inventory cost flow alternative whereby the cost of goods sold and the ending inventory are determined to be an average cost of all merchandise on hand at the end of the period.

_____ 2. Purchases minus purchase returns and purchase discounts plus freight-in.

_____ 3. A method of valuing inventory and determining cost of goods sold whereby the actual costs of inventory items are assigned to specific units of inventory on hand and to those units that have been sold.

_____ 4. Cost of goods sold divided by average inventory.

_____ 5. An inventory cost flow alternative whereby the first goods purchased determine the cost of goods sold and the last goods purchased determine the ending inventory.

_____ 6. Manufactured units not yet finished.

_____ 7. Inventory ready for resale in a manufacturing firm.

_____ 8. An inventory cost flow alternative whereby the last goods purchased determine the cost of goods sold and the first goods purchased determine the ending inventory.

_____ 9. Inventory used in the manufacture of products.

_____ 10. The expenses incurred to purchase the merchandise sold during a period.

_____ 11. Beginning inventory plus net purchases.

_____ 12. A method of recording inventory in which detailed records of the number of units and the cost of each purchase and sales transaction are prepared throughout the accounting period.

_____ 13. Goods held for sale to customers.

_____ 14. A method of recording inventory in which cost of goods sold is determined and inventory is adjusted at the end of the accounting period, not when merchandise is purchased or sold.

_____ 15. The amount of net income (earnings) related to each share of stock; computed by dividing net income by the number of shares of stock outstanding during the period.

_____ 16. Money collected from customers for sales taxes that must be remitted to local governments and other taxing authorities.

_____ 17. Payments made in advance for items eventually charged to expense.

_____ 18. Items incurred or earned from activities that are outside, or peripheral to, the normal operations of a firm.

_____ 19. Compensation received by employees after they have retired.

_____ 20. A company's ability to meet current obligations with cash or other assets that can be quickly converted to cash.

_____ 21. Benefits incurred after an employee has ceased to work for an employer but before the employee retires.

_____ 22. The amount expected to be paid to the federal and state governments based on the income before taxes as reported on the income statement.

_____ 23. Nonoperating gains and losses that are unusual in nature, infrequent in occurrence, and material in amount.

_____ 24. A measure of the liquidity of a business; equal to current assets divided by current liabilities.

_____ 25. Sick pay and other missed work that must be paid for by employers.

_____ 26. A measure of a firm's ability to meet current liabilities; computed by dividing net quick assets (all current assets, except inventories and prepaid expenses) by current liabilities; more restrictive than current ratio.

True/False

Instructions: Place a check mark in the appropriate column to indicate whether each of the following statements is true or false.

	True	False
1. During a period of rising prices, firms using FIFO will report higher profits than will firms using LIFO.	_____	_____
2. With the periodic inventory method, cost of goods sold is calculated as ending inventory plus purchases minus beginning inventory.	_____	_____
3. Under generally accepted accounting principles, it is necessary for a firm that has a FIFO flow of goods to use the FIFO inventory costing alternative.	_____	_____
4. When using the perpetual inventory method, the account Purchase Discounts is not used.	_____	_____
5. Under the perpetual inventory method, a current record of inventory on hand is maintained.	_____	_____
6. A credit entry to the Inventory account is made each time merchandise is sold when the perpetual inventory method is used.	_____	_____
7. The cost of shipping merchandise into a firm (freight-in) is added to cost of goods sold for a period.	_____	_____
8. Under the average cost—periodic inventory costing alternative, the amount recorded as cost of goods sold is the average cost of all inventory available for sale multiplied by the number of units sold.	_____	_____
9. The FIFO cost flow alternative produces the same inventory and cost of goods sold numbers under both the perpetual and the periodic inventory methods.	_____	_____
10. In a period of increasing prices, LIFO results in the paying of higher taxes than does FIFO.	_____	_____
11. The Inventory Shrinkage account is a real account that is not closed.	_____	_____
12. A physical count of inventory under the periodic inventory method usually provides only a confirmation that the recorded inventory count is correct.	_____	_____
13. With the periodic inventory method, a Cost of Goods Sold account is maintained throughout the period.	_____	_____
14. A credit entry to the Inventory account is made each time merchandise is sold when the periodic inventory method is used.	_____	_____
15. After all adjusting entries are made and assuming FIFO inventory, the amounts shown as Inventory on the balance sheet and as Cost of Goods Sold on the income statement are the same under the perpetual and the periodic inventory methods.	_____	_____
16. State and federal income taxes are usually withheld from employees' checks.	_____	_____
17. Both the employer and the employee must pay FICA taxes.	_____	_____

	True	False
18. Compensated absences are usually recognized as expenses when sick days are taken.	_____	_____
19. A liability for bonuses payable must be recorded when the target figure or trigger for the bonus has been reached.	_____	_____
20. A defined contribution pension plan pays a set amount to employees when they retire, usually based on the number of years worked.	_____	_____
21. Sales taxes payable are usually considered long-term liabilities............................	_____	_____
22. Recurring gains and losses are classified as extraordinary items on the income statement.	_____	_____
23. Extraordinary items are separately classified on the income statement because they are (a) infrequent in occurrence, (b) unusual in nature, and (c) material in amount....	_____	_____
24. Earnings per share is equal to net income divided by total assets.	_____	_____
25. Common-size income statements allow a better comparison between firms of different sizes than do regular financial statements.	_____	_____
26. When number of days' sales in accounts payable is subtracted from number of days' sales in inventory plus number of days' sales in receivables, the amount of time the vendor is financing the operating cycle is determined.	_____	_____

Multiple Choice

Instructions: Circle the letter that best completes each of the following statements.

1. Which of the following inventory costing alternatives usually results in the highest cost of goods sold amount during a period of continuous inflation?
   a. FIFO
   b. LIFO
   c. Average cost
   d. None of the above

Use the following information to answer Questions 2-5.
Transactions of DEF Company, January 2000

Jan.	1	Beginning inventory	8 snowmobiles at $2,000 each
	5	Purchased	5 snowmobiles at $2,500 each
	13	Sold	9 snowmobiles at $3,000 each
	18	Sold	3 snowmobiles at $3,000 each
	23	Purchased	7 snowmobiles at $2,600 each
	25	Sold	3 snowmobiles at $3,200 each

2. Total sales for DEF Company in January 2000 amounted to
   a. $36,000.
   b. $45,600.
   c. $40,000.
   d. None of the above

3. The total number of snowmobiles available for sale in January 2000 was
   a. 22.
   b. 20.
   c. 18.
   d. None of the above

4. The number of snowmobiles left in ending inventory at the end of January was

   a. 15.
   b. 20.
   c. 5.
   d. 8.

5. The cost of ending inventory using the periodic LIFO inventory alternative was

   a. $12,000.
   b. $12,500.
   c. $10,000.
   d. $13,000.

6. The Cost of Goods Sold account is

   a. an expense.
   b. an asset.
   c. a revenue.
   d. a liability.

7. A Cost of Goods Sold account is

   a. maintained when the perpetual inventory method is used.
   b. debited when merchandise is sold, with the perpetual inventory method.
   c. credited when merchandise is returned by customers, with the perpetual inventory method.
   d. All of the above

8. Net Purchases is equal to

   a. Gross Purchases + Purchase Returns + Purchase Discounts – Freight-In.
   b. Gross Purchases + Purchase Returns + Purchase Discounts + Freight-In.
   c. Gross Purchases – Purchase Returns – Purchase Discounts + Freight-In.
   d. Gross Purchases – Purchase Returns – Purchase Discounts – Freight-In.

9. A firm that has a LIFO inventory goods flow

   a. must use the periodic LIFO inventory alternative.
   b. must use the perpetual LIFO inventory alternative.
   c. must use a FIFO inventory alternative.
   d. can use any inventory costing method.

Use the following information to answer Questions 10-12.
Transactions of DEF Company, January 2000

Jan.	1	Beginning inventory	8 snowmobiles at $2,000 each
	5	Purchased	5 snowmobiles at $2,500 each
	13	Sold	9 snowmobiles at $3,000 each
	18	Sold	3 snowmobiles at $3,000 each
	23	Purchased	7 snowmobiles at $2,600 each
	25	Sold	3 snowmobiles at $3,200 each

10. The cost of ending inventory using the periodic FIFO inventory alternative was

   a. $10,000.
   b. $12,000.
   c. $12,500.
   d. $13,000.

11. The cost of goods sold using the periodic LIFO inventory alternative was

    a. $38,000.

    b. $32,500.

    c. $36,700.

    d. $21,850.

12. The ending inventory using the average cost—periodic inventory alternative was

    a. $12,500.

    b. $10,000.

    c. $11,675.

    d. $12,125.

Use the following information to answer Questions 13 and 14.

Beginning Inventory	$20,000
Purchases	40,000
Purchases Returns	3,000
Purchase Discounts	4,000
Freight-In	?
Cost of Goods Available for Sale	55,000
Ending Inventory	?
Cost of Goods Sold	23,000

13. The amount of Freight-In must be

    a. $3,000.

    b. $4,000.

    c. $2,000.

    d. $1,000.

14. The amount of Ending Inventory must be

    a. $23,000.

    b. $32,000.

    c. $33,000.

    d. $22,000.

15. Which of the following accounts is not maintained throughout the period when the periodic inventory method is used?

    a. Purchases

    b. Cost of Goods Sold

    c. Purchase Discounts

    d. Purchase Returns

16. Which of the following is the correct calculation for cost of goods sold with the periodic inventory method?

    a. Beginning Inventory + Purchases + Ending Inventory

    b. Beginning Inventory + Purchases – Ending Inventory

    c. Ending Inventory + Purchases – Beginning Inventory

    d. Ending Inventory + Purchases + Beginning Inventory

17. Which of the following taxes is *not* a payroll tax expense of the employer?

    a. FICA taxes

    b. Federal unemployment tax

    c. State unemployment tax

    d. Federal withholding tax

Use the following information to answer Questions 18 and 19.
During the first week of January, Tamara McKeon had gross earnings of $100. FICA taxes are 7.65 percent of wages up to $20,000 for both employer and employee, state unemployment tax is 5.0 percent of wages up to $13,000, and federal unemployment tax is 0.8 percent of wages up to $13,000. Voluntary withholding is $10 (in addition to taxes); federal and state income taxes are $12 and $4, respectively.

18. What amount is the check, net of all deductions, that Tamara received for the week's pay?

    a. $60.55
    b. $65.55
    c. $66.35
    d. $77.85

19. What is the employer's payroll tax expense, assuming that Tamara McKeon is the only employee?

    a. $6.15
    b. $9.55
    c. $8.95
    d. $13.45

20. Accrued expenses for future sick days that will be taken are referred to as

    a. compensated absences.
    b. post-employment benefits.
    c. post-retirement benefits.
    d. current period salary expense.

21. Which of the following is true of defined contribution plans?

    a. Payments are made to retired employees on the basis of years worked.
    b. Payments are made to retired employees on the basis of ending salary.
    c. Payments are made to retired employees based on a fixed formula.
    d. Payments are made to employees depending on the earnings of funds set aside while the employees worked.

22. Extraordinary items are

    a. unusual types of events.
    b. infrequent types of events.
    c. separately classified on the income statement.
    d. All of the above

23. The earnings per share computation includes

    a. the gross margin amount.
    b. total revenues.
    c. net income.
    d. total expenses.

24. Which of the following is *not* an income statement account?

    a. Sales Revenue
    b. Salary Expense
    c. Purchase Discounts
    d. Accounts Receivable

25. The current ratio is calculated by dividing current assets by

    a. current liabilities.
    b. total liabilities.
    c. stockholder's equity.
    d. total assets.

26. Number of days' sales in inventory plus number of days' sales in receivables minus number of days' sales in accounts payable identifies
    a. the number of days the vendor is financing the operating cycle.
    b. the number of days the company is financing the operating cycle.
    c. the operating cycle turnover for the year.
    d. the amount of cash that must be paid during the next period.

Exercises

E5-1   Periodic Inventory Alternatives

During December 2000, Alpha Company (which sells air conditioners and uses a periodic inventory method) had the following inventory transactions and records.

Dec.	1	Beginning inventory	9 units at $400 each
	4	Purchased	6 units at $440 each
	11	Sold	10 units at $700 each
	18	Purchased	4 units at $500 each
	23	Sold	6 units at $800 each
	27	Purchased	2 units at $520 each

Instructions: Compute both the cost of goods sold and ending inventory balances, using the following alternatives.

1. Periodic FIFO inventory alternative
2. Periodic LIFO inventory alternative
3. Average-cost—periodic inventory alternative

E5-2   Closing Entries—The Periodic Inventory Method

Peterson Incorporated, which uses the periodic inventory method, has the following trial balance as of December 31, 2000.

Peterson Inc.
Trial Balance
December 31, 2000

	Debits	Credits
Cash	$ 3,000	
Accounts Receivable	3,500	
Inventory (1/1/00)	12,000	
Equipment	26,000	
Accounts Payable		$ 3,000
Notes Payable		9,200
Capital Stock		14,500
Retained Earnings (1/1/00)		6,300
Sales Revenue		68,000
Sales Discounts	2,100	
Purchases	31,000	
Purchase Discounts		1,000
Freight-In	900	
Salary Expense	9,800	
Rent Expense	7,500	
Income Tax Expense	3,400	
Miscellaneous Expenses	2,800	
Totals	$102,000	$102,000

Instructions: Given this trial balance and assuming ending inventory of $10,000:

1. Prepare closing entries for the revenue accounts.

2. Prepare closing entries for salary, rent, income tax, and miscellaneous expenses.

3. Prepare entries to adjust the inventory balance and to close the inventory-related nominal accounts.

4. Prepare a post-closing trial balance.

Part 4

Peterson Inc.

Post-Closing Trial Balance

December 31, 2000

		DEBIT	CREDIT

Parts 1 through 3

		JOURNAL			PAGE	
DATE		DESCRIPTION	POST. REF.	DEBIT	CREDIT	

E5-3   Preparing an Income Statement

The following information is available for GSM Foods, Inc. for the year ending December 31, 2000.

Income Tax Expense	$ 48,000
Property Tax Expense	4,550
Miscellaneous Office Expense	2,850
Gross Sales Revenue	973,500
Insurance Expense	1,900
Advertising Expense	7,500
Sales Salaries Expense	113,500
Delivery Expense	14,800
Sales Returns and Allowances	13,500
Beginning Inventory	120,000
Ending Inventory	145,000
Purchase Discounts	22,000
Office Salaries Expense	50,000
Purchases	700,000
Number of Shares of Stock Outstanding	10,000

Instructions: Prepare an income statement for GSM Foods, Inc. for the year ending December 31, 2000, using the form on page 71.

E5-4   Ratio Analysis

The following information is available for the Mill Meadow Company:

Total Quick Assets	$25,000
Total Current Assets	$40,000
Total Current Liabilities	$30,000
Total Days in Receivables	42
Total Days in Inventory	38
Cost of Goods Sold	$80,000
Average Accounts Payable	$16,000

Instructions: Based on this information, calculate the following:

1. Current ratio

2. Quick ratio

3. Number of days' sales in accounts payable

4. Number of days the company finances its operating cycle

GSM Foods, Inc.

Income Statement

For the Year Ended December 31, 2000

ANSWERS

Matching

1.	e	10.	d	19.	x
2.	l	11.	c	20.	w
3.	k	12.	b	21.	v
4.	j	13.	a	22.	u
5.	i	14.	n	23.	t
6.	h	15.	o	24.	s
7.	g	16.	q	25.	r
8.	f	17.	z	26.	p
9.	m	18.	y		

True/False

1.	T	10.	F	19.	T
2.	F	11.	F	20.	F
3.	F	12.	F	21.	F
4.	T	13.	F	22.	F
5.	T	14.	F	23.	T
6.	T	15.	T	24.	F
7.	F	16.	T	25.	T
8.	T	17.	T	26.	F
9.	T	18.	F		

Multiple Choice

1.	b	11.	c (7 units @ $2,600;	18.	c
2.	b		5 units @ $2,500;	19.	d
3.	b		3 units @ $2,000)	20.	a
4.	c	12.	c (5 units @ $2,335)	21.	d
5.	c (5 units @ $2,000)	13.	c	22.	d
6.	a	14.	b	23.	c
7.	d	15.	b	24.	d
8.	c	16.	b	25.	a
9.	d	17.	d	26.	b
10.	d (5 units @ $2,600)				

Exercises

E5-1   Periodic Inventory Alternatives

Units available	21
Units sold	16
Ending inventory	5

Cost of goods available for sale:

Beginning inventory, 9 units at $400 each	$3,600
December 4, purchase 6 units at $440 each	2,640
December 18, purchase 4 units at $500 each	2,000
December 27, purchase 2 units at $520 each	1,040
	$9,280

1. Periodic FIFO Inventory Alternative

   Ending inventory:

2 units at $520 each	$1,040
3 units at $500 each	1,500
	$2,540

Cost of goods available for sale	$9,280
Ending inventory	2,540
Cost of goods sold	$6,740

2. Periodic LIFO Inventory Alternative

Ending Inventory:

5 units at $400 each	$2,000

Cost of goods available for sale	$9,280
Ending inventory	2,000
Cost of goods sold	$7,280

3. Average-Cost—Periodic Inventory Alternative

Average cost:
$9,280 \div 21 = \$441.90$

5 units at $441.90	$2,209.50

Cost of goods available for sale	$9,280.00
Ending inventory	2,209.50
Cost of goods sold	$7,070.50

E5-2   Closing Entries—The Periodic Inventory Method

1. Sales Revenue	68,000	
Sales Discounts		2,100
Retained Earnings		65,900
To close revenue accounts.		
2. Retained Earnings	23,500	
Salary Expense		9,800
Rent Expense		7,500
Income Tax Expense		3,400
Miscellaneous Expenses		2,800
To close expense accounts (other than Cost of Goods Sold).		
3. Inventory	30,900	
Purchase Discounts	1,000	
Freight-In		900
Purchases		31,000
To close inventory-related accounts.		
Cost of Goods Sold	32,900	
Inventory		32,900
To establish ending inventory balance. ($12,000 beginning inventory + $30,900 net purchases – $10,000 ending inventory)		
Retained Earnings	32,900	
Cost of Goods Sold		32,900
To close Cost of Goods Sold to Retained Earnings.		

4.

Peterson Inc.
Post-Closing Trial Balance
December 31, 2000

	Debits	Credits
Cash	3,000	
Accounts Receivable	3,500	
Inventory	10,000	
Equipment	26,000	
Accounts Payable		3,000
Notes Payable		9,200
Capital Stock		14,500
Retained Earnings ($6,300 + $9,500)		15,800
Totals	42,500	42,500

E5-3   Preparing an Income Statement

GSM Foods, Inc.
Income Statement
For the Year Ended December 31, 2000

Gross sales revenue			$973,500
Less sales returns and allowances			(13,500)
Net sales revenue			$960,000
Cost of Goods Sold:			
Beginning inventory		$120,000	
Purchases	$700,000		
Less purchase discounts	(22,000)	678,000	
Cost of goods available for sale		$798,000	
Ending inventory		(145,000)	
Cost of goods sold			653,000
Gross margin			$307,000
Selling Expenses:			
Sales salaries expense	$113,500		
Delivery expense	14,800		
Advertising expense	7,500		
Total selling expenses		$135,800	
General and Administration Expenses:			
Office salaries expense	$ 50,000		
Insurance expense	1,900		
Property tax expense	4,550		
Miscellaneous office expense	2,850		
Total general and administrative expenses		59,300	
Total expenses			195,100
Income before taxes			$111,900
Income taxes			48,000
Net income			$ 63,900

Earnings per share:
$63,900 ÷ 10,000 = $6.39 per share

E5-4   Ratio Analysis

1. Current ratio: $40,000/$30,000 = 1.33
2. Quick ratio: $25,000/$30,000 = .83
3. Number of days' sales in accounts payable: 365/ ($80,000/$16,000) = 73 days
4. Number of days the company finances its operating cycle: 42 + 38 – 73 = 7 days

Chapter 6
Financing Activities

LEARNING OBJECTIVES

After studying this chapter, you should be able to:

1. Use present value concepts to measure long-term liabilities.

2. Account for long-term liabilities, including notes payable, mortgages payable, and lease obligations.

3. Account for bonds, including the original issuance, the payment of interest, and the retirement of bonds.

4. Distinguish between debt and equity financing and describe the advantages and disadvantages of organizing a business as a proprietorship or a partnership.

5. Describe the basic characteristics of a corporation and the nature of common and preferred stock.

6. Account for the issuance and repurchase of common and preferred stock.

7. Understand the factors that impact retained earnings, describe the factors determining whether a company can and should pay cash dividends, and account for cash dividends.

8. Compute the common ratios that are used to evaluate the capital structure of a company.

CHAPTER REVIEW

Measuring Long-Term Liabilities

1. Money borrowed for a period longer than one year is classified as a long-term liability on the balance sheet. Some common long-term liabilities are:

   Notes payable: Regular borrowing from a bank or other lending institution. Terms, payments, collateral, and other debt requirements are negotiated.

   Mortgage payable: Money borrowed to purchase a specific asset. (Usually the asset is pledged as collateral, and monthly or yearly payments are made.)

   Lease obligations: The present value of money owed on long-term rental of property or equipment. Since such assets are often leased for periods that approximate their useful life, leasing can be essentially equivalent to purchasing.

   Deferred income taxes payable: The delayed payment of taxes by using tax-planning devices. In theory, deferred taxes must be paid to the government sometime. By delaying payments, one is really "borrowing from the government" without interest.

   Pension liabilities: Liabilities for obligations to pay future retirement benefits to employees.

   Bonds payable: A long-term liability consisting of a periodic interest payment (an annuity) and a repayment of the principal (a lump sum).

2. Money has a time value. That is, since money can be invested and earn a return over time, current dollars are worth more than dollars received in the future.

3. Because money has a time value, its value today is equal to its future value minus the amount of interest that the money could earn. The value today of dollars to be received in the future is called present value.

4. An annuity is a series of equally spaced, equal-amount payments to be received or paid at the end of each period. Because of the time value of money, the dollars paid or received at the various intervals are not of equal value. Therefore, to find the value of an annuity, it is necessary to find the value of all payments on a common date. The present value of an annuity is its value today (when all payments are discounted back to today's value).

Accounting for Long-Term Liabilities

5. The most common long-term liability is notes payable. Long-term notes payable are obligations to pay money at future dates at least one year hence.

6. A mortgage payable is similar to a note payable, except that proceeds from a note payable can often be used for any business purpose; however, mortgage money is usually related to a specific asset. Assets purchased with a mortgage are usually pledged as security. Mortgages generally require monthly or periodic payments over the life of the mortgage. During the early years of a mortgage, a large percentage of each payment is interest; in later years, most of the payment reduces the mortgage payable account balance.

7. A lease must be capitalized if it meets the definition of a capital lease, which generally means that it is a long-term, noncancelable contract to rent property from a lessor. The amount of liability to be recorded in accounting for a capital lease is the present value of all future lease payments (discounted at the market rate of interest). The difference between the present value and the total cost paid on the lease is charged as interest expense over the lease's life.

The Nature of Bonds

8. Conceptually, the price of a bond is the present value of all future payments required to pay it off in full.

   a. If a long-term bond pays approximately the market rate of interest, its present value is approximately equivalent to the stated amount of the debt.

   b. If a long-term bond pays either no interest or an interest rate significantly lower than the current market rate, the present value is less than the stated amount of the bonds. In this case, the stated amount of the bonds plus the contractual interest rate are discounted to a lower present value, using the market rate of interest. The difference between this lower present value and the face value is called a discount.

   c. If a long-term bond pays interest at a higher rate than the effective (current market) rate, the present value of the bond is more than the stated face value of the bond after discounting the face value of the bonds and the interest payments, using the effective (current) rate of interest. The excess above the face value is called a premium.

Accounting for Bonds Payable

9. Bonds are issued at face value, at a discount, or at a premium. Premiums and discounts on bonds are amortized over the life of the bonds.

10. When bonds issued at face value are retired at maturity, a journal entry is required to close the Bonds Payable account with a cash payment to the bondholders for the face value of the bonds.

11. When bonds are retired before maturity, the typical entry to retire bonds on an interest date (assuming that the entry for the interest payments has been made) would be:

Bonds Payable................. xxx
Loss on Bond Retirement.   xx
    Cash............................   xxx

The loss (or gain on retirement) is reported on the income statement as an extraordinary loss (or gain).

Raising Equity Financing

12. When companies obtain money by borrowing from financial institutions or by issuing bonds, it is called debt financing. When companies raise money by selling stock, it is called equity financing. Debt financing results in liabilities on the balance sheet; equity financing transactions affect the stockholders' equity section of the balance sheet.

13. There are three different types of business organizations: (a) proprietorships, (b) partnerships, and (c) corporations. A proprietorship is an unincorporated business owned by one person. A partnership is an unincorporated busi-

ness owned by two or more persons or entities. A major disadvantage of proprietorships and partnerships is the unlimited liability of the owner or partners.

14. A corporation is an entity, distinct from its owners, that can conduct business, sue, and enter into contracts. Stockholders are held responsible for the debts and actions of a corporation only to the extent of their investment.

15. Corporations are given life (incorporated) by a state and have a continuity of existence.

16. Corporations differ from proprietorships and partnerships in the following ways.

    a. Shareholders have limited liability.
    b. Ownership interests are easily transferred.
    c. They have the ability to raise large amounts of capital.
    d. They are separately taxed.
    e. They are often closely monitored and regulated by various government agencies.

17. Owners of a corporation are called stockholders (or shareholders), and those who operate a corporation are called managers. (Managers do not necessarily have to be shareholders; they are often hired by shareholders because of their managerial expertise.) A board of directors is annually elected by the shareholders to monitor management and govern the corporation.

18. Because the stocks of large corporations are traded daily on stock exchanges, shareholders can increase or decrease their ownership interest in the firm by selling or buying shares of stock.

19. The two most typical types of stock are common and preferred. Common stock usually provides owners with voting rights (to elect directors and decide other matters), while preferred stock allows other privileges.

Accounting for Stock

20. Most stock has a par value, that is, a nominal value written on the face of each stock certificate. Although the par value does not relate to the issuance price of the stock (the price of most stocks is much higher than par value), it becomes the amount of legal capital of a business. This legal capital (number of shares outstanding times par value) is the minimum amount of owners' equity a company must maintain.

21. The entries to record the original issuance of stock are:

Par value stock:

Cash...............................	xxx	
Common (Preferred) Stock (par value × number of shares)		xxx
Paid-In Capital in Excess of Par (excess cash received)		xxx

No-par stock:

Cash (amount received) ...	xxx	
Common (Preferred) Stock		xxx

These entries show that proceeds received from the issuance of stock are divided into the amount attributable to par value and the excess.

22. Stock that has been repurchased by a company is known as treasury stock. This stock is usually recorded at cost and is not separated into par value and excess paid. The entry to record the repurchase of treasury stock is:

Treasury Stock (cost)	xxx	
Cash		xxx

The account Treasury Stock is a contra-stockholders' equity account. Treasury stock is treated like unissued stock in that it possesses no voting, dividend, or other rights.

23. When treasury stock is reissued, it is credited at cost, and any excess of cash received over cost is credited to an account entitled Paid-In Capital, Treasury Stock. If the stock is sold for an amount less than cost, the Paid-In Capital, Treasury Stock account is usually debited to the extent it exists, and excesses are debited to Retained Earnings.

24. The owners' equity section must show the different types of stock separately, the par value of the stocks, excess over par value, other paid-in capital sources, retained earnings, and treasury stock.

Retained Earnings

25. Retained Earnings is increased by earnings and decreased by losses and dividends.

26. The distribution of corporate profits to shareholders is accomplished by paying dividends. Dividends can be paid in cash, other property, or additional shares of company stock.

27. The following three dates are important regarding dividends.

    a. *Declaration date*—date the dividend is declared payable by the board of directors. (This is the date a dividend becomes a liability.)

b. *Record date*—date that identifies who will receive dividends.

c. *Payment date*—date dividends are actually paid.

The entries to account for cash dividends are shown below.

Declaration Date:

Dividends xxx
   Dividends Payable........   xxx

Record Date:
No entry.

Payment (Distribution) Date:

Dividends Payable............ xxx
   Cash.............................   xxx

28. The following types of dividend preferences can be associated with preferred stock.

a. *Current-dividend preference*—the right to receive current dividends before common shareholders.

b. *Cumulative-dividend preference*—the right to receive undistributed dividends from past years before the common shareholders receive any dividends for the current year.

The percentage usually associated with preferred stock indicates the amount of dividends preferred stockholders are to receive before common shareholders receive any dividends. This percentage multiplied by the number of outstanding shares at par value is their rightful share. The current-dividend preference allows this amount per year; the cumulative-dividend preference allows this amount for every year.

Using Financing Ratios to Evaluate Capital Structure

29. There are a number of stockholders' equity-related ratios that provide information about how an organization is financing its business and how obligated a company is by these financing decisions. The most common ratios are (a) the debt ratio, which is total liabilities divided by total assets; (b) the debt-equity ratio, which is total liabilities divided by total stockholders' equity; and (c) the dividend payout ratio, which is cash dividends divided by net income.

COMMON ERRORS

The most common errors and most difficult areas to understand in this chapter are:

1. The discounting of long-term liabilities.

2. The accounting for leases.

3. Miscalculating the issuance price of the bond.

4. Failure to adjust the number of shares of stock when completing comprehensive stockholders' equity problems.

5. Recognizing a gain on the reissuance of treasury stock.

1. **Discounting of Long-Term Liabilities**

It is sometimes very difficult to understand conceptually why long-term liabilities must often be discounted. To help you understand, think of liabilities this way. Suppose you were buying a new car. You went to one dealer and he offered you the car for $12,000, including a $2,000 down payment and 13 percent interest on the balance, to be paid over a period of 4 years. The second dealer advertised 4 percent interest, but upon visiting that dealership you found that the car could only be purchased for $14,000, including a $2,000 down payment and the balance at 4 percent over 4 years. The final dealer offered an even better deal—no interest on the unpaid balance. You couldn't believe it; however, when you visited that dealer, you found that he would only sell the car for $16,000. What is really happening? Probably all the dealers are charging approximately 13 percent interest, but the last two are hiding part or all of the interest in the purchase price.

Because of the potential for this kind of abuse, accounting rule makers have decided that for liabilities where there is either no interest or an unreasonably low interest rate, part of the liability is really interest. If they didn't impose this requirement, debt would often be disclosed without associated interest expense, and net income would be artificially high.

Because the calculations and entries required for discounted liabilities are difficult, it is very important that you read carefully the section of the chapter dealing with the measurement of liabilities.

2. **The Accounting for Leases**

The only exposure most of you have to leases is the apartment lease you sign for one year at a time. The term is short, and you will not have any financial interest in the apartment at the conclusion of the lease; you are merely renting under a fixed rental agreement. These rental-type leases differ from a lease where the lessee has the leased asset for most of its useful life or where it is purchased for a nominal amount at the end of the lease term. This latter kind of lease is very much like a purchase, and so it must be capitalized—recorded as both an asset and a liability. And, since this type of lease is similar to a "noninterest-bearing note," it is recorded at its discounted present value. Then as each lease payment is made, part of it is interest and part is a reduction of the lease liability. Similarly, since the leased asset is "owned," it must be depreciated (amortized) over the lease period. Don't let the term lease confuse you. Rather, think of a lease as either a rental agreement (noncapitalizable lease) or as a noninterest-bearing note payable (capitalized lease).

3. The Bond Issuance Price

The issuance price is often miscalculated because the wrong number of periods is used in computing the present value, because the cash interest payments used in the calculation are wrong, or because the interest rate used in discounting the principal and interest is incorrect.

a. Bonds usually are based on semiannual compounding. This means that a 10-year bond will have 20 interest payments. Therefore, as a general rule, the number of periods you use in determining a bond's present value will be double its life (a 5-year bond will have 10 periods, a 20-year bond will have 40 periods, and so on).

b. The cash interest payments are based on the stated (contract) rate of the interest, not on the effective rate. For example, if a $100,000 bond has a stated rate of 8 percent and an effective rate of 10 percent, the cash payments will be $8,000 per year (8% × $100,000), or $4,000 every 6 months. Do not use $10,000 (10% × $100,000), and be sure to remember that the interest is paid twice a year at half the stated rate times the face value of the bonds (for example, 4% × $100,000 = $4,000).

c. In computing the issuance price of a bond, the principal and the interest payments are discounted at the effective rate, not the stated (contract) rate. Since the compounding is semiannual, the principal and the interest must be discounted for the number of semiannual periods (see a.) at the 6-months' effective rate. Thus, a $100,000 10-year bond with a contract rate of 8 percent and an effective rate of 10 percent would be discounted for 20 periods at 5%.

To illustrate the correct computation of the issuance price of a bond, assume that $200,000 face value bonds with a 5-year life and a stated rate of 10 percent are issued on January 1, when the effective rate of interest is 12 percent.

To calculate the issuance price, you first determine the following facts:

a. The principal is $200,000.

b. The semiannual interest payments are $10,000 (5% × $200,000), payable January 1 and July 1.

c. The number of amortization periods is 10 (5 years × 2).

d. The discount rate is 6 percent (12% ÷ 2).

e. The present value factor to discount the principal of $200,000 is 0.5584 (see Table I on text page 475—6 percent for 10 periods). Note: Do not use the stated rate in determining the present value factor.

f. The present value factor to discount the interest payments of $10,000 is 7.3601 (see Table II—6 percent for 10 periods). Note: Do not use 5 percent or 5 periods.

Based on this information, the issuance price of the bonds would be computed as follows:

Discounting the principal:
$200,000 × 0.5584...................... $111,680
Discounting the interest payments:
$10,000 × 7.3601......................... 73,601
Issuance price (total present value) . $185,281

4. Adjusting the Number of Shares of Stock

A common type of homework problem in this chapter involves journalizing a series of stockholders' equity transactions and then preparing the stockholders' equity section of a balance sheet. Some journal entries involve issuing additional shares of either preferred or common stock, with a later entry involving the declaration of dividends. Since the dividends are usually declared and paid on a per-share basis, it is important to remember to update the number of shares of stock for each transaction.

The easiest way to eliminate this problem is to keep a running balance of the number of shares and the par values of preferred and common stock after each stockholders' equity transaction. This approach will also help you when you prepare the stockholders' equity section, because you will already know the correct numbers of shares of stock and par values, and you can check to see whether shares times par value equals the amount recorded in your stock accounts.

5. The Reissuance of Treasury Stock

You have just studied chapters on property, plant, and equipment and on long-term investments. In those chapters, when an asset was sold, any excess over book value was recognized as a gain. Now we tell you in this chapter that excess received over the cost of treasury stock is not a gain but additional paid-in capital. To avoid confusion over this apparent discrepancy, you should recognize that when a company reissues treasury stock, it is "selling" its own stock. When it sells an investment, it is selling stock or bonds of other corporations, and when it sells property, plant, and equipment, it is selling assets that have ready market values.

Companies cannot recognize gains when selling their own stock. If they could, they could easily manipulate earnings by buying their own stock and strategically selling it at a later date. And since companies have some control over their stock prices, gains could be recognized on nonindependent transactions—which violates the arm's-length transaction rule.

SELF-TEST

Matching

Instructions: Write the letter of each of the following terms in the space to the left of its appropriate definition.

a.	annuity	p.	issued stock
b.	term bonds	q.	common stock
c.	lessee	r.	current-dividend preference
d.	lessor	s.	legal capital
e.	note payable	t.	contributed capital
f.	present value	u.	stockholders
g.	market rate of interest	v.	preferred stock
h.	face value	w.	treasury stock
i.	stated rate of interest	x.	no-par stock
j.	callable bonds	y.	par value stock
k.	debentures	z.	prospectus
l.	convertible bonds	aa.	proprietorship
m.	serial bonds	bb.	partnership
n.	bond payable	cc.	unlimited liability
o.	cumulative-dividend preference		

_____   1.   An entity that agrees to make periodic rental payments for the use of leased property.

_____   2.   A debt owed to a creditor, evidenced by an unconditional written promise to pay a sum of money on or before a specified future date.

_____   3.   Bonds that all mature on one day.

_____   4.   A landlord or owner of leased property.

_____   5.   The value today of money to be received at some future date, given a specified interest rate.

_____   6.   A series of equal amounts to be received or paid at the ends of equal time intervals.

_____   7.   The nominal amount printed on the face of a bond.

_____   8.   A long-term debt, evidenced by an unconditional written promise to pay interest regularly plus a sum of money on a specified future date.

_____   9.   The actual rate of return earned or paid on a bond.

_____   10.   Bonds that mature in a series of installments.

_____   11.   Bonds that can be redeemed by the issuer over specified periods before maturity at a designated price.

_____   12.   Bonds that have no specific assets as security to guarantee payment.

_____   13.   The rate of interest specified on the bond indenture to be paid annually to a bondholder.

_____   14.   Bonds that can be converted to other securities, such as stocks, after a specified period, at the option of the bondholder.

_____   15.   The portion of owners' equity invested by owners through the issuance of stock.

_____   16.   The right of preferred shareholders to receive current dividends before common shareholders receive any dividends.

_____   17.   Stock that does not have a value assigned by the corporate charter and printed on the face of the stock certificate.

_____   18.   An unincorporated business owned by two or more persons or entities.

_____   19.   A class of stock most frequently issued by corporations; it usually confers a voting right in the corporation; its dividend and liquidation rights are usually inferior to those of preferred stock.

_____   20.   The owners of a corporation.

_____   21.   The right of preferred shareholders to receive dividends for all past years in which no dividends were paid before common shareholders receive any dividends.

_____   22.   Authorized stock originally issued to stockholders, which may or may not still be outstanding.

_____ 23. A class of stock issued by corporations, usually having dividend and liquidation preferences over common stock.

_____ 24. Issued stock that has subsequently been reacquired and not retired by the corporation.

_____ 25. Stock that has a nominal value assigned to it in the corporation's charter and printed on the face of each share of stock.

_____ 26. The amount of contributed capital not available for dividends as restricted by state law for the protection of creditors.

_____ 27. A report provided to potential investors that explains a company's business plan, sources of financing, and significant risks, and contains financial statements.

_____ 28. The absence of a ceiling on a proprietor's or partner's responsibility for the debts of the business.

_____ 29. An unincorporated business owned by one person.

True/False

Instructions: Place a check mark in the appropriate column to indicate whether each of the following statements is true or false.

	True	False
1. The issuance price of bonds is usually a function of the stability of the organization issuing the bonds and the stated interest rate on the bonds.	_____	_____
2. The present value of a long-term liability is usually greater than the stated amount of the liability.	_____	_____
3. A note payable is a written promise to pay a stated amount of money in the future.	_____	_____
4. During the early years of a mortgage, most of the mortgage payment goes toward reducing the principal mortgage balance.	_____	_____
5. A person or company leasing an asset from another company is called a lessor.	_____	_____
6. A lease that is essentially equivalent to a purchase must be recorded both as an asset and as a liability.	_____	_____
7. Interest expense on a lease is usually recognized on a straight-line basis.	_____	_____
8. All leases must be capitalized.	_____	_____
9. Coupon bonds and callable bonds are the same thing.	_____	_____
10. Because interest expense is tax deductible, the real cost of borrowing money by issuing bonds (in a profitable company) is less than the stated rate of interest.	_____	_____
11. The bond principal is the same as the face value of a bond.	_____	_____
12. The debt ratio and the debt-equity ratio both measure the relative quantities of debt and equity in a firm's capital structure.	_____	_____
13. A corporation is a legal entity that is separate and distinct from its owners.	_____	_____
14. A disadvantage of a corporation is its unlimited liability.	_____	_____
15. The owners of a corporation are called shareholders, or stockholders.	_____	_____
16. Corporate income is not taxed separately from the income of the owners.	_____	_____
17. Stock that has been issued and bought back by a corporation is called outstanding stock.	_____	_____
18. Under the cumulative-dividend preference, preferred shareholders share any excess dividends equally with common shareholders.	_____	_____
19. When no-par common stock is sold, Common Stock is credited for the total proceeds of the sale.	_____	_____
20. Treasury stock should be classified as an asset.	_____	_____
21. When treasury stock is purchased, it is recorded at cost.	_____	_____
22. The account Retained Earnings is never credited when accounting for treasury stock.	_____	_____

	True	False
23. Dividends are the distribution of profits to shareholders.	_____	_____
24. The date that identifies who will receive a dividend is known as the declaration date.	_____	_____

Multiple Choice

Instructions: Circle the letter that best completes each of the following statements.

1. Which of the following is a characteristic of a mortgage payable?

   a. The liability is usually secured with some kind of collateral.
   b. The liability usually requires regular periodic repayments.
   c. The liability is usually evidenced by a mortgage document.
   d. All of the above

2. The balances in the Leased Asset and Lease Liability accounts will be equal

   a. throughout the life of the lease.
   b. never.
   c. at the inception of the lease.
   d. at the end of each year during the lease term.

3. An investor who thought a company would be extremely profitable in the future and that the company's stock price would increase significantly would be most interested in which of the following?

   a. Secured bonds
   b. Serial bonds
   c. Callable bonds
   d. Convertible bonds

4. Bonds payable must be discounted to their present value for balance sheet presentation when

   a. they are issued between interest dates at par.
   b. the bonds' stated rate of interest equals the market rate of interest.
   c. the bonds' stated rate of interest is less than the market rate of interest.
   d. Both *b* and *c*

5. If the market rate of interest is 12 percent and a company issues 10 percent long-term bonds, what interest rate would be used in the tables to discount the bonds (assuming semiannual compounding)?

   a. 6 percent
   b. 5 percent
   c. 10 percent
   d. 12 percent

6. The effective interest rate will be lower than the stated interest rate

   a. if bonds are sold at a premium.
   b. if bonds are sold at a discount.
   c. if bonds are sold at par.
   d. at no time.

7. The effective rate of interest on bonds would be higher than the stated rate if

   a. bonds sold at par.
   b. bonds sold at a premium.
   c. bonds sold at a discount.
   d. bonds sold at face value.

8. Assume the market interest rate of 12 percent. Bonds that have a stated interest rate of 10 percent will probably be issued at

   a. a discount.
   b. par.
   c. a premium.
   d. face value.

9. Which of the following would differ most between a partnership and a corporation?

   a. Asset section of a balance sheet
   b. Expense section of an income statement
   c. Liability section of a balance sheet
   d. Owners' equity section of a balance sheet

10. Which of the following is *not* a feature of a corporation?

    a. Limited liability
    b. Easy transferability of ownership interests
    c. Separate taxation
    d. Unlimited liability

11. Stock that has been issued but not repurchased is called

    a. issued and outstanding stock.
    b. treasury stock.
    c. authorized but unissued stock.
    d. issued but not outstanding stock.

12. Excess paid-in capital would never be associated with

    a. no-par stock.
    b. par value stock.
    c. treasury stock.
    d. All of the above

13. Contributed capital that cannot be impaired is called

    a. paid-in capital.
    b. legal capital.
    c. stated capital.
    d. retained earnings.

14. The entry for the issuance of common stock at par includes a

    a. credit to Cash.
    b. debit to Common Stock.
    c. credit to Common Stock.
    d. credit to Paid-In Capital.

15. Mammoth Company has 2,000 shares of $10 par value common stock outstanding. If it purchased 100 shares of its stock at $15, the entry would include a debit to Treasury Stock of

    a. $1,500.
    b. $1,000.
    c. Neither *a* nor *b*
    d. Either *a* or *b*

16. Treasury stock is

    a. an asset.
    b. a liability.
    c. a contra-stockholders' equity account.
    d. a revenue.

17. The account Paid-In Capital, Treasury Stock is credited when

    a. treasury stock is purchased at a price above par.
    b. treasury stock is sold at a price above cost.
    c. treasury stock is sold at a price below cost.
    d. treasury stock is purchased at a price below par.

18. The declaration and payment of a cash dividend

    a. increases Retained Earnings.
    b. decreases Retained Earnings.
    c. increases Contributed Capital.
    d. increases Cash.

19. The board of directors of a corporation first announces a dividend on the

    a. date of record.
    b. declaration date.
    c. payment date.
    d. dividend date.

20. The right of preferred shareholders to receive undistributed dividends from past years is called the

    a. current-dividend preference.
    b. cumulative-dividend preference.
    c. past year's preference.
    d. liquidation right.

21. Which of the following ratios are used to assess the capital structure of a firm?

    a. Current ratio
    b. Price-earnings ratio
    c. Debt-equity ratio
    d. All of the above

Exercises

E6-1   Notes Payable

On December 15, 2000, Audubon Company borrowed $21,000 for 60 days from Second National City Bank at 12 percent interest. Assume that Audubon's accounting period ends on December 31.

Instructions: Make the necessary journal entries to account for the note on the following dates (use a 365-day year):
    1. December 15, 2000
    2. December 31, 2000
    3. February 13, 2001 (payment date).

	JOURNAL			PAGE	
DATE	DESCRIPTION	POST. REF.	DEBIT	CREDIT	

E6-2   Mortgages Payable

Assume that a company signs a mortgage agreement to borrow $150,000 to build an addition to its research lab. The company pledges the lab as collateral for the loan. The mortgage is for 20 years at 12 percent and the annual payment is $20,081.93, (150,000/7.4694 (Table II) = 20,081.93).

Instructions: Prepare the entries to record the acquisition of the mortgage and the first annual payment.

	JOURNAL			PAGE	
DATE	DESCRIPTION	POST. REF.	DEBIT	CREDIT	

E6-3   Lease Accounting

Ledbetter Company leased a computer for 10 years from Diamond Corporation. The fair market value of the computer is $94,528, which is equal to the present value of the lease payments. The annual lease payment is $17,000.

Instructions: 1. Record the lease, assuming that it should be capitalized.
2. Record the annual payment of the lease and interest expense (assuming 12 percent interest) and the amortization (depreciation) expense, using the straight-line method of amortization.
3. Record the annual lease payment, assuming that the lease does not need to be capitalized.

JOURNAL   PAGE

DATE	DESCRIPTION	POST. REF.	DEBIT	CREDIT

E6-4 Issuance of Stock

Embarcadero Company was organized in 2000. During the first year of operations, it had the following stock transactions.

1. Issued 15,000 shares of $10 par value common stock to investors at $11.25 per share.
2. Issued 6,000 shares of $5 par value preferred stock to investors for $23 per share.
3. Issued 1,500 shares of no-par common stock for $8 per share.
4. Traded 4,000 shares of $5 par value preferred stock for a building. The market value of the building was $100,000.

Instructions: Prepare journal entries to record these transactions.

JOURNAL   **PAGE**

DATE	DESCRIPTION	POST. REF.	DEBIT	CREDIT

E6-5   Treasury Stock Transactions

Little John Company has 250,000 shares of $10 par value company stock outstanding. During 2000, the company had the following transactions.

1. January 15: Purchased 6,000 shares of its own stock at $20 per share.

2. February 2: Sold 1,500 shares of stock purchased in item 1 for $22 per share.

3. November 15: Sold 2,000 shares of stock purchased in item 1 for $18 per share.

Instructions: Prepare journal entries to record these transactions.

	JOURNAL			PAGE	
DATE	DESCRIPTION	POST. REF.	DEBIT	CREDIT	

E6-6   Analysis of Stockholders' Equity

The stockholders' equity section of Green Bay Corporation at the end of 2000 showed the following.

Preferred stock (8%, $20 par, 15,000 shares
   authorized, 9,000 shares issued and outstanding).................. $ X

Common stock ($10 par value, 90,000 shares authorized,
   60,000 issued, including 1,000 shares of treasury stock)....... 600,000

Common stock (no-par, 9,000 shares authorized,
   8,000 shares issued)... 72,000

Paid-in capital in excess of par value, preferred stock.............. X

Paid-in capital in excess of par value, common stock 120,000

    Total contributed capital .... $ X

Retained earnings.. 720,000

Less cost of treasury stock.. (10,000)

    Total stockholders' equity .... $ X

Instructions: 1. What is the dollar amount in the Preferred Stock account?

2. What is the average price for which the $10 par value common stock was issued?

3. If the preferred stock was issued at an average price of $22 per share, what amount should appear in the Paid-In Capital in Excess of Par Value, Preferred Stock account?

4. What is the average cost per share of treasury stock?

5. Assuming that the $10 par value common stock and preferred stock were sold for average prices of $12 and $22, respectively, what is the total amount of contributed capital (including no-par common stock)?

6. Given the assumption in item 5, what is the total amount of stockholders' equity?

E6-7   Dividend Transactions

Ghiardelli Company had 20,000 shares of $10 par value common stock outstanding on January 1, 2000. The following dividend transactions occurred during the year.

Jan. 15:   Declared a $0.50-per-share cash dividend, payable on March 15 to shareholders of record on February 15.
Feb. 15:   Date of record.
Mar. 15:   Payment of cash dividend.

Instructions: Record the above transactions.

JOURNAL   **PAGE**

DATE	DESCRIPTION	POST. REF.	DEBIT	CREDIT

E6-8   Dividend Calculations

White Plains Corporation has the following stock outstanding:

   a. Common stock ($10 par, 10,000 shares outstanding)

   b. Preferred stock (6%, $5 par, 10,000 shares outstanding)

During the years 1998–2001, White Plains Corporation had net income of $20,000, $18,000, $5,000, and $30,000, respectively. The company has a policy of paying 50 percent of its income to shareholders as dividends, and no dividends are in arrears as of January 1, 1998.

Instructions: Compute the total amount of dividends that common and preferred shareholders would receive in each of the four years, assuming the following:
      1. The preferred stock is noncumulative.
      2. The preferred stock is cumulative.

ANSWERS

Matching

1.	c	11.	j	21.	o
2.	e	12.	k	22.	p
3.	b	13.	i	23.	v
4.	d	14.	l	24.	w
5.	f	15.	t	25.	y
6.	a	16.	r	26.	s
7.	h	17.	x	27.	z
8.	n	18.	bb	28.	cc
9.	g	19.	q	29.	aa
10.	m	20.	u		

True/False

1.	T	9.	F	17.	F
2.	F	10.	T	18.	F
3.	T	11.	T	19.	T
4.	F	12.	T	20.	F
5.	F	13.	T	21.	T
6.	T	14.	F	22.	T
7.	F	15.	T	23.	T
8.	F	16.	F	24.	F

Multiple Choice

1.	d	8.	a	15.	a
2.	c	9.	d	16.	c
3.	d	10.	d	17.	b
4.	c	11.	a	18.	b
5.	a	12.	a	19.	b
6.	a	13.	b	20.	b
7.	c	14.	c	21.	c

Exercises

E6-1   Notes Payable

1. Dec. 15, 2000   Cash 21,000

    Notes Payable 21,000

    Borrowed $21,000 from Second National City Bank.

2. Dec. 31, 2000   Interest Expense 110

    Interest Payable 110

    *To record the interest expense on note to Second National
    City Bank for 16 days ($21,000 × 0.12 16/365 = $110).*

3. Feb. 13, 2001   Interest Expense 304
   (payment date)   Interest Payable 110

    Note Payable 21,000

    Cash 21,414

    *Paid $21,000 note to Second National City Bank
    ($21,000 × 0.12 × 60/365 = $414; $414 – $110 = $304).*

E6-2   Mortgages Payable

Acquisition of Mortgage:

Cash	150,000	
Mortgage Payable		150,000

Borrowed $150,000 to build an addition to the research lab.

First Annual Payment:

Mortgage Payable	2,081.93	
Interest Expense...	18,000.00	
Cash		20,081.93

*To make the first annual mortgage payment on the addition
to the research lab.($150,000 × 0.12 = $18,000)*

E6-3   Lease Accounting

1.
Leased Computer	94,528	
Lease Liability..		94,528

   To record 10-year lease of a computer (discounted at 12%).

2.
Lease Liability..	5,657	
Interest Expense	11,343	
Cash..		17,000

   Paid for first year of lease of computer
   ($94,528 × 0.12 = $11,343; $17,000 – $11,343 = $5,657).

Amortization (Depreciation) Expense......................................	9,453	
Accumulated Amortization (Depreciation)—Leased Computer		9,453

   To record amortization on leased computer for the first year
   ($94,528/10 = $9,453).

3.
Rent Expense..	17,000	
Cash..		17,000

   To record annual lease expense on computer.

E6-4   Issuance of Stock

1.
Cash...	168,750	
Common Stock..		150,000
Paid-In Capital in Excess of Par Value, Common Stock...........................		18,750

   Issued 15,000 shares of $10 par value common stock at $11.25.

2.
Cash...	138,000	
Preferred Stock..		30,000
Paid-In Capital in Excess of Par Value, Preferred Stock		108,000

   Issued 6,000 shares of $5 par value preferred stock at $23.

3.
Cash...	12,000	
Common Stock..		12,000

   Issued 1,500 shares of no-par common stock at $8.

4.
Building..	100,000	
Preferred Stock..		20,000
Paid-In Capital in Excess of Par Value, Preferred Stock........................		80,000

   Issued 4,000 shares of $5 par value preferred stock for a building.

E6-5   Treasury Stock Transactions

1. January 15

Treasury Stock	120,000	
Cash		120,000

Purchased 6,000 shares of treasury stock at $20 per share.

2. February 2

Cash...	33,000	
Treasury Stock		30,000
Paid-In Capital, Treasury Stock		3,000

Resold 1,500 shares of treasury stock at $22 per share.

3. November 15

Cash...	36,000	
Paid-In Capital, Treasury Stock	3,000	
Retained Earnings	1,000	
Treasury Stock		40,000

Resold 2,000 shares of treasury stock at $18 per share.

E6-6   Analysis of Stockholders' Equity

1. $180,000 (9,000 shares × $20).
2. $12 per share [($600,000 + $120,000)/60,000 shares].
3. $18,000 [$180,000 + X)/9,000 shares = $22].
4. $10 per share ($10,000/1,000 shares).
5. $990,000 ($180,000 + $600,000 + $72,000 + $18,000 + $120,000).
6. $1,700,000 ($990,000 + $720,000 − $10,000).

E6-7   Dividend Transactions

January 15

Dividends	10,000	
Dividends Payable..		10,000

Declared $0.50-per-share dividend on 20,000 shares.

February 15   No entry

March 15

Dividends Payable...	10,000	
Cash..		10,000

Paid $0.50-per-share cash dividend.

E6-8   Dividend Calculations

1. Preferred Stock—Noncumulative

Year	Common	Preferred	Total
1998	$ 7,000	$3,000	$10,000
1999	6,000	3,000	9,000
2000	—	2,500	2,500
2001	12,000	3,000	15,000

2. Preferred Stock—Cumulative

Year	Common	Preferred	Total
1998	$ 7,000	$3,000	$10,000
1999	6,000	3,000	9,000
2000	—	2,500	2,500
2001	11,500	3,500	15,000

Note: In this case, preferred stockholders get 6 percent every year, and since only $2,500 was paid in 2000, the $500 deficiency must be made up in 2001.

Chapter 7
Investing Activities

LEARNING OBJECTIVES

After studying this chapter, you should be able to:

1. Identify the two major categories of long-term operating assets: property, plant, and equipment and intangible assets.

2. Understand the factors important in deciding whether to acquire a long-term operating asset.

3. Record the acquisition of property, plant, and equipment through a simple purchase and as part of the purchase of several assets at once.

4. Compute straight-line and units-of-production depreciation expense for plant and equipment.

5. Record the discarding and selling of property, plant, and equipment.

6. Account for the acquisition and amortization of intangible assets and understand the special difficulties associated with accounting for intangibles.

7. Understand why companies invest in other companies.

8. Understand the different classifications for securities.

9. Account for the purchase, recognition of revenue, and sale of trading and available-for-sale securities.

10. Account for changes in the value of securities.

CHAPTER REVIEW

Nature of Long-Term Operating Assets

1. Property, plant, and equipment and intangible assets are assets that are used in the business, are not held for sale, and benefit several periods. Property, plant, and equipment are tangible assets; intangible assets have no physical existence.

2. The major elements in accounting for property, plant, and equipment are:

   a. Accounting for its acquisition.
   b. Accounting for the allocation of its cost over its useful life.
   c. Accounting for expenditures (post-acquisition costs) that either increase its capacity or lengthen its life.
   d. Accounting for its disposal.

Deciding Whether to Acquire a Long-Term Operating Asset

3. Long-term assets such as property, plant, and equipment should only be purchased if they will generate sufficient future cash flows to make the investment profitable.

4. It is difficult to accurately assess how much the future cash flows of an asset will be. When making asset acquisition decisions, future cash flows must be discounted to their present values.

Accounting for Acquisition of Property, Plant, and Equipment

5. Long-term operating assets are originally recorded at cost. When cash is paid for the assets,

the cost is the cash given up. When two or more long-term assets are purchased for a lump sum (known as a basket purchase), cost is apportioned by using the relative fair market value method.

6. The relative fair market value method apportions a lump-sum amount for two or more assets to the individual assets on the basis of their market values. For example, if $200,000 was paid for land and a building with fair market values of $80,000 and $160,000, respectively, the cost would be apportioned as shown below.

Assets	Fair Market Values	Percentage of Total Value	Cost
Land	$ 80,000	1/3*	1/3 x $200,000 = $ 66,667
Building	160,000	2/3**	2/3 x $200,000 = 133,333
Total	$240,000		$200,000

$$* \frac{\$80,000}{\$240,000} \qquad ** \frac{\$160,000}{\$240,000}$$

Calculating and Recording Depreciation Expense

7. Assets become expenses when they are used up or when they are deemed to have no future value. Since plant and equipment assets benefit many periods, their costs are apportioned over their useful lives.   This apportioning of the costs of assets is called depreciation for plant and equipment, depletion for natural resources, and amortization for intangible assets. Property (land) is usually not depreciated.

8. The two methods of depreciating property, plant, and equipment that were discussed in the chapter are: (1) the straight-line method, which charges an equal percentage of the cost to each period benefited; and (2) the units-of-production method, which uses some measure of output to apportion the costs.

9. The salvage or residual value of an asset is an estimated amount for which the asset can be sold at the end of its useful life.

10. The formula for straight-line depreciation is:

$$\frac{\text{cost - salvage value}}{\text{estimated useful life of asset (years)}}$$

11. The formula for the units-of-production method of depreciation is:

$$\frac{\text{cost - salvage value}}{\text{total estimated life (units)}} \times \frac{\text{number of units}}{\text{produced during year}}$$

12. As an example of the two depreciation methods, we will assume that on January 1, 2000,

TIP Corporation purchased a truck for $65,000. The truck's estimated useful life is 5 years, and its salvage value is $5,000. The truck will be driven 100,000 miles over its life (14,000 miles in the first year, 26,000 miles in the second, 28,000 miles in the third, 12,000 in the fourth, and 20,000 miles in the fifth). The depreciation for the truck would be calculated as shown below.

COMPARISON OF DEPRECIATION METHODS

Year	Straight-Line	Units-of-Production
Basis for formula	5 years	Total units (100,000 miles)
2000	$12,000	$8,400
	$\dfrac{\$60,000\,*}{5}$	$\dfrac{\$60,000\,*}{100,000} \times 14,000$
2001	$12,000	$15,600
		$\dfrac{\$60,000\,*}{100,000} \times 14,000$

Year	Straight-Line	Units-of-Production
2002	$12,000	$16,800
		$\dfrac{\$60,000\,*}{100,000} \times 28,000$
2003	$12,000	$7,200
		$\dfrac{\$60,000\,*}{100,000} \times 12,000$
2004	$12,000	$12,000
		$\dfrac{\$60,000\,*}{100,000} \times 20,000$

*($65,000 – $5,000)

13. The entry to record depreciation expense for the year involves a debit to Depreciation Expense and a credit to a contra-asset account called Accumulated Depreciation. The difference between the cost of an asset and its accumulated depreciation is called the book value of the asset.

14. When a long-term operating asset is purchased during a year, depreciation is taken for a partial year only. The amount of depreciation is usually calculated as a percentage of the year; that is, if an asset is purchased on April 1, nine-twelfths of a full year's depreciation is taken, no matter which depreciation method is used.

15. Long-term operating assets, such as oil wells, timber tracts, and coal mines, are referred to as natural resources, and the process of writing off the costs of such assets is called depletion. Depletion is usually computed on a basis similar to the units-of-production method. That is, a

portion of the cost is depleted as each ton, pound, gallon, and so forth is extracted. The formula for computing depletion is:

cost number of tons, pounds, gallons	=	depletion per ton, pound, gallon	×	number of tons, pounds, gallons extracted in current year	=	current year's depletion expense

16. Just as a contra account (Accumulated Depreciation) is maintained for property, plant, and equipment, there may also be a contra account for natural resources. If used, the contra account is called Accumulated Depletion.

Disposal of Property, Plant, and Equipment

17. Long-term operating assets can be disposed of in three ways: (1) they can be discarded or scrapped, (2) they can be sold, or (3) they can be traded for new assets. When an asset is scrapped before it has been fully depreciated and no cash is involved, a loss is recognized. When the net sales price of an asset being sold is less than the asset's book value, a loss is recognized; if the net price is more than book value, a gain is recognized.

18. When an asset is disposed of, the entry always involves a debit to Accumulated Depreciation and a credit to the asset account. The other accounts (gain or loss and cash received) depend on the amount at which the asset is sold. The different types of entries are summarized below.

Cash (if received).................................	xxx	
Loss on Disposal (if net sales price is less than book value).............	xxx	
Accumulated Depreciation	xxx	
Asset		xxx (cost)
Gain on Disposal (if net sales price is more than book value)......		xxx

Accounting for Intangible Assets

19. Intangible assets are assets that have no physical substance. Common examples are patents, franchises, licenses, trademarks, and goodwill. The process of writing off the cost of intangible assets over their useful or legal lives is called amortization. Most assets are amortized on a straight-line basis.

Why Companies Invest in Other Companies

20. Firms often invest in other companies to earn a return through either interest/dividends or through increases in the value of the invest-

ment. Firms also invest in other companies to diversify their operations.

Classifying a Security

21. Firms can invest in both equity and debt securities. Debt securities are instruments issued by a company that carry a promise of repayment of interest and principal. Equity securities represent actual ownership in a corporation.

22. Investments in other companies are classified in four categories: (a) held-to-maturity, (b) equity method, (c) trading, and (d) available-for-sale.

Held-to-maturity—Debt securities that are purchased with the intent of being held until maturity of the instrument. These investments are reported at amortized cost, and changes in fair value are not recorded on the financial statements.

Equity Method—Equity securities that represent ownership of 20 to 50 percent of the total stock outstanding of the investee. Equity method investments are recorded at cost, and adjusted for changes in the investee's net assets. Changes in fair value of the investment are not recorded on the financial statements.

Trading securities—Debt and equity securities purchased with the intent of being resold in the short run. Trading securities are recorded at fair value and the change in value is reported on the income statement.

Available-for-sale—Debt and equity securities not classified as any of the above. These securities are recorded at fair value, but the change in value is not reported on the income statement; rather it is reported directly to equity.

Accounting for Trading and Available-for-Sale Securities

23. All investments, regardless of their classification, are initially recorded at their cost. This cost includes the price of the security plus any additional related expenditures. The most common additional expenditure is broker's fees.

24. As noted, both trading securities and available-for-sale securities are reported at fair value. Therefore the accounting treatment is similar for these two categories.

25. The amount of cash received by an investor is recorded as dividend or revenue income on the income statement.

26. Gains or losses resulting from the sale of an investment are recorded as income on the income statement. A gain or loss is the difference between the book value of the investment and the proceeds of the sale. For example, if Company A sells equity securities for $10,000 and the value of the securities on the accounting records is $9,000, the recorded gain on the sale would be $1,000.

Accounting for Changes in the Value of Securities

27. The changes in value of a trading security are recorded as income even though the security has not been sold. For example, a trading security purchased at $1,000 is now worth $1,200. This increase in value of the trading security would be recorded as follows.

Market-Adjustment—
Trading Securities 200
   Unrealized Gain on Trading
     Securities—Income 200

The market adjustment account is an asset account if it has a debit balance or a contra-asset account if it has a credit balance.

28. Changes in value of available-for-sale securities are not recorded as income but are rather an adjustment made directly to equity.

29. The market adjustment account is a balance sheet account. Therefore, if the value changes again, the account is adjusted to the new balance. For example, if the securities in item 27 were subsequently worth $900, the needed adjustment would be $300 since the balance in

the market adjustment account is now $200 debit and it should have a $100 credit balance. The entry would be as follows:

Unrealized Loss on Trading
Securities—Income 300
   Market-Adjustment—
     Trading Securities 300

COMMON ERRORS

The most common errors made by students in trying to learn the material in this chapter involve:

1. Depreciation expense calculations.

2. Trading and Available-for-Sale Securities.

1. Calculating Depreciation Expense

The most common error made in calculating depreciation expense is taking a full year of depreciation in the year of acquisition when the asset was used for only part of a year. It is extremely important that you note the date of acquisition before you do anything else.

2. Trading and Available-for-Sale Securities

In accounting for trading and available-for-sale securities, the most common errors made relate to adjusting securities to their market values. For trading and available-for-sale securities, securities are adjusted to their fair values using a market adjustment account. The difference between the two types of securities relates to the offset to the market adjustment account. For trading securities, the offset goes through the income statement. For available-for-sale securities, the offset to market adjustment is to a stockholders' equity account.

SELF-TEST

Matching

Instructions: Write the letter of each of the following terms in the space to the left of its appropriate definition.

a.   depletion
b.   goodwill
c.   franchise
d.   intangible asset
e.   salvage value
f.   amortization

g.   property, plant, and equipment
h.   book value
i.   straight-line depreciation method
j.   units-of-production depreciation method
k.   patent

_____   1.   The process of cost allocation that assigns the original cost of a natural resource to the periods benefited.

_____   2.   An exclusive right granted for 17 years by the federal government to manufacture and sell an invention.

_____   3.   Tangible, long-lived assets acquired for use in the operation of a business and not intended for resale.

_____   4.   An intangible asset showing that a business is worth more than the value of its net assets; equal to the excess of the cost over the fair market value of the net assets purchased.

_____   5.   The process of cost allocation that assigns the original cost of an intangible asset to the periods benefited.

_____   6.   A long-lived asset that does not have physical substance and is not held for resale.

_____   7.   A depreciation method in which the cost of an asset is allocated to each period on the basis of its productive output during the period.

_____   8.   The net amount shown in the accounts for an asset, a liability, or an owners' equity item.

_____   9.   An exclusive right to sell a product or offer a service in a certain geographical area.

_____   10.   A depreciation method in which the cost of an asset is allocated equally over the periods of its estimated useful life.

_____   11.   The estimated value or actual price of an asset at the conclusion of its useful life, net of disposal costs.

True/False

Instructions: Place a check mark in the appropriate column to indicate whether each of the following statements is true or false.

	True	False
1. Long-term operating assets are assets held for resale.	_____	_____
2. Land is usually considered to be an intangible asset.	_____	_____
3. The relative fair market value method is usually used to allocate the cost of two or more assets when they are purchased for a lump-sum payment.	_____	_____
4. The residual value of an asset is usually the same as the book value of an asset.	_____	_____
5. Generally accepted accounting principles allow for the expensing of the cost of an asset over a period that is generally shorter than the asset's useful life.	_____	_____
6. When an asset is sold for an amount less than its book value, a gain on the sale is realized.	_____	_____
7. Accumulated Depreciation is debited when an asset is sold.	_____	_____
8. The process of writing off the cost of an intangible asset is referred to as depletion accounting.	_____	_____
9. In accounting for an investment as a trading or available-for-sale security, the entry to record the receipt of dividends includes a credit to the Investment account.	_____	_____

	True	False
10. Trading securities are not recorded at fair value.	_____	_____
11. When investments in debt securities are sold before maturity at amounts greater than their carrying value, a gain is realized.	_____	_____
12. Securities that are held with the intent of selling them should the need for cash arise are properly classified as available-for-sale securities.	_____	_____
13. The account Market Adjustment—Trading Securities is disclosed on the balance sheet.	_____	_____
14. Held-to-maturity securities can include both debt and equity investments.	_____	_____
15. All investments in debt and equity securities are valued at their market value.	_____	_____
16. Unrealized gains and losses result from changes in the price of securities while the security is still being held.	_____	_____

Multiple Choice

Instructions: Circle the letter that best completes each of the following statements.

1. Which of the following does *not* apply to intangible assets?

   a. They are capitalized—recorded as assets rather than expenses.
   b. Their cost is amortized over their lives.
   c. They can suffer an impairment of value.
   d. Their cost is depreciated over their lives.

2. If land and a building with respective market values of $20,000 and $30,000 were purchased for a lump-sum payment of $60,000, the land should be recorded at

   a. $20,000.
   b. $24,000.
   c. $30,000.
   d. $36,000.

3. The cost of an asset less its accumulated depreciation is called its

   a. book value.
   b. residual value.
   c. salvage value.
   d. either *b* or *c*.

4. The entry to record the depreciation expense on a piece of equipment for a year includes a

   a. debit to Accumulated Depreciation.
   b. credit to Equipment.
   c. credit to Depreciation Expense.
   d. debit to Depreciation Expense.

5. The first-year straight-line depreciation expense on an asset with a cost of $42,000, a residual value of $6,000, and a life of 6 years is

   a. $7,000.
   b. $6,000.
   c. $5,000.
   d. $10,000.

6. A truck was purchased for $50,000, is expected to have no salvage value, and has an estimated useful life of 75,000 miles. If the truck was driven 18,000 miles in a year, the units-of-production annual depreciation expense would be

   a. $18,000.
   b. $15,000.
   c. $12,000.
   d. $9,000.

7. The entry to record the sale of equipment would probably include a

   a. credit to Cash.
   b. debit to Accumulated Depreciation.
   c. debit to Equipment.
   d. credit to Accumulated Depreciation.

8. Which of the following intangible assets is most often amortized over a 40-year period?

   a. A patent
   b. A license
   c. A franchise
   d. Goodwill

9. When an investment in stock is considered available-for-sale, the entry to record the receipt of a dividend includes a

   a. credit to Dividend Revenue.
   b. credit to Investment in Stock.
   c. credit to Cash.
   d. debit to Investment in Stock.

10. The account Market Adjustment is credited when which of the following types of investments is reduced to market value?

    a. Held-to-maturity securities
    b. Investments in stocks accounted for on the equity basis
    c. Trading securities
    d. None of the above

11. Which of the following is a stockholders' equity account?

    a. Unrealized Decrease in Value of Available-For-Sale Securities
    b. Market Adjustment—Available-For-Sale Securities
    c. Unrealized Loss on Trading Securities
    d. Realized Gain on Sale of Securities

12. Available-for-sale securities are securities that are

    a. purchased with the intent of selling them should the need for cash arise.
    b. purchased with the intent of holding them until they mature.
    c. purchased with the intent of taking advantage of short-term increases in price.
    d. not classified as trading, held-to-maturity, or equity method securities.

13. The account Market Adjustment—Trading Securities is

    a. a stockholders' equity account.
    b. a nominal account that contains the current period's increase or decrease in value of trading securities.
    c. an account that adjusts trading securities from cost to market.
    d. a balance sheet account that tracks the change in value of the trading securities for the current period.

Exercises

E7-1   Acquiring Long-Term Operating Assets

During 2000 Fishkill Company had the following transactions.

1. Purchased a delivery truck for $8,000 cash.
2. Purchased land and a building for $200,000. The fair market values of the land and building are $82,510 and $140,490, respectively. The company paid $20,000 down and borrowed the other $180,000 from a local bank with a promissory note.

Instructions: Journalize these transactions.

		JOURNAL			PAGE
DATE	DESCRIPTION	POST. REF.	DEBIT	CREDIT	

E7-2   Depreciation Calculations

On July 1, 2000, Aspen Manufacturing Company purchased a new helicopter for $1,260,000. The helicopter is estimated to have a useful life of 6 years, or 5,400 hours, and a salvage value of $180,000.

Instructions: Compute the depreciation expense for 2000 using the following methods.
1. Straight-line depreciation.
2. Units-of-production depreciation (assuming that the helicopter was flown 600 hours in 2000).

E7-3   Disposal of Long-Term Operating Assets

During 2000, APT Company had the following transactions involving long-term operating assets.

1. Sold for $4,000 cash equipment that cost $14,000 and had a book value of $5,000.
2. Took a worn-out, fully depreciated truck that cost $6,000 to the junkyard and received $120.

Instructions: Journalize these transactions.

JOURNAL   PAGE

DATE		DESCRIPTION	POST. REF.	DEBIT	CREDIT

E7-4   Intangible Assets

On December 31, 2000, ZAP Corporation had the following three intangible assets on its books.

a. Patent: This patent was purchased from another company on January 1, 1998, for $24,000. At the time of purchase, it was deemed to have a remaining useful life of 12 years.

b. License: This license was acquired from the U.S. Department of Transportation on January 1, 1999, for $45,000. At the time of purchase, it was deemed to have a remaining useful life of 15 years.

c. Goodwill: On January 1, 2000, ZAP Corporation purchased the assets of RTC Company for $265,000. It was determined at the time of purchase that the fair market value of RTC Company's individual assets totaled $225,000. ZAP intends to amortize the goodwill over the maximum allowable period.

Instructions: Complete the following:
1. Record the purchase of each asset.
2. Record the amortization of each asset for 2000.
3. Compute the book values of these assets on December 31, 2000.

		JOURNAL			PAGE	
DATE		DESCRIPTION	POST. REF.	DEBIT	CREDIT	

E7-5   Investments in Stock (No Significant Influence Exercised)

The following transactions relate to the investment activities of Jordan Company during 2000 and 2001.

1. (2000) Purchased as an available-for-sale security 800 shares of Dog Corporation stock at $22 per share plus $400 brokerage fees.

2. (2000) Purchased as a trading security 500 shares of RST Corporation stock at $20 per share plus $200 brokerage fees.

3. (2000) Received a $3-per-share dividend on the Dog Corporation stock.

4. (2000) The market values of the stocks on the last day of the year were:
   a. Dog Corporation stock: $24 per share
   b. RST Corporation stock: $16 per share

5. (2001) Sold all 800 shares of Dog Corporation stock at $25 per share.

Instructions: Journalize these transactions.

JOURNAL **PAGE**

DATE		DESCRIPTION	POST. REF.	DEBIT	CREDIT

ANSWERS

Matching

1.	a	5.	f	9.	c	
2.	k	6.	d	10.	i	
3.	g	7.	j	11.	e	
4.	b	8.	h			

True/False

1.	F	7.	T	12.	F	
2.	F	8.	F	13.	T	
3.	T	9.	F	14.	F	
4.	F	10.	F	15.	F	
5.	F	11.	T	16.	T	
6.	F					

Multiple Choice

1.	d	6.	c	10.	c	
2.	b	7.	b	11.	a	
3.	a	8.	d	12.	d	
4.	d	9.	a	13.	c	
5.	b					

Exercises

E7-1   Acquiring Long-Term Operating Assets

1. Truck 8,000
      Cash 8,000
   Purchased a new delivery truck.

2. Building 126,000
      Land 74,000
         Cash 20,000
         Notes Payable 180,000
   Purchased land and building.

Asset	Market Values	Percent	Cost
Building	$140,490	0.63	$126,000*
Land	82,510	0.37	74,000**
	$223,000	1.00	$200,000

*$200,000 x 0.63
**$200,000 x 0.37

E7-2   Depreciation Calculations

1. ($1,260,000 – $180,000)/6 years = $180,000 per year
   Depreciation for 2000 is $90,000 ($180,000 x ½)

2. $\dfrac{(\$1,260,000 - \$180,000)}{5,400} \times 600 = \$120,000.$

E7-3   Disposal of Long-Term Operating Assets

1. Cash.. 4,000
   Accumulated Depreciation... 9,000
   Loss on Sale of Equipment.. 1,000
      Equipment   14,000
   Sold equipment.

Cost	$14,000	Book value	$5,000
Book value	5,000	Cash received................................	4,000
Accumulated depreciation..........................	$ 9,000	Loss...	$1,000

2. Cash.. 120
   Accumulated Depreciation... 6,000
      Truck   6,000
      Gain on Disposal of Truck   120
   Discarded truck.

E7-4   Intangible Assets

1. Jan. 1, 1998   Patent.. 24,000
        Cash..   24,000
       Purchased patent.

   Jan. 1, 1999   License 45,000
        Cash..   45,000
       Purchased license.

   Jan. 1, 2000   Assets (Various) 225,000
        Goodwill... 40,000
        Cash..   265,000
       Purchased RTC Company.

2. Amortization Expense—Patent 2,000
      Patent..   2,000
   Amortized patent ($24,000 ÷ 12 years).

   Amortization Expense—License.. 3,000
      License   3,000
   Amortized license ($45,000 ÷ 15 years).

   Amortization Expense—Goodwill.. 1,000
      Goodwill..   1,000
   Amortized goodwill [($265,000 − $225,000) ÷ 40 years].

3.

	Patent	License	Goodwill
Cost	$24,000	$45,000	$40,000
Amortization	6,000	6,000	1,000
Book value on December 31, 2000	$18,000	$39,000	$39,000

E7-5   Investments in Stock (No Significant Influence Exercised)

1. Investment in Available-for-Sale Securities, Dog Corporation Stock............. 18,000
      Cash..   18,000
   Purchased 800 shares of Dog Corporation stock at $22 per share plus
   $400 brokerage fees.

2. Investment in Trading Securities, RST Corporation Stock   10,200
    Cash...   10,200
    Purchased 500 shares of RST Corporation stock at $20 per share plus
    $200 brokerage fees.

3. Cash...   2,400
    Dividend Revenue...   2,400
    Received a $3-per-share dividend on 800 shares of Dog Corporation stock.

4. a.   Market Adjustment—Available-for-Sale Securities   1,200
          Unrealized Increase in Value of Available-for-Sale Securities—Equity   1,200
   b.   Unrealized Loss on Trading Securities—Income   2,200
          Market Adjustment—Trading Securities   2,200

5. Cash...   20,000
    Investment in Available-for-Sale Securities, Dog Corporation Stock.........   18,000
    Gain on Sale of Investment in Available-for-Sale Securities......................   2,000
    Sold 800 shares of Dog Corporation stock at $25 per share.

Chapter 8
Statement of Cash Flows

LEARNING OBJECTIVES

After studying this chapter, you should be able to:

1. Understand the purpose of a statement of cash flows.

2. Recognize the different types of information reported in the statement of cash flows.

3. Prepare a simple statement of cash flows.

4. Analyze financial statements to prepare a statement of cash flows.

5. Use information from the statement of cash flows to make decisions.

CHAPTER REVIEW

What's the Purpose of a Statement of Cash Flows?

1. The primary purpose of the statement of cash flows is to provide information about the cash receipts and payments of an entity during a period of time. This information can be used to evaluate a company's ability to generate positive net cash flows in the future to meet its obligations and to pay dividends.

2. A statement of cash flows also explains the changes in the balance sheet accounts and the cash effects of the accrual-basis amounts reported in the income statement. The cash flow statement complements the balance sheet and income statement and is one of the three primary financial statements.

What Information Is Reported in the Statement of Cash Flows?

3. When preparing a statement of cash flows, cash should include cash equivalents, which are short-term, highly liquid investments (Treasury bills, money market funds, and commercial paper) that can be converted easily to cash.

4. On a statement of cash flows, the inflows and outflows of cash must be classified into three main categories: operating activities, investing activities, and financing activities.

5. Operating activities include all cash flows that enter into the determination of net income. Major operating cash inflows are cash receipts from sales and other cash revenues; major operating cash outflows are cash payments to purchase inventory and pay operating expenses.

Dividend receipts and interest receipts and payments are included in operating activities.

6. Investing activities include cash outflows to purchase stocks and bonds of other companies (except cash equivalents) not classified as trading securities; property, plant, and equipment, and other assets to be used in the business, and the making and collecting of loans. Investing activities also include cash inflows from the sale of these same investments.

7. Financing activities include transactions and events where resources are obtained from or repaid to owners (equity financing) and creditors (debt financing). The payment of dividends and the purchase of treasury stock are financing activities.

8. The format of the statement of cash flows should provide a reconciliation of the beginning and ending balances of cash (and cash equivalents).

9. Noncash investing and financing transactions, such as purchasing land by issuing stock or paying off long-term debt by issuing stock, are not shown in the statement of cash flows but are reported in a note or in a separate schedule.

Preparing a Statement of Cash Flows—A Simple Example

10. If detailed cash flow information is readily available from the cash account, the preparation of a statement of cash flows is straightforward. The cash inflows and outflows merely need to be classified according to type of activity—operating, investing, and financing.

11. By properly coding information when input into a computerized accounting system, accounting software can make the preparation of a cash flow statement very easy.

Analyzing the Other Primary Financial Statements to Prepare a Statement of Cash Flows

12. If detailed cash flow information is not readily available, a statement of cash flows can be prepared by analyzing the income statement and comparative balance sheets.

13. By analyzing the change in balance sheet accounts in relation to income statement data, cash flows for the period can be determined. For example, the beginning accounts receivable balance plus sales for the period less the ending accounts receivable balance equals the amount

of cash collected from customers, which would be reported as an operating item on the statement of cash flows. A similar analysis is required for each balance sheet account and related income statement amounts.

14. A six-step process can be used in preparing a statement of cash flows, as follows:

   a. Compute the change in the cash and cash-equivalent accounts for the period of the statement. This is a check figure.

   b. Convert income statement amounts from an accrual-basis to a cash-basis summary of operations. This is done by (a) eliminating any income statement expenses that do not involve cash (e.g., depreciation); (b) eliminating any effects of non-operating activities (e.g., gain or loss on sale of equipment); and (c) adjusting current asset and liability operating accounts (other than cash) to a cash basis.

   c. Analyze long-term assets to identify the cash flow effects of investing activities.

   d. Analyze long-term debt and stockholders' equity accounts to determine cash flow effects of financing activities.

   e. Prepare a formal statement of cash flows by classifying all cash inflows and outflows according to operating, investing, and financing activities. The net cash flow for the period should be the same amount computed in the first step (a.). The net increase (decrease) in cash for the period is then added (subtracted) to the beginning cash balance to reconcile to the ending cash balance.

   f. Report any significant noncash investing or financing transactions (e.g., purchasing land by issuing stock) in a narrative explanation or on a separate schedule to the statement of cash flows.

15. The statement of cash flows can be prepared using either the direct or the indirect method. The difference between the two methods is in the way the cash flows from operating activities are presented; the format for presenting cash flows from investing and financing activities is the same for both methods.

16. The indirect method involves a reconciliation between net income and net cash flows from operations. With the indirect method, net income is adjusted for items that do not affect cash, such as depreciation, and for differences between reported (accrual) revenues and expenses and cash received and spent for those revenues and expenses. The indirect method is

favored by most accountants and companies because it is easier to prepare.

17. When using the indirect method, net cash received (paid) from operating activities is determined by adjusting accrual-based net income to cash received from (paid for) operations. When adjusting net income, decreases in receivables and other current operating assets, increases in payables and other current operating liabilities, and noncash expenses, such as depreciation, are added to net income; increases in current operating assets and decreases in current operating liabilities are deducted from net income. This calculation is shown below (with arbitrary numbers):

Cash Flows from Operating Activities:

Net income $60,400

Add (deduct) adjustments to cash basis:

Increase in accounts receivable	(8,000)
Decrease in interest receivable	2,000
Decrease in inventory	18,000
Decrease in prepaid insurance	2,400
Increase in accounts payable	5,500
Increase in wages payable	2,000
Decrease in interest payable	(3,000)
Decrease in taxes payable	(5,000)
Depreciation	12,000
Net cash flow provided by (used in) operating activities	$86,300

18. Increases in receivables and other current operating assets are subtracted from net income because less cash was received (some of it is still owed and will be collected next period) than was reported as a revenue; increases in payables are added to net income because they have not yet been paid, and thus less cash was spent than was reported as an expense on the income statement. The opposite logic explains why decreases in receivables and other assets are added and why decreases in payables are subtracted. Depreciation and other noncash expenses are added because even though they decreased net income, they did not require any cash. Adjustments must also be made for gains and losses on the sale of assets.

19. The direct method shows separately the major classes of operating cash receipts, such as cash collected from customers and cash received from interest or dividends, and cash payments, such as cash paid to suppliers for goods and services, to creditors for interest, and to the government for taxes. With the direct method, the difference between operating cash receipts and cash payments is the net cash flow provided by (used in) operations. The direct method is favored by many user groups because it is straightforward and is not likely to be misunderstood.

20. Accrual-based revenues can be converted to cash received by adding the appropriate beginning receivable balances and subtracting the ending receivable balances as follows (with arbitrary numbers):

Income statement amount (sales, interest revenue, or dividend revenue)	$300,000
+ Beginning receivable amount (accounts receivable, interest receivable, or dividend receivable) .	12,000
– Ending receivable amount (accounts receivable, interest receivable, or dividend receivable) .	(8,000)
= Cash collected from revenue (sales, interest, or dividends)	$304,000

21. Cost of goods sold can be converted to cash paid for inventory by first determining purchases for the period and then determining the amount of cash paid for purchases during the period as follows (with arbitrary numbers):

Determining Purchases:

Cost of goods sold	$200,000
+ Ending inventory	15,000
– Beginning inventory	(18,000)
= Purchases during the period	$197,000

Determining Cash Paid for Purchases:

Purchases during the period	$197,000
+ Beginning accounts payable	22,000
– Ending accounts payable	(15,000)
= Cash paid for inventory	$204,000

22. Cash paid for expenses such as wages, rent, insurance, and taxes can be determined by adding appropriate beginning payables and ending prepaid balances and subtracting ending payables and beginning prepaid balances, as shown below (with arbitrary numbers):

Reported expenses (wages, insurance, taxes, etc.)	$100,000
+ Beginning payable balance (wages payable, etc.)	5,000
+ Ending prepaid balance (prepaid wages, etc.)	0
– Ending payable balance (wages payable, etc.)	(4,000)
– Beginning prepaid balance (prepaid wages, etc.)	0
= Cash paid for expenses	$101,000

Obviously, some expenses will have balances in the prepaid accounts, while some will have balances in the liability accounts. Only on rare occasions will there be balances in both for the same expenses.

23. When using the direct method, noncash items such as depreciation, amortization, and the like are ignored and therefore omitted from the statement of cash flows.

24. Regardless of which method is used, the formal statement of cash flows is always divided into three parts: cash flows from operating activities, cash flows from investing activities, and cash flows from financing activities.

Using Information From the Statement of Cash Flows to Make Decisions

25. By highlighting cash inflows and outflows during a period, the statement of cash flows helps investors and creditors assess the timing, amounts, and uncertainty of future cash flows. It helps users compare the financial policies of different firms and answers such questions as whether or not a company is expanding or retrenching, increasing or decreasing its reliance on operating income, debt, or equity financing, and how new buildings, other investments, and even dividends are being paid for.

26. We can learn a great deal about a company by analyzing patterns that appear among the three cash flow categories in a statement of cash flows.

COMMON ERRORS

The three most difficult aspects of this chapter, and hence the reasons for the most common student errors, are:

1. Properly classifying cash flows as operating, investing, or financing activities.

2. Adjusting reported net income to cash flow provided by (used in) operations when using the indirect method.

3. Converting revenues and expenses to cash inflows and outflows when using the direct method.

1. **Properly Classifying Cash Flows as Operating, Investing, or Financing Activities**

Text Exhibit 8-3 will help you learn the proper classification of cash flows. Basically, any cash inflows from activities whose revenue would

be reported on the income statement are operating activities. Included in this category are interest revenue and dividend revenue, which students may be tempted to classify as financing activities. Cash outflows are the expenses reported on the income statement, except for depreciation and similar noncash expenses.

Included in investing activities are purchases and sales of all noncurrent assets and investments other than trading securities and the making or collecting of loans. Sometimes students are tempted to include cash flows from the non-trading securities transactions in operating activities, but they should be classified as investing activities.

Finally, financing activities include all borrowing and repayments, the issuance or purchase of stock, and the payments of dividends. Be careful to include the proceeds of short-term as well as long-term debt as a financing activity.

2. **Adjusting Reported Net Income to Cash Flow Provided by (Used in) Operations When Using the Indirect Method**

The best way to understand how to adjust net income to cash flow provided by (used in) operations is to consider the following.

a. Decreases in accounts receivable are added to net income because some of the receivable balance from last period has been collected during the current period. Therefore, cash collected is greater than reported revenue. Similarly, decreases in other current assets are added because some of the assets purchased last period have been used this period. Therefore, the reported expenses are greater than cash paid for expenses.

b. Increases in accounts receivable are subtracted from net income because some of this period's sales are not yet collected. Similarly, increases in other current assets are subtracted because cash has been spent to buy assets that have not yet been used in operations and therefore have not yet been recognized as expenses.

c. Increases in current operating payables are added to net income because the liability for expense has not yet been paid. Therefore, the reported expense exceeds cash paid. Conversely, decreases in current operating payables mean more cash was spent than had been reported as an expense, and so net income must be reduced to determine cash inflow from operations.

d. All noncash items such as depreciation and amortization must be added back to net income because they were expenses that did not require any cash.

e. The adjustments needed can be summarized as follows:

Net income	xxxx
+ Noncash expenses (e.g., depreciation)......................	xx
− Increases in current operating assets...........................	(xx)
+ Decreases in current operating assets...........................	xx
+ Increases in current operating payables......................	xx
− Decreases in current operating payables......................	(xx)
= Net cash flow provided by (used in) operating activities	xxxx

3. Converting Revenues and Expenses to Cash Inflows and Outflows When Using the Direct Method

Be sure to understand the logic of converting from accrual to cash amounts before relying on the guidelines given in the chapter. For example, in trying to understand how sales revenue is converted to cash receipts from customers, use logic such as sales for the period plus beginning receivables is all that could have been collected. And if there were no receivables at the end of the period, then all the cash would have been collected during the period. However, the amount of receivables at the end of the period must be subtracted (because it wasn't collected), so sales plus beginning receivables minus ending receivables equals cash receipts from customers. Similar logic can be used for expenses. For example, reported interest expense plus the beginning balance in Interest Payable is the total amount of interest that could have been paid during the period. And if there were no ending Interest Payable, all the cash would have been paid. If there is an ending balance in Interest Payable, interest expense plus the beginning payable balance minus the ending payable balance equals cash payments for interest. All other revenues and expenses would be similarly converted, except insurance expense, which is usually purchased (and is an asset) before it is an expense, and cost of goods sold, which must be converted to purchases and then to cash paid for inventory purchased.

SELF-TEST

Matching

Instructions: Write the letter of each of the following terms in the space to the left of its appropriate definition.

a. cash equivalents
b. operating activities
c. statement of cash flows
d. cash flows

e. direct method
f. indirect method
g. financing activities

_____ 1. The financial resources that flow into and out of a company.

_____ 2. A method of reporting the net cash flow from operations that converts accrual net income to a cash basis.

_____ 3. Transactions and events whereby resources are obtained from or repaid to owners and creditors.

_____ 4. The primary financial report that shows the inflows and outflows of cash for a given period.

_____ 5. Transactions and events that are used in the determination of net income.

_____ 6. Highly liquid investments that are easily converted to cash.

_____ 7. A method of reporting the net cash flow from operations that shows the main classes of cash receipts and cash payments.

True/False

Instructions: Place a check mark in the appropriate column to indicate whether each of the following statements is true or false.

	True	False
1. The statement of cash flows is a primary financial statement, along with the income statement and the balance sheet.	_____	_____
2. The statement of cash flows is the connecting link between two income statements.	_____	_____
3. The statement of cash flows is usually prepared for the same time period covered by the corresponding income statement.	_____	_____
4. Dividend receipts would be included in the amount of cash provided by operating activities.	_____	_____
5. The primary purpose of the statement of cash flows is to provide information about the profitability of an entity for a given period of time.	_____	_____
6. Cash generated by operations is equal to the net income for the period less dividends paid or declared.	_____	_____
7. When the direct method is used to prepare a statement of cash flows, depreciation is added back to net income.	_____	_____
8. The issuance of stock for the purchase of land is reported as a financing activity on the statement of cash flows.	_____	_____
9. The indirect method of preparing a statement of cash flows involves adding back noncash expenses to net income in arriving at net cash flow provided by (used in) operations.	_____	_____
10. An increase in the Accounts Payable balance over the year is added to net income when the statement of cash flows is prepared using the direct method.	_____	_____
11. The statement of cash flows provides investors with information that helps users assess the amounts, timing, and uncertainty of future cash flows.	_____	_____
12. The statement of cash flows is not covered by the auditor's opinion.	_____	_____
13. Cash generated by operations will be the same under both the indirect and the direct methods of preparing a statement of cash flows.	_____	_____

	True	False
14. A decrease in the Inventory balance for the period is added to net income in computing cash generated from operations with the indirect method.	_____	_____
15. A decrease in the Accounts Receivable balance is subtracted from net income in computing cash generated from operations by the indirect method.	_____	_____
16. Since the statement of cash flows uses the same information found in comparative balance sheets and income statements, it is always the least useful of the three primary financial statements.	_____	_____

Multiple Choice

Instructions: Circle the letter that best completes each of the following statements.

1. Which of the following is *least* likely to be classified as a cash equivalent?
   a. Commercial paper
   b. Investments in short-term bonds
   c. U.S. Treasury bills
   d. Certificates of deposit

2. Which of the following would *not* be reported on a statement of cash flows prepared using the indirect method?
   a. The amortization of patents
   b. Fully depreciated machinery that was scrapped during the year
   c. Treasury stock that has been purchased from a stockholder
   d. Depreciation expense for the year

3. Which of the following groups of business activities is *not* a required classification on the statement of cash flows?
   a. Operating activities
   b. Financing activities
   c. Cash activities
   d. Investing activities

4. When the indirect method is used to prepare a statement of cash flows, depreciation is treated as an adjustment to reported net income because it
   a. is a source of cash.
   b. reduces reported net income but does not involve an outflow of cash.
   c. reduces reported net income and involves an inflow of cash.
   d. is an inflow of cash to a reserve account for the replacement of assets.

5. Which of the following would be reported on a statement of cash flows prepared using the direct method?
   a. Total wages paid during the year
   b. Depreciation expense for the year
   c. Accrual-basis net income
   d. An increase in the Accounts Receivable balance for the year

6. Which of the following is considered an operating activity?
   a. The purchase of a building
   b. The payment of dividends to stockholders
   c. The repayment of the principal on a loan
   d. The payment of interest to creditors

7. The direct method of preparing a statement of cash flows

   a. is usually the easiest method to implement.
   b. is usually more straightforward than the indirect method and thus may be easier to understand.
   c. generally produces a higher net cash flow figure than the indirect method.
   d. involves a reconciliation between net income and net cash flows from operating activities.

Use the following information to answer Questions 8–10.
Following are the Machinery and Accumulated Depreciation—Machinery accounts as they looked after transactions for the year had been reported. (Note that some entries were intentionally omitted.)

Machinery

Beg. Bal.	120,000	Sale of Machinery	40,000
End. Bal.	160,000		

Accumulated Depreciation—Machinery

Sale of Machinery	26,000	Beg. Bal.	38,000
		End. Bal.	64,000

8. The cost of machinery acquired during the period (assuming cash purchases) was

   a. $38,000.
   b. $64,000.
   c. $120,000.
   d. $80,000.
   e. $200,000.

9. The book value of machinery sold during the period was

   a. $14,000.
   b. $28,000.
   c. $38,000.
   d. $40,000.
   e. $64,000.

10. The depreciation expense that would be added back to net income in computing cash from operations under the indirect method was

   a. $26,000.
   b. $38,000.
   c. $40,000.
   d. $52,000.
   e. $120,000.

11. Which of the following transactions would *not* appear on a statement of cash flows prepared by the direct method?

   a. A net loss from operations
   b. The amount paid to acquire treasury stock
   c. Payment of last year's federal income tax liability
   d. The payment of cash dividends that were declared last year

12. Baker Company issued stock to Taylor Company in exchange for equipment. This transaction would be reflected in

   a. a narrative explanation or in a separate schedule.
   b. the operating activities section of a statement of cash flows.
   c. the financing activities section of a statement of cash flows.
   d. the investing activities section of a statement of cash flows.

13. The statement of cash flows discloses changes in the cash and cash-equivalent accounts during the year and
    a. summarizes the operating, financing, and investing activities of an entity.
    b. includes transactions that affect an entity's prior financial position.
    c. reports significant changes in net income.
    d. measures the overall profitability of an entity.

14. Clark Company had the following operating results for 2000:

Beginning Inventory	$ 200,000
Ending Inventory	180,000
Cost of Goods Sold	1,150,000
Beginning Accounts Payable	45,000
Ending Accounts Payable	65,000

How much cash did Clark pay for inventory in 2000?
    a. $1,170,000
    b. $1,110,000
    c. $1,150,000
    d. $1,190,000

Use the following financial information to answer Questions 15–17.

	2000	1999
Cash	$ 35,000	$ 20,000
Other current assets	175,000	130,000
Equipment	400,000	320,000
Accumulated depreciation	(140,000)	(120,000)
Land	40,000	36,000
Current liabilities	60,000	40,000
Bonds payable	100,000	50,000
Common stock	300,000	270,000
Retained earnings	50,000	26,000

Additional information:
   • No equipment was sold during the year.
   • Dividends for the year 2000 were $12,000.
   • Retained Earnings was affected only by net income and dividends.
   • All changes in the current accounts were from operating activities.

15. Cash provided by operating activities amounted to
    a. $11,000.
    b. $76,000.
    c. $31,000.
    d. $56,000.

16. Cash provided by (used in) investing activities amounted to
    a. $84,000.
    b. $(84,000).
    c. $80,000.
    d. $(80,000).

17. Cash provided by financing activities amounted to:
    a. $80,000.
    b. $38,000.
    c. $18,000.
    d. $68,000.

Exercises

E8-1   Statement of Cash Flows Classifications

Sound Company had the following transactions during 2000.

Cash sales totaled $750,000.
Purchased land and building for $200,000.
Paid $25,000 of cash dividends that were declared in 1999.
Issued long-term bonds of $250,000.
Paid interest on long-term bonds of $25,000.
Purchased inventory for $75,000 cash.
Received $50,000 worth of inventory in exchange for common stock.
Paid taxes of $32,000 for the year.
Purchased treasury stock for $15,000.

Instructions: Based on the above transactions, compute the amount of cash provided by operating, investing, and financing activities for 2000.

E8-2   Converting Accrual Amounts to Cash Basis

The 2000 and 1999 balance sheets and additional information for Suarez Company are presented below.

Suarez Company
Balance Sheets
As of December 31, 2000 and 1999

Assets	2000	1999
Cash and cash equivalents	$ 8,000	$ 5,000
Accounts receivable.....................................	65,000	45,000
Interest receivable.......................................	1,500	2,000
Inventory...	50,000	40,000
Equipment..	150,000	100,000
Accumulated depreciation	(60,000)	(40,000)
Total assets...	$214,500	$152,000

Liabilities and Stockholders' Equity	2000	1999
Accounts payable...	$ 32,000	$ 18,000
Wages payable...	24,000	12,000
Capital stock	100,000	100,000
Retained earnings..	58,500	22,000
Total liabilities and stockholders' equity..	$214,500	$152,000

Additional information:
  a. 2000 sales totaled $521,500.

  b. Interest revenue was $20,000.

  c. Cost of goods sold was $350,000.

  d. Wages expense was $125,000.

  e. No equipment was retired during the year.

  f. Dividends of $10,000 were paid in December 2000.

Instructions: Compute the following for 2000.

  1. Cash collected from customers.

  2. Cash received as interest revenue.

  3. Cash paid for inventory.

4. Cash wages paid to employees.

E8-3   Cash Flows from Operations (Direct Method)

Partial 2000 and 1999 financial statements for White Company are presented below.

White Company
Partial Balance Sheets
December 31, 2000 and 1999

	2000	1999
Current Assets		
Cash	$ 40,000	$ 30,000
Accounts receivable	70,000	66,000
Inventory	60,000	66,000
Prepaid insurance	4,000	3,000
Total current assets	$174,000	$165,000
Current Liabilities		
Accounts payable	$150,000	$145,000
Notes payable	25,000	0
Wages payable	12,000	14,000
Total current liabilities	$187,000	$159,000

White Company
Partial Income Statement
For the Year Ending December 31, 2000

Sales revenue		$150,000
Cost of goods sold:		
Beginning inventory	$ 66,000	
Purchases	80,000	
Cost of goods available for sale	$146,000	
Ending inventory	60,000	
Cost of goods sold		86,000
Gross margin		$ 64,000
Wages expense	$ 50,000	
Insurance expense	9,000	
Depreciation expense	10,000	69,000
Net income (loss)		$ (5,000)

Instructions: 1. Compute the cash received from sales.

2. Compute the cash paid for inventory, insurance, and wages.

3. Using the direct method, compute the total cash inflow (outflow) from operating activities.

E8-4   Cash Flows from Operations (Indirect Method)

Use the information for White Company in E8-3 to compute by the indirect method the net cash inflow (outflow) from operating activities.

E8-5   Cash Flow Provided by (Used in) Operating Activities (Indirect Method)

Income statement data for Crane Corporation for the year are as follows.

Net income before depreciation	$60,000
Depreciation expense	(22,000)
	$38,000
Gain on sale of long-term investments	3,000
	$41,000
Loss on sale of equipment	(8,000)
Income before taxes	$33,000
Income taxes	(12,000)
Net income	$21,000

Instructions: Prepare the cash flow provided by (used in) operating activities section of the statement of cash flows using the indirect method.

E8-6   Cash Flow Provided by (Used in) Operating Activities (Direct Method)

Michelle Oxborrow is the proprietor of a small bakery. Below are shown the results of last year's operations and selected balance sheet data.

Sales revenue	$300,000	
Cost of goods sold	170,000	
Gross margin		$130,000
Operating expenses:		
Salaries expense	$ 55,000	
Insurance expense	5,000	
Rent expense	17,000	
Utilities expense	3,000	80,000
Net income		$50,000

	Beginning of Year	End of Year
Accounts receivable	$15,000	$23,000
Inventory	20,000	17,500
Prepaid insurance	5,000	3,500
Accounts payable	10,000	20,000
Salaries payable	8,000	6,000

Instructions: From the information provided, determine the amount of net cash flow provided from operations, using the direct method. (Use the form on page 194 for your answer.)

E8-7   Cash Flow Provided by (Used in) Operating Activities (Indirect Method)

Given the data in E8-6, show how the amount of net cash flow from operating activities would be calculated using the indirect method.

E8-6

ANSWERS

Matching

1.	d		4.	c		6.	a
2.	f		5.	b		7.	e
3.	g						

True/False

1.	T		7.	F		12.	F
2.	F		8.	F		13.	T
3.	T		9.	T		14.	T
4.	T		10.	F		15.	F
5.	F		11.	T		16.	F
6.	F						

Multiple Choice

1.	b		7.	b		13.	a
2.	b		8.	d		14.	b
3.	c		9.	a		15.	c
4.	b		10.	d		16.	b
5.	a		11.	a		17.	d
6.	d		12.	a			

Exercises

E8-1   Statement of Cash Flows Classifications

<u>**Cash Flow from Operating Activities**</u>

Receipts:

Sales..		$ 750,000

Payments:

Inventory..	$(75,000)	
Interest..	(25,000)	
Taxes...	(32,000)	(132,000)
Total		$ 618,000

<u>**Cash Flow from Investing Activities**</u>

Payments:

Land and building...		$(200,000)

<u>**Cash Flow from Financing Activities**</u>

Receipts:

Long-term bonds...		$ 250,000

Payments:

Dividends..	$(25,000)	
Treasury stock..	(15,000)	(40,000)
Total...		$ 210,000

E8-2   Converting Accrual Amounts to Cash Basis

1. Cash collected from customers:

2000 Sales	$521,500
Beginning accounts receivable	45,000
Ending accounts receivable	(65,000)
Cash collected from sales	$501,500

2. Cash received from interest revenue:

Interest revenue	$ 20,000
Beginning interest receivable	2,000
Ending interest receivable	(1,500)
Cash collected from interest	$ 20,500

3. Cash paid for inventory:

Cost of goods sold	$350,000
Ending inventory	50,000
Beginning inventory	(40,000)
Purchases	$360,000
Beginning accounts payable	18,000
Ending accounts payable	(32,000)
Cash paid for inventory	$346,000

4. Cash wages paid to employees:

Wages expense	$125,000
Beginning wages payable	12,000
Ending wages payable	(24,000)
Cash paid for wages	$113,000

E8-3   Cash Flows for Operations (Direct Method)

1.

Sales revenue	$150,000
+ Beginning accounts receivable balance	66,000
− Ending accounts receivable balance	(70,000)
Cash received from sales	$146,000

2.

Cost of goods sold	$ 86,000
+ Ending inventory balance	60,000
− Beginning inventory balance	(66,000)
= Purchases	$ 80,000
+ Beginning accounts payable balance	145,000
− Ending accounts payable balance	(150,000)
Cash payments for inventory	$ 75,000

Insurance expense	$ 9,000
+ Ending prepaid insurance balance	4,000
− Beginning prepaid insurance balance	(3,000)
Cash payments for insurance	$ 10,000

Wages expense	$ 50,000
+ Beginning wages payable balance	14,000
− Ending wages payable balance	(12,000)
Cash paid for wages	$ 52,000

3.
White Company
Cash Flow from Operating Activities

Cash receipts from sales		$146,000
Cash payments for:		
Inventory	$75,000	
Insurance	10,000	
Wages	52,000	137,000
Net cash flow provided by operating activities		$ 9,000

E8-4 Cash Flows form Operations (Indirect Method)

White Company
Cash Flow from Operating Activities

Net income (loss)		$(5,000)
Add (deduct) adjustments to cash basis:		
Depreciation expense	$10,000	
Increase in accounts receivable	(4,000)	
Decrease in inventory	6,000	
Increase in prepaid insurance	(1,000)	
Increase in accounts payable	5,000	
Decrease in wages payable	(2,000)	14,000
Net cash flow provided by operating activities		$ 9,000

E8-5 Cash Flow Provided by (Used in) Operating Activities (Indirect Method)

Net income		$21,000
Add: Depreciation expense	$22,000	
Loss on sale of equipment	8,000	30,000
Subtract: Gain on sale of long-term investments		(3,000)
Net cash flow provided by operating activities		$48,000

E8-6   Cash Flow Provided by (Used in) Operating Activities (Direct Method)

Sales Revenue	$300,000	
+ Beginning accounts receivable	15,000	
− Ending accounts receivable	(23,000)	
Total cash receipts		$292,000
Cost of goods sold	$170,000	
+ Ending inventory	17,500	
− Beginning inventory	(20,000)	
Purchases	$167,500	
+ Beginning accounts payable	10,000	
− Ending accounts payable	(20,000)	
Cash paid to suppliers for inventory	$157,500	
Salaries expense	$ 55,000	
+ Beginning salaries payable	8,000	
− Ending salaries payable	(6,000)	
Cash paid to employees	$ 57,000	
Utilities expense (no adjustment required)	$ 3,000	
Rent expense (no adjustment required)	$ 17,000	
Insurance expense	$ 5,000	
+ Ending prepaid insurance	3,500	
− Beginning prepaid insurance	(5,000)	
Cash paid for insurance	$ 3,500	
Total cash payments		238,000
Net cash flow provided from operations		$ 54,000

E8-7   Cash Flow Provided by (Used in) Operating Activities (Indirect Method)

Net income	$ 50,000

Add (deduct) adjustments to cash basis:

Increase in accounts receivable	(8,000)
Decrease in inventory	2,500
Decrease in prepaid insurance	1,500
Increase in accounts payable	10,000
Decrease in salaries payable	(2,000)
Net cash flow provided from operations	$ 54,000

Chapter 9
Introduction to Management Accounting

LEARNING OBJECTIVES

After studying this chapter, you should be able to:

1. Describe some of the history that defines modern management accounting.

2. Discuss the major differences in managing manufacturing, merchandising, and service companies.

3. Define the common terms and measures found in modern management accounting.

4. Understand that successfully planning, controlling, and evaluating a business requires effective management of cost, quality, and time.

5. Describe the professional environment of management accountants today.

CHAPTER REVIEW

1. Chapter 9, the first chapter on management accounting, is introductory in nature. In this chapter you learn a little about the history and development of management accounting. In addition, you are introduced to a host of new terms that are unique to management accounting.

2. The purpose of management accounting is to provide information for decision making by those inside an organization. Organizations must have accounting information that allows for decisions relating to planning, controlling, and evaluating business processes and opportunities.

A Little History

3. In the early 1800s, most American business focused on individuals specializing at selected tasks. Beginning in 1812, the introduction of large cotton mills changed the production process from one individual starting and finishing a product to multiple individuals working on a product at various stages in the production process. This new way of doing business changed the accounting process and required additional information for managers.

4. The next major change in management accounting resulted from the proliferation of railways. Managers required information that would allow them to manage others and measure performance from long distances. New methods of measurement were developed to evaluate costs and performance.

5. With the emergence of mass production, businesses began to specialize in distribution and sales rather than solely in production. Whole-

salers and retailers purchased and delivered finished products. The challenge for these businesses was to monitor and control their levels of inventory. Accounting measurements, such as inventory turnover, were developed to assist in this task.

6. DuPont changed the way businesses and divisions within a business are evaluated with the development of the DuPont ROI formula. This formula allows differing investments to be evaluated and compared. The DuPont formula breaks down the return on investment to allow users to identify why investments provide a given return.

Business Organizations

7. Businesses can be partitioned into three distinctly different types: manufacturing, merchandising, and service. Manufacturing businesses invest in raw materials, production facilities, and labor to produce finished products. Merchandising businesses purchase inventory from manufacturers and make it available to customers. These firms specialize in logistics — getting the right product to the right place at the right time at the right price. Service firms provide a service. Like manufacturers and merchandisers, service firms must carefully monitor and control costs.

Traditional Management Accounting Terminology

8. Because management accounting is less structured and rigid than financial accounting, the vocabulary of management accounting is less specified. Terms are often used that require a detailed understanding if one is to understand the message being conveyed. Because some terms can be used interchangeably, it is important for you to gain a basic understanding of the management accounting vocabulary.

9. The term *cost* has many meanings. Cost generally represents the amount paid for an item (thought of as an asset). But cost can also represent the amount of an item that has been used up (thought of as an expense). If an expenditure has no future value, it is often referred to as a cost (thought of as a loss). As you can see, the term cost can be used in many ways to represent completely different things. The point — know which definition of cost someone is using when they refer to the term.

10. Costs can be broken down into two general categories: product and period. Product costs are those costs associated with producing inventory (in a manufacturing company), purchasing inventory and preparing it for resale (in a merchandising company), or providing services (in a service firm). Period costs are those costs that cannot be associated with or assigned to a product or service. These costs are generally not associated with inventory but instead are associated with a time period.

11. Product costs can be further partitioned into three categories: direct materials, direct labor, and manufacturing overhead. Direct materials are those materials that become part of the product and are traceable to it. Direct labor costs are those wages that are paid to employees who actually work on the direct materials to convert those materials into inventory. Manufacturing overhead includes all other product costs that are not classified as direct materials or direct labor. Examples include the cost of the production equipment, utilities, and supervision associated with production.

12. Product costs are those costs associated with inventory. There are three different types of inventory for a manufacturing firm. Raw materials is the term used for materials that have yet to be put into the production process. Work in process, as you can guess, is the term used for inventory that is in the production process but not yet complete. Once the inventory is finished, it is termed finished goods inventory.

13. Product and period costs can be either fixed in nature or variable. Variable costs are those costs that vary in proportion to an activity level. For example, sales commissions vary with the number of units sold. Raw materials vary with the number of units produced. Fixed costs are those costs that remain constant regardless of the level of activity, at least within a relevant range of activity.

14. The terms direct and indirect costs are used when evaluating the performance of a particular business division or segment. Direct costs are those costs that can be traced to a business unit. Indirect costs are costs that are normally incurred to benefit several segments. The distinction between direct and indirect costs is important when evaluating performance, because managers and employees should be evaluated based on those costs directly traceable to their areas of responsibility.

15. Differential costs are those costs that differ between alternatives being evaluated. These

are future costs that may or may not be incurred depending on the decision made. Sunk costs are past costs that will not change based on which alternative is selected.

16. Out-of-pocket costs are those costs that require an outlay of cash or other assets while opportunity costs are costs that are forgone because a different alternative was selected.

Management Accounting Today and in the Future

17. In the past, cost was the primary measure of success. If costs were kept at a minimum, then profits would follow. The changing business environment has required management to focus on two additional performance measures: quality and time. Quality relates to the characteristics of the product or service being delivered. Consumers require products whose quality is commensurate with the price being paid. Additionally, those products must be delivered in a timely fashion. These new dimensions require additional information, and management accounting must respond to that need.

18. As mentioned earlier, the purpose of management accounting is to provide information for decision making. Decision making consists of three parts; planning, controlling, and evaluating. Management accounting provides information relating to each of these three dimensions of the decision-making process.

The Management Accounting Profession

19. The management accountant provides information to support decision making. The top accountant in most organizations is called the controller. The controller plays a key role in planning, controlling, and evaluating information and business processes.

20. Technology has changed the way in which information is collected and analyzed. With technology, management accountants are now able to collect data that just ten years ago would have been impossible. This new information allows companies to make better business decisions and also allows managers and employees to be evaluated using numerous measurements.

21. The management accountant is often confronted with ethical dilemmas. Because management accountants deal with estimates, the opportunity to exercise professional judgment

often presents itself. Since these judgments can influence outcomes, one must be careful to ensure that all information is considered carefully and without bias.

COMMON ERRORS

This chapter deals mostly with conceptual and definitional material. It is designed to set the stage for the study of management accounting. Students frequently have difficulty orienting themselves to two new perspectives required for the study of management accounting:

1. Future time focus
2. The plan-control-evaluate cycle

1. Future Time Focus

After studying financial accounting, you have become familiar with accounting for completed business transactions. In this chapter, we drop this focus on the past and ask you to take a future focus. This is difficult to do, because old habits die hard. With practice, however, you will learn to consider each decision-making situation carefully in terms of future implications. For example, should you accept a customer's rush order? For financial accounting, you would compare what it cost to produce the product in the past with the sales price and decide whether or not to accept the order. For management accounting, to make the decision you must compare what it will cost to produce the product in the future with the sales price. Remember that for a rush order the future labor cost may be higher because of overtime or the future materials cost may be higher because the material must be shipped air freight.

2. Plan-Control-Evaluate Cycle

Financial accounting has the accounting equation to provide a framework. Students can relate individual accounting issues to this equation, which helps them to understand how each issue is part of a coordinated system. Unfortunately, management accounting does not have such an obvious framework, so it is often seen as a group of unrelated concepts. One major purpose of this chapter is to demonstrate that a framework also exists for the study of management accounting. All management accounting concepts and techniques can be viewed as methods of providing information to management for making decisions related to its planning, controlling, and evaluating functions. Subsequent chapters will follow this cycle for the routine operations of an organization. We take the perspective that accountants provide information to assist management with decisions e.g., budgeting, measuring actual activity by segments, and performance reporting.

SELF-TEST

Matching

Instructions: Write the letter of each of the following terms in the space to the left of its appropriate definition.

a.	asset	**k.**	manufacturing overhead
b.	differential costs	**l.**	opportunity costs
c.	direct labor	**m.**	out-of-pocket costs
d.	direct materials	**n.**	period costs
e.	expenses	**o.**	product costs
f.	finished goods	**p.**	raw materials
g.	indirect costs	**q.**	sunk costs
h.	indirect labor	**r.**	variable costs
i.	indirect materials	**s.**	work-in-process inventory
j.	manufacturing costs		

_____   1.   A cost that has a future value.

_____   2.   Completed inventory that is ready for sale.

_____   3.   The sum of direct labor, direct materials, and manufacturing overhead.

_____   4.   Costs that can be assigned to products or services.

_____   5.   Past costs that do not change as a result of a future action.

_____   6.   Miscellaneous material costs (such as supplies) that are included in manufacturing overhead.

_____   7.   Product costs that cannot be assigned directly to products.

_____   8.   Costs that change in total with changes in volume of activity.

_____   9.   Material costs that are directly traceable to specific products.

_____ 10.   Benefits lost or forfeited as a result of selecting one alternative over another.

_____ 11.   Costs whose benefits have expired.

_____ 12.   Costs that change as the result of a future decision.

_____ 13.   Labor costs that are included in manufacturing overhead.

_____ 14.   Inventory in the process of being manufactured.

_____ 15.   Costs that are not associated with products but are charged to the income statement in the period incurred.

_____ 16.   Costs that require an outlay of cash.

_____ 17.   Labor costs that are directly traceable to specific products.

_____ 18.   Materials that have not yet been placed in production.

_____ 19.   All manufacturing costs except direct labor and direct materials.

True/False

Instructions: Place a check mark in the appropriate column to indicate whether each of the following statements is true or false.

	True	False
1. External financial statements are usually too aggregated to be the only output of the accounting system to be relied upon by managers.	_____	_____
2. The terms *costs* and *expenses* are sometimes used interchangeably, but are distinguishable.	_____	_____

		True	False
3.	Management accounting is primarily concerned with reporting to those inside the organization (i.e., managers).	_____	_____
4.	Product costs in a manufacturing firm are often referred to as manufacturing costs...	_____	_____
5.	Service companies generally do *not* have manufacturing overhead costs.	_____	_____
6.	Manufacturing overhead is *not* a product cost.	_____	_____
7.	Manufacturing overhead is directly traceable to specific products.	_____	_____
8.	Indirect materials are not considered product costs.	_____	_____
9.	Indirect labor is included as part of manufacturing overhead.	_____	_____
10.	Raw materials are not considered an inventory cost.	_____	_____
11.	Financial accounting statements report past performance.	_____	_____
12.	Inventory is really a buffer that may hide inefficient operations.	_____	_____
13.	Per-unit fixed costs vary as activity level changes.	_____	_____
14.	Total variable costs vary as activity level changes.	_____	_____
15.	Indirect costs are specifically traceable to a unit of business.	_____	_____
16.	Management accounting reports are required to use GAAP.	_____	_____
17.	Costs that are already committed and will not benefit new projects are called sunk costs.	_____	_____
18.	The first step in the management process is decision making.	_____	_____
19.	Opportunity costs do not involve an outlay of cash.	_____	_____
20.	Opportunity costs are not important and do not need to be considered unless there is a limited amount of resources.	_____	_____

Multiple Choice

Instructions: Circle the letter that best completes each of the following statements.

1. Expenditures that have future value are called

   a. assets.
   b. costs.
   c. expenses.
   d. losses.

2. Costs associated with products or services are called

   a. manufacturing costs.
   b. service costs.
   c. product costs.
   d. None of the above

3. Depreciation on a factory building could be considered part of

   a. manufacturing costs.
   b. product costs.
   c. manufacturing overhead costs.
   d. All of the above

4. Advertising would be considered which of the following?

   a. Nonmanufacturing cost
   b. Sunk cost
   c. Manufacturing cost
   d. Indirect cost

5. Which of the following usually is *not* considered part of manufacturing overhead?

   a. Indirect labor
   b. Depreciation on factory
   c. Factory foreman's salary
   d. Delivery costs

6. Which of the following is a product cost that is *not* traceable to specific products?

   a. Direct materials
   b. Advertising
   c. Direct labor
   d. Manufacturing overhead

7. Wages paid to factory maintenance workers normally are classified as

   a. direct labor.
   b. period cost.
   c. indirect labor.
   d. nonmanufacturing cost.

8. Which of the following would *not* include any manufacturing overhead costs?

   a. Raw materials inventory
   b. Work-in-process inventory
   c. Finished goods inventory
   d. Cost of goods sold

9. Which of the following is *not* a characteristic of management accounting?

   a. Makes substantial use of estimates
   b. Reports in accordance with GAAP
   c. Does not require reporting
   d. Reports primarily to those inside the organization

10. The direct costs of operating a Pizza Hut franchise include

    a. the store manager's salary.
    b. the franchise fees paid to the corporation.
    c. the cost of advertising in the local telephone directory.
    d. All of the above

11. The indirect costs of operating a Sears store are

    a. the store's billing for corporate computer usage.
    b. the store's billing for utility costs.
    c. the store's employee benefit costs.
    d. All of the above

12. Which nonfinancial information would probably be of least interest to a factory manager?

    a. The general rate of inflation
    b. Units produced of a product
    c. Pounds of scrap material
    d. Hours worked by factory employees

13. Direct materials are usually considered

    a. variable costs.
    b. fixed costs.
    c. period costs.
    d. opportunity costs.

14. Which of the following is *not* a difference between financial and management accounting?

    a. The time focus

    b. The reporting unit focus

    c. Influence of GAAP

    d. Use of ratios

15. Costs directly traceable to a unit are referred to as

    a. sunk costs.

    b. opportunity costs.

    c. direct costs.

    d. expenses.

16. The typical order of the steps in the management process is

    a. controlling, planning, evaluating.

    b. evaluating, controlling, planning.

    c. planning, evaluating, controlling.

    d. planning, controlling, evaluating.

17. Which of the following does *not* involve an outlay of cash?

    a. Variable costs

    b. Fixed costs

    c. Opportunity costs

    d. Relevant costs

18. Which of the following need *not* be considered when making a decision?

    a. Opportunity costs

    b. Relevant costs

    c. Out-of-pocket costs

    d. Sunk costs

Exercises

E9-1   Cost Terms

Instructions: Below are a number of costs that might be incurred in a service, merchandising, or manufacturing company. Place an X in the appropriate column for each cost to indicate whether the cost involved would be variable or fixed.

Cost	Variable	Fixed
1. Needles used in a hospital	_____	_____
2. Depreciation of marketing center	_____	_____
3. Senior executive salaries	_____	_____
4. Cost of electricity to run machines	_____	_____
5. Advertising of products	_____	_____
6. Sales commissions	_____	_____
7. Wood used to make baseball bats	_____	_____
8. Wages of assembly employees in plant	_____	_____
9. Rent on an office facility	_____	_____
10. Insurance for CPA's office	_____	_____

E9-2   Use of Cost Terms

Instructions: Given the cost terms introduced in the chapter, choose the most appropriate term to complete each of the following sentences.

1. You should not consider the amount you paid for opera tickets in deciding whether or not to go to a basketball game. They are a(n) _____.

2. If you build a wedding reception center on a piece of property, you will not be able to build a bowling alley. Profits lost from not building the bowling alley are a(n) _____.

3. A friend of yours asks for advice. She has $80,000 in cash and is thinking about two alternative investments. First, she wants to spend the money to buy a beach condominium for personal use. Second, she thinks that maybe she should invest the money in the stock market. The dividends and stock price increases she will forgo if she buys the condominium are known as a(n) _____.

4. Most of the costs associated with the home office of an organization, including officers' salaries, would be accounted for as _____.

5. Jane wants to buy a new car for her business. The interest she will pay on the car loan is known as a(n) _____ associated with the decision to buy the car.

ANSWERS

Matching

1.	a	8.	r	15.	n
2.	f	9.	d	16.	m
3.	j	10.	l	17.	c
4.	o	11.	e	18.	p
5.	q	12.	b	19.	k
6.	i	13.	h		
7.	g	14.	s		

True/False

1.	T	8.	F	15.	F
2.	T	9.	T	16.	F
3.	T	10.	F	17.	T
4.	T	11.	T	18.	F
5.	T	12.	T	19.	T
6.	F	13.	T	20.	F
7.	F	14.	T		

Multiple Choice

1.	a	7.	c	13.	a
2.	c	8.	a	14.	d
3.	d	9.	b	15.	c
4.	a	10.	d	16.	d
5.	d	11.	a	17.	c
6.	d	12.	a	18.	d

Exercises

E9-1   Cost Terms

1. Variable
2. Fixed
3. Fixed
4. Variable
5. Could be either; usually fixed
6. Variable
7. Variable
8. Variable
9. Fixed
10. Fixed

E9-2   Use of Cost Terms

1. Sunk cost
2. Opportunity cost
3. Opportunity cost
4. Period costs
5. Differential cost

Chapter 10
Cost Systems

LEARNING OBJECTIVES

After studying this chapter, you should be able to:

1. Explain the flow of goods in a manufacturing firm.

2. Understand the difficulty, yet importance, of having accurate product cost information.

3. Identify and compare conventional product costing systems.

4. Describe and apply job order costing procedures for a manufacturing firm.

5. Understand how merchants manage cost information in their organizations.

6. Understand how service organizations manage their cost information.

CHAPTER REVIEW

The Flow of Goods In a Manufacturing Firm

1. In a manufacturing operation, raw materials are converted into finished products by factory workers. The costs of raw materials and direct labor are fairly easily assigned to products; other manufacturing costs (e.g., manufacturing overhead) are more difficult to track and to assign to specific products.

2. Managers need accurate product cost information to plan for the future, control current operations, and evaluate past performance. This information is also needed so that high quality products can be delivered to customers at the lowest price and fastest speed.

Why Having Accurate Product Costs Is So Difficult, Yet Important

3. The costs of manufacturing can be categorized into three elements: Direct Materials, Direct Labor, and Manufacturing Overhead. The major problem in determining accurate product costs deals with this allocation of manufacturing overhead.

4. Without accurate cost information, managers can easily over- or under-price products and make other poor management decisions.

5. Because conventional cost systems have been designed primarily to provide information needed for external reporting, they have not necessarily provided the best information for management decisions. Recently, a number of innovative approaches to product costing have been developed that appear to offer significant potential benefit to

manufacturing companies in helping to reduce costs and improve productivity.

Conventional Product Cost Accumulation Systems

6. Job order costing and process costing are the two conventional systems for accumulating product costs and assigning them to individual products. Job order costing is used by firms that produce custom-ordered goods; that is, the costs of each product, job, or small group of products are separately accumulated. Job order costing is especially useful for tracking the costs of high-cost, low volume and special-ordered materials when the cost of each separate product must be known.

   Process costing is used to accumulate the costs of basically identical products that pass through a series of uniform steps or processes. Because such products are basically indistinguishable, the costs of large numbers of products can be accumulated, and the cost of the individual products is an average of the total. Process costing is useful in mass production industries such as the brick, lumber, rubber, and gasoline industries.

The Job Order Cost System

7. With job order costing, the costs of each job must be carefully accumulated. The basic document or computer file for accumulating these costs is the job cost sheet. It identifies the various operations involved in manufacturing a product, as well as the direct materials, direct labor, and manufacturing overhead costs of each operation. The job cost sheet also serves as a basis for determining the cost of the completed job, which is then transferred to Finished Goods Inventory.

8. In job order costing it is important to account accurately for all direct materials, direct labor, and manufacturing overhead costs.

9. The costs of materials used in production are accounted for in two ways in a job order costing system: (1) The costs of materials used directly in manufacturing the product are separately identified as direct materials costs; (2) the costs of miscellaneous inexpensive items, such as glue and nails, which benefit many products, are charged to products indirectly by including them in the manufacturing overhead costs of a period. The latter are called indirect materials costs.

10. The accounting for labor costs under a job order costing system is similar to the accounting for materials costs. There are two types of labor: direct and indirect. The costs of direct labor used in production are separately accumulated on a computer or on time tickets and charged directly to particular jobs, whereas the costs of indirect labor are accumulated in the Manufacturing Overhead account.

11. The third type of product cost, manufacturing overhead, must also be accurately accounted for. Unlike direct materials and direct labor costs, manufacturing overhead costs represent miscellaneous items that are difficult to trace to specific products. Therefore, manufacturing overhead costs must be applied to products in some predetermined manner. The most common way is as follows:

   a. Choose an equitable base, called a *cost driver*, that influences the overhead costs. For example, if all items are made on a certain machine, the number of machine hours might be an appropriate measure of volume of activity; if all items involve all production personnel, the number of direct labor hours might be best.
   b. Estimate the total variable and fixed manufacturing overhead costs for the period.
   c. Divide the estimated total manufacturing overhead costs by the allocation base to get a predetermined overhead rate by hour, job, etc.
   d. Multiply the predetermined overhead rate by the expected volume of activity.

   Note that the allocation scheme described above applies an estimated amount of manufacturing overhead to each job. Actual manufacturing overhead, which will be known only when the jobs are completed, may be quite different.

12. As a job is being completed in a job order cost system, the costs of direct materials, direct labor, and manufacturing overhead are accounted for separately. When the job is completed, these costs are transferred from Work-in-Process Inventory to Finished Goods Inventory by the following entry:

   Finished Goods Inventory   xxx
       Work-in-Process Inventory   xxx

13. At the completion of each job, its unit cost is computed by adding the direct materials, direct labor, and applied manufacturing overhead costs and dividing the total cost by the number of units produced.

14. When a product is sold, the costs assigned to it are transferred to the Cost of Goods Sold account by the following entry:

Cost of Goods Sold   xxx
    Finished Goods Inventory   xxx

With this entry, two major steps have been accomplished: (1) the total cost of producing an item has been summarized on the job cost sheet, and (2) the proper entries have been made to account for production costs.

15. The flow of product costs through a firm is summarized in Exhibit 10-1.

16. As Exhibit 10-1 reflects, actual manufacturing overhead costs are recorded on the debit side of the Manufacturing Overhead account, and applied manufacturing overhead costs are recorded on the credit side of the Manufacturing Overhead account.

17. At the end of the year, the difference between actual and applied manufacturing overhead is accounted for in one of two ways: (1) the difference is debited/credited directly to Cost of Goods Sold, or (2) the difference is prorated and allocated to Work-in-Process Inventory, Finished Goods Inventory, and Cost of Goods Sold. The first method is easier and more commonly used; the second method is more theoretically accurate. The entry to transfer the difference to Cost of Goods Sold, assuming that applied manufacturing overhead is less than actual manufacturing overhead, is:

Cost of Goods Sold   xxx
    Manufacturing Overhead..........   xxx

Exhibit 10-1   The Flow of Product Costs

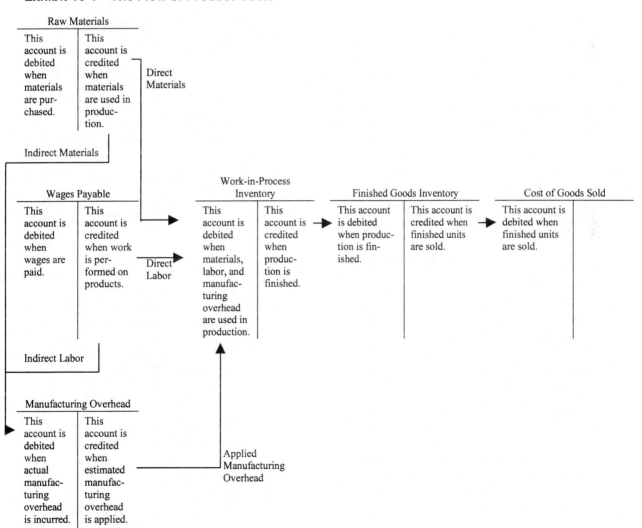

18. The job cost sheet summarizes the costs of a specific product or job; all production costs for a period are summarized on a cost of goods manufactured schedule. This schedule provides the backup information needed for calculating cost of goods sold in a manufacturing firm.

Cost Accumulation in Merchandising Organizations

19. The inventory flow in a merchandising organization is much simpler than that of a manufacturing organization; there are no raw materials, work-in-process, or finished goods in merchandising. There is just one inventory account, Merchandise Inventory. As inventory is sold, the cost of inventory is credited to the Merchandise Inventory account and debited to Cost of Goods Sold.

20. Merchandisers try to avoid carrying too much and too little inventory.

    a. Carrying too much inventory exposes merchandisers to holding costs (opportunity costs associated with having money tied up in inventory) and inventory shrinkage (theft, spoilage, damage, etc.).

    b. Carrying too little inventory puts merchandisers at risk of not having sufficient inventory to meet sales demand and of being vulnerable to excess ordering costs and sudden price increases.

21. Two measures of inventory management are inventory asset turnover, which is equal to revenue divided by average inventory, and net operating profit, which is equal to gross revenues less the costs associated with purchasing inventory. (Note: Stockturn, traditionally measured as cost of goods sold divided by average inventory, provides similar information as the inventory asset turnover measure.)

Cost Accumulation in Service Organizations

22. In performing services for clients, service firms incur costs for labor, supplies, and overhead. Service firms accumulate these costs in an account called Work-in-Process Services, which is very similar to a manufacturing firm's Work-In-Process Inventory account.

23. Like manufacturing firms, service firms apply overhead by using a predetermined overhead rate, which is calculated by dividing total estimated overhead costs for the period by an appropriate activity measure (such as direct labor hours). As the appropriate overhead activities actually take place, overhead is allocated to the Work-in-Process Services account.

24. When the firm finishes a job and bills the client, it recognizes revenue and transfers the associated Work-in-Process Services costs on the balance sheet to Cost of Services (similar to Cost of Goods Sold) on the income statement.

COMMON ERRORS

The most common errors made by students in trying to learn the material in this chapter involve:

1. Determining the manufacturing overhead rate.

2. Recording the appropriate manufacturing overhead cost on the job cost sheet.

1. Determining the Manufacturing Overhead Rate

The predetermined overhead rate is the estimated annual manufacturing overhead costs divided by an activity base, such as machine hours or direct labor hours. Generally, the activity base should reflect the major activity of the department. A department of assembly line operations, for example, would use machine hours as its base; direct labor hours would not provide an accurate picture of that department's activity.

2. Recording the Appropriate Manufacturing Overhead Cost on the Job Cost Sheet

The manufacturing overhead cost assigned (applied) to each department involved in a job is the units of activity performed on that job (direct labor hours, machine hours, etc.) multiplied by the predetermined overhead rate, computed as described in No. 1. The amounts assigned to the departments are added together to make the total manufacturing overhead cost. The actual manufacturing overhead is not recorded in Work-in-Process Inventory or on the job cost sheet; instead, this applied cost is recorded both in Work-in-Process and on each job cost sheet. At the end of the accounting year, the difference between actual and applied manufacturing overhead is computed and reflected in Cost of Goods Sold.

SELF-TEST

Matching

Instructions: Write the letter of each of the following terms in the space to the left of its appropriate definition.

a. overapplied manufacturing overhead
b. job cost sheet
c. product cost
d. predetermined overhead rate
e. process costing
f. underapplied manufacturing overhead
g. job order costing
h. work-in-process services
i. inventory shrinkage
j. lead time
k. holding costs

_____ 1. The sum of direct materials, direct labor, and manufacturing overhead.

_____ 2. A rate at which estimated manufacturing overhead costs are assigned to products throughout the year; equals total estimated manufacturing overhead costs divided by a suitable allocation base, such as direct labor hours or direct materials used.

_____ 3. The excess of actual manufacturing overhead over the applied manufacturing overhead costs for a period.

_____ 4. A document prepared for each manufacturing job that is job order costed; summarizes direct materials, direct labor, and manufacturing overhead costs.

_____ 5. A method of product costing whereby costs are accumulated by process or work centers and averaged over all products manufactured in those centers.

_____ 6. A method of product costing whereby each job, product, or batch of products is costed separately.

_____ 7. The excess of applied manufacturing overhead (based on a predetermined overhead rate) over the actual manufacturing overhead costs for a period.

_____ 8. The financial opportunity costs of keeping inventory on hand.

_____ 9. Can be caused by theft or spoilage of inventory.

_____ 10. The amount of time that passes between placing an order and receipt of the order.

_____ 11. Services in the process of being completed for a client.

True/False

Instructions: Place a check mark in the appropriate column to indicate whether each of the following statements is true or false.

	True	False
1. Job order costing is most appropriate in industries such as the rubber, brick, textile, and gasoline industries.	_____	_____
2. Both job order and process costing are cost accumulation methods that compute unit costs by dividing the total number of units produced into total manufacturing costs.	_____	_____
3. The job cost sheet or computer job form is the basic document for keeping track of costs in a job order costing system.	_____	_____
4. The major problem in determining accurate product cost information is with assigning manufacturing overhead.	_____	_____
5. The Work-in-Process Inventory account is credited when materials are used in production.	_____	_____
6. Indirect materials and indirect labor are usually classified as manufacturing overhead costs.	_____	_____

147

	True	False
7. Managers need accurate product cost information for pricing and other important management decisions.	_____	_____
8. The entry to recognize actual indirect labor costs includes a debit to the Work-in-Process Inventory account.	_____	_____
9. The application of manufacturing overhead to the Work-in-Process Inventory account results in a credit to the Manufacturing Overhead account.	_____	_____
10. Actual manufacturing overhead costs usually are not directly assigned to products as they are manufactured.	_____	_____
11. When the debit balance in the Manufacturing Overhead account exceeds the credit balance in the Manufacturing Overhead account, manufacturing overhead was overapplied.	_____	_____
12. A manufacturing firm typically has three types of inventory on hand.	_____	_____
13. Total cost of goods manufactured will be less than total cost of goods sold if ending finished goods inventory exceeds beginning finished goods inventory.	_____	_____
14. The easiest way to dispose of over- or underapplications of manufacturing overhead is to assign them equitably to work-in-process and finished goods inventories and cost of goods sold.	_____	_____
15. Depreciation expense is always a product cost.	_____	_____
16. Employee wages are always product costs.	_____	_____
17. Nonmanufacturing costs are treated as period expenses.	_____	_____
18. The best way to minimize holding costs is to maintain a large amount of inventory on site.	_____	_____
19. An example of inventory shrinkage is when grocery items spoil or become stale.	_____	_____
20. It is always beneficial to carry a very small amount of inventory.	_____	_____
21. Inventory asset turnover (or stockturn) measures how well a company manages its inventory.	_____	_____
22. A service business is any organization whose main economic activity involves producing a non-physical product that provides value to a customer.	_____	_____
23. Both manufacturing companies and service companies have overhead costs.	_____	_____
24. One way to calculate an overhead rate is by subtracting total estimated direct labor hours from total estimated overhead costs.	_____	_____
25. Unlike manufacturing companies, most service companies' main product costs are associated with labor.	_____	_____
26. A service company's direct labor account is much like a manufacturing company's work-in-process inventory account in that it is used to collect all the different product costs that eventually end up in the cost of services.	_____	_____
27. An audit in its final stages is an example of something that might be in a CPA firm's Work-in-Process Services account.	_____	_____

Multiple Choice

Instructions: Circle the letter that best completes each of the following statements.

1. Accurate product cost data are needed so that

   a. management can price its products intelligently.
   b. management can make decisions about operations.
   c. net income can be determined accurately.
   d. All of the above

2. Product cost information is used to

   a. plan, control, and evaluate operations.
   b. report financial results (e.g., cost of goods sold and inventory balances).
   c. Both *a* and *b*
   d. Neither *a* nor *b*

3. Job order costing would probably *not* be used by a

   a. textile manufacturer.
   b. building contractor.
   c. furniture manufacturer.
   d. printer.

4. Which of the following supports the cost of goods sold calculation for the income statement?

   a. A job cost sheet
   b. A materials requisition form
   c. A cost of goods manufactured schedule
   d. None of the above

5. A job cost sheet identifies all of the following except

   a. production departments.
   b. direct labor hours.
   c. actual manufacturing overhead costs.
   d. applied manufacturing overhead costs.

6. Which of the following would be least likely to be included in manufacturing overhead?

   a. Direct labor
   b. Indirect materials
   c. Indirect labor
   d. Rent on plant

7. Which of the following is *not* an inventory account?

   a. Raw Materials
   b. Cost of Goods Sold
   c. Work-in-Process
   d. Finished Goods

8. Management would want to determine cost of goods manufactured on a

   a. product-by-product basis.
   b. period-by-period basis.
   c. department-by-department basis.
   d. All of the above

9. Which of the following would *not* be a very good base for allocating manufacturing overhead costs to products?

   a. Direct labor hours required to produce each item
   b. Machine hours required to produce each item
   c. An equal allocation of overhead costs to each item
   d. Direct labor costs required to produce each item

10. Which of the following statements is false?

    a. Actual manufacturing overhead costs are debited to the Manufacturing Overhead account.
    b. Applied manufacturing overhead costs are credited to the Manufacturing Overhead account.
    c. The debit balance in the Manufacturing Overhead account exceeds the credit balance in that account when manufacturing overhead is underapplied.
    d. The credit balance in the Manufacturing Overhead account exceeds the debit balance in that account when manufacturing overhead is underapplied.

11. Total cost of goods manufactured

    a. is equal to total cost of goods sold if beginning and ending work-in-process inventories are the same.
    b. is equal to total cost of goods sold if beginning and ending raw materials inventories are the same.
    c. is equal to total cost of goods sold if beginning and ending finished goods inventories are the same.
    d. exceeds cost of goods sold if ending work-in-process inventory exceeds beginning work-in-process inventory.

12. Why do retailers want to keep a small amount of inventory on hand?

    a. The financial opportunity costs of holding inventory can be significant
    b. To be prepared for sudden, unexpected shifts in sales demand
    c. To maintain good relationships with suppliers
    d. To minimize return on investment in inventory

13. A retailer's main inventory account is

    a. Manufacturing Overhead.
    b. Work-in-Process.
    c. Raw Materials.
    d. Merchandise Inventory.

14. All the following are examples of events that may cause inventory shrinkage *except*

    a. theft.
    b. spoilage.
    c. goods being damaged.
    d. goods being sold.

15. Retailers generally try not to carry too little inventory for all the following reasons *except*

    a. they become susceptible to sudden price increases.
    b. it forces them to rely on suppliers to *always* meet delivery commitments.
    c. they may not have sufficient inventory to meet customer demand.
    d. it causes their inventory asset turnover to be too low.

16. The following information is available for Kayman Corporation for 2000 and 2001:

Revenue, 2000	$200,000
Revenue, 2001	300,000
Inventory, December 31, 2000	50,000
Inventory, December 31, 2001	70,000

    What is Kayman Corporation's inventory asset turnover for 2001?

    a. .20
    b. 5.00
    c. 4.00
    d. 4.29

17. Which of the following attributes is *not* common to both service and manufacturing firms?

    a. They identify needs for which customers are willing to pay.
    b. They always require large investments in expensive capital equipment and buildings.
    c. They allocate overhead as work is performed.
    d. All the above are common attributes.

18. Which of the following is *not* a difference between service and manufacturing firms?

    a. Service firms rely much less on the distribution channel.
    b. Service firms generally deal directly with the end-user customer.
    c. Service firms do much more customization than do manufacturing firms.
    d. Service firms do not use direct labor.

19. Using the following forecasted information for Hoffsteader Attorneys' 2000 operations, calculate Hoffsteader's predetermined overhead rate. Hoffsteader allocates overhead based on direct labor hours.

Total forecasted overhead costs	$1 million
Total forecasted jobs	200
Total forecasted direct labors hours	10,000
Total forecasted purchases of supplies	$5,000

    a. $5,000 per direct labor hour
    b. $100 per direct labor hour
    c. $200 per direct labor hour
    d. $80 per direct labor hour

20. Which of the following costs is an example of an overhead cost?

    a. Direct labor
    b. Support staff salaries
    c. Supplies/materials traceable to specific jobs
    d. All of the above

21. All the following costs are put *directly* into the work-in-process services account *except*

    a. direct labor.
    b. supplies/materials.
    c. utilities.
    d. applied overhead.

Exercises

E10-1   Job Order Costing: Journal Entries

Instructions: Using the journal form on the following page, prepare journal entries to account for the following transactions of Dustin Corporation.

   1. Purchased $2,000 of raw materials on account from Supply Company.
   2. Incurred $1,200 of direct labor costs; paid in cash.
   3. Issued $1,300 of raw materials into production.
   4. Recorded depreciation expense of $300 on the plant.
   5. Used $100 of indirect materials on several jobs.
   6. Incurred $300 of indirect labor costs; paid in cash.
   7. Paid $400 of property taxes on the plant.
   8. Applied manufacturing overhead at the rate of $1 for each $1 of direct labor cost.
   9. Transferred finished goods costing $3,000 to the warehouse.
  10. Sold goods costing $2,700 for $3,600.

JOURNAL **PAGE**

DATE	DESCRIPTION	POST. REF.	DEBIT	CREDIT

E10-2   Applying Manufacturing Overhead Cost

Eureka Company has three subsidiaries: X, Y, and Z. Each company keeps a separate set of accounting records. Forecasts of manufacturing costs for 2000 are shown below.

	COMPANY		
	X	Y	Z
Material to be used (ft)	10,000 ft	12,000 ft	15,000 ft
Direct labor hours	8,000 hr	12,000 hr	12,000 hr
Machine hours	16,000 hr	10,000 hr	7,000 hr
Direct labor costs	$40,000	$72,000	$49,000
Manufacturing overhead	$15,000	$22,000	$19,000

Predetermined overhead rates for the application of manufacturing overhead costs to work-in-process inventory are determined on the following basis:

Company X: machine hours
Company Y: direct labor costs
Company Z: direct labor hours

Instructions: 1. Compute the predetermined overhead rate to be used by each subsidiary.
2. If Company Z has 12,500 direct labor hours and $18,500 of manufacturing overhead December 2000, will overhead be over- or underapplied? By how much?

E10-3   Service Cost Flows

Pace CPA Firm incurred the following costs in July:

Use of supplies*..	$ 3,500
Utilities	8,000
Property tax...	12,000
Direct labor...	100,000
Support staff salaries..	35,000

* $2,000 was directly related to specific client accounts.

Instructions: Using the general journal form below, prepare the journal entries to account for the above costs. Pace does not allocate overhead costs until the client project is completed. No client projects were completed and billed during July.

JOURNAL   PAGE

DATE	DESCRIPTION	POST. REF.	DEBIT	CREDIT

E10-4   Service Cost Flows

Pierce Engineering Firm estimated its total overhead costs for 2000 to be $2 million. It allocates overhead based on direct labor hours. Pierce has a total of 9 engineers, each of whom work an average of 2,500 hours per year. Pierce pays its engineers $50 per hour. Pierce engineers worked a total of 30 hours and used $300 of supplies in doing work for Mr. Carson, one of Pierce's clients. Pierce charged Mr. Carson $7,000 for the work performed.

Instructions: 1. What is Pierce's overhead rate?
                     2. Using the general journal form below, prepare the journal entries to record the following:
                           a. overhead for the Carson job.
                           b. the cost of supplies for the Carson job.
                           c. the cost of labor for the Carson job.
                           d. completion of the Carson job.

JOURNAL   **PAGE**

DATE		DESCRIPTION	POST. REF.	DEBIT	CREDIT

ANSWERS

Matching

1.	c	5.	e	9.	i		
2.	d	6.	g	10.	j		
3.	f	7.	a	11.	h		
4.	b	8.	k				

True/False

1.	F	10.	T	19.	T
2.	T	11.	F	20.	F
3.	T	12.	T	21.	T
4.	T	13.	F	22.	T
5.	F	14.	F	23.	T
6.	T	15.	F	24.	F
7.	T	16.	F	25.	T
8.	F	17.	T	26.	F
9.	T	18.	F	27.	T

Multiple Choice

1.	d	8.	d	15.	d
2.	c	9.	c	16.	b
3.	a	10.	d	17.	b
4.	c	11.	c	18.	d
5.	c	12.	a	19.	b
6.	a	13.	d	20.	b
7.	b	14.	d	21.	c

Exercises

E10-1   Job Order Costing: Journal Entries

1. Raw Materials Inventory 2,000
     Accounts Payable 2,000
   Purchased raw materials.

2. Work-in-Process Inventory 1,200
     Cash 1,200
   Incurred direct labor costs.

3. Work-in-Process Inventory 1,300
     Raw Materials Inventory 1,300
   Used raw materials in production.

4. Manufacturing Overhead 300
     Accumulated Depreciation—Plant 300
   To record depreciation on the plant.

5. Manufacturing Overhead 100
     Raw Materials Inventory 100
   Used indirect materials in production.

6. Manufacturing Overhead 300
     Cash 300
   Incurred indirect labor costs.

7. Manufacturing Overhead... 400

    Cash...   400

    Paid property taxes.

8. Work-in-Process Inventory 1,200

    Manufacturing Overhead.. 1,200

    To record application of manufacturing overhead.

9. Finished Goods Inventory 3,000

    Work-in-Process Inventory 3,000

    Transferred work-in-process to finished goods inventory.

10. Accounts Receivable.. 3,600

    Sales Revenue 3,600

    Cost of Goods Sold 2,700

    Finished Goods Inventory 2,700

    Sold goods costing $2,700 for $3,600.

E10-2   Applying Manufacturing Overhead Cost

1.

Company X	=	$\dfrac{\$15,000}{16,000}$	=	$0.9375 per machine hour
Company Y	=	$\dfrac{\$22,000}{72,000}$	=	$0.3056 per direct labor dollar
Company Z	=	$\dfrac{\$19,000}{12,000}$	=	$1.5833 per direct labor hour

2. At 12,500 direct labor hours, $19,791.25 ($1.5833 x 12,500) would be applied. Since actual manufacturing overhead costs were only $18,500, manufacturing overhead would be overapplied by $1,291.25 ($19,791.25 – $18,500). This overapplied manufacturing overhead would be closed to (and thus would decrease) Cost of Goods Sold or a combination of Work-in-Process, Finished Goods, and Cost of Goods Sold.

E10-3   Service Cost Flows

Work-in-Process Services... 2,000

    Supplies 2,000

To record the direct cost of supplies used during July.

Overhead... 1,500

    Supplies 1,500

To record the indirect cost of supplies used during July.

Overhead... 8,000

    Utilities Payable... 8,000

To record the cost of utilities for July.

Overhead... 12,000

    Property Tax Payable... 12,000

To record the cost of property tax for July.

| Work-in-Process Services.. | 100,000 | |
| Salaries and Wages Payable.. | | 100,000 |

To record direct labor costs for July.

| Overhead.. | 35,000 | |
| Salaries and Wages Payable.. | | 35,000 |

To record the cost of support staff salaries for July.

E10-4   Service Cost Flows

1. Overhead Rate = $2 million/(9 × 2,500 hours) = $88.89 per direct labor hour

| 2. a. Work-in-Process Services .... | 2,667 | |
| Overhead .... | | 2,667 |

To apply overhead costs to the Bailey job ($88.89 × 30=$1,882).

| b. Work-in-Process Services .... | 300 | |
| Supplies .... | | 300 |

To record the cost of supplies used in doing the Bailey job.

| c. Work-in-Process Services .... | 1,500 | |
| Salaries and Wages Payable .... | | 1,500 |

To record the cost of direct labor for the Bailey job ($50 × 30=$1,500).

| d. Accounts Receivable .... | 7,000 | |
| Sales Revenue... | | 7,000 |

To record the billing of the Carson job.

| Cost of Services.. | 4,467 | |
| Work-in-Process Services.. | | 4,467 |

To transfer the Carson job costs from Work-in-Process Services to Cost of Services.

Chapter 11
Analyzing Cost-Volume-Profit Relationships

LEARNING OBJECTIVES

After studying this chapter, you should be able to:

1. Understand the key factors involved in cost-volume-profit (CVP) analysis and why CVP is such an important tool in management decision making.

2. Explain and analyze the basic cost behavior patterns—variable and fixed.

3. Describe the behavior patterns of mixed costs and stepped costs.

4. Analyze mixed costs using the scattergraph and high-low methods.

5. Analyze CVP relationships using the contribution margin, equation, and graphic approaches.

6. Describe potential changes in CVP variables and the effect these changes have on company profitability; identify the limiting assumptions of CVP analysis.

7. Explain the effects of sales mix on profitability.

8. Explain the issues of quality and time on CVP decisions.

CHAPTER REVIEW

Understanding Why Cost-Volume-Profit (CVP) Analysis Is Important

1. Understanding the interrelationships of key variables in CVP analysis can assist management in planning and in making critical control and evaluation decisions.

2. Key factors involved in CVP analysis include: (a) revenues derived from the prices charged for products and services; (b) fixed and variable costs; (c) level of activity; (d) mix of products or services; (e) effect on speed and quality of making changes in costs and prices; and (f) profits resulting from various combinations of the other factors.

Basic Cost Behavior Patterns

3. There are two basic cost behavior patterns—variable and fixed; other patterns are variations of these.

4. A cost is classified as variable or fixed by the way it reacts to changes in level of activity.

5. Level of activity may be measured in terms of output (for example, number of items produced or service hours billed) or in terms of input (for example, number of hours worked).

6. Variable costs change in total in direct proportion to changes in the level of activity, within a relevant range (the normal operating level of activity). Variable costs are, therefore, constant per unit over this range.

7. Within the relevant range, we can assume that variable costs rise in direct proportion with activity level. In reality, however, costs are often curvilinear.

8. The nonlinearity of costs makes it important to identify carefully the relevant range. Within the relevant range, even curvilinear costs can be closely approximated with straight lines.

9. Fixed costs do not change in total with changes in level of activity. Because total fixed costs remain constant within the relevant range, the per-unit fixed cost decreases as activity level increases.

10. More and more costs have become fixed versus variable, primarily due to increased automation. With increased fixed costs, management is less likely or less able to reverse a decision (to produce a particular product, for example). It simply becomes too costly.

Other Cost Behavior Patterns

11. Mixed costs contain both fixed and variable elements. Each of these elements must be identified before meaningful cost and profit planning can take place.

12. Stepped costs are those that change in total in a stair-step fashion with changes in activity level. Costs that change in relatively wide steps compared with the relevant range are classified and treated as fixed costs. If the steps are relatively narrow compared with the relevant range, the costs are approximated as variable costs.

Analysis of Mixed Costs

13. There are two common methods of analyzing mixed costs: the scattergraph and the high-low methods. In each case, a pool of mixed costs is related to some activity (such as labor hours or number of units produced), and the behavior of the cost elements determines which are fixed and which are variable.

14. With the scattergraph method, the total mixed costs for each level of activity are plotted on a graph, and a line is fitted visually through the points. Fixed costs are estimated to be that point where the line crosses the cost axis, and the per-unit variable cost is estimated to be equal to the slope of the line of averages (called a regression line).

15. The high-low method is an analytical approach in which the changes in activity between the highest and the lowest cost points are used to estimate the per-unit variable cost (change in cost divided by change in activity level). The fixed cost is then total costs minus activity times variable cost rate. This method is extremely simple, but it can also be very wide of the mark if the high and low points are not representative of all cost points.

Methods of CVP Analysis

16. There are three common and related ways to perform CVP analysis: (a) the contribution margin approach, (b) the equation approach, and (c) the graphic approach.

17. Contribution margin is the amount of sales revenue that can be applied to cover fixed costs and provide a profit after variable costs have been deducted from sales. It is equal to sales revenue minus variable costs.

18. One of the most common applications of the fixed and variable cost classification is a contribution margin income statement. A contribution margin income statement uses the following relationships:

Sales revenue – Variable costs = Contribution margin – Fixed costs = Net income (Profit)

This type of income statement is more useful for management decision making than a functional statement, which assigns costs to a product or period. A contribution margin income statement reveals the amount of revenue left after variable costs have been deducted (the contribution margin) to cover fixed costs and provide a profit. This format allows management to calculate profits at various levels of activity.

19. The contribution margin can also be expressed as a ratio. Management should always emphasize those units with the highest contribution margin ratio, assuming that other factors are equal.

20. CVP analysis can also be expressed in an equation format:

Revenues – Costs = Profit

Revenues – Variable costs – Fixed costs = Profit

(Sales price × Units) – (Variable cost × Units) – Fixed costs = Profit

21. The break-even point is that level of sales where total revenues equal total fixed and variable costs. It can be computed by dividing fixed costs by the per-unit contribution margin. Once the break-even point is realized, profits will increase by the amount of the per-unit

contribution margin for each additional unit of sales.

22. The graphic approach allows managers simultaneously to examine cost and revenue data over wide ranges of activity rather than at single volumes, as with the other two approaches.

23. The following graphic approach is the most common.

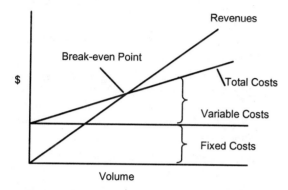

24. A profit graph allows managers to see how profits change as volume changes. The following is an example of a profit graph.

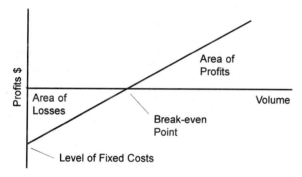

25. The three CVP approaches are simply alternative representations of the same calculation. They can be used to calculate target incomes as well as to compute break-even points. Target income can be expressed as an absolute amount or as a percentage of revenues. The equation would be:

Sales revenues = Variable costs + Fixed costs + Target income

The Effect of Changes in Costs, Prices, and Volume on Profitability

26. In analyzing the effects of changes in volume, variable costs, or fixed costs, the changed variable is inserted and a new calculation is made, as shown, where X equals the number of units.

Revenues	=	Variable costs	+	Fixed costs
Selling price	Number of units (X)	=	Variable costs (X)	+	Fixed costs
Changed to examine effect of changes in selling price	Changed to examine effect of changes in volume		Changed to examine effect of changes in variable costs		Changed to examine effect of changes in fixed costs

27. Increases in variable or fixed costs and decreases in sales price or sales volume result in decreases in profits. Changes in the opposite direction result in increases in profits.

Limiting Assumptions of CVP Analysis

28. Two main assumptions of CVP analysis are that (a) the behavior of revenues and costs is linear, and (b) all costs can be divided into fixed and variable categories.

29. Another assumption deals with the sales mix, which is the proportion of total units sold represented by each of a company's products. If a company's products have different contribution margin ratios, a change in the sales mix results in a change in the break-even point, and hence in profit.

30. Notwithstanding these and other implicit assumptions, CVP analysis provides a good model for predicting future operating results when specific relationships are defined.

Sales Mix

31. Changes in sales mix can change profits because not all products have the same contribution margin. A company's profits are maximized when the products with the highest contribution margin ratio are emphasized.

Issues of Quality and Time

32. It is important to consider the effect of changes in costs, prices, and volume on the quality of goods and services and the speed at which products and services are delivered to customers.

COMMON ERRORS

The three most common mistakes made by students learning how to analyze cost behavior patterns are:

1. Confusing fixed and variable costs in terms of their behavior in total or per unit.

2. Differentiating between the functional and contribution margin income statements.

3. Understanding that the methods of analyzing CVP relationships are simply alternative ways of looking at the same situation.

1. Variable and Fixed Costs

Students often make the mistake of thinking that because variable costs are referred to as "per unit," the unit amount changes with changes in activity level. In fact, variable costs change in total, while fixed costs change per unit. For example, suppose variable costs are $10 per unit at a production level of 500 units. Total variable costs are $5,000. If production doubles from 500 to 1,000 units, total variable costs will double ($10 × 1,000 = $10,000), but the variable cost per unit will remain the same ($10 in this case). Total fixed costs, on the other hand, remain constant over the relevant range; as a result, per-unit fixed costs change with activity level. If fixed costs are $24,000 at a production level of 500 units, the fixed cost per unit is $48 ($24,000 ÷ 500). When production increases to 1,000 units, the fixed cost per unit is $24 (assuming that we are still within the relevant range), because total fixed costs remained constant at $24,000.

2. Functional versus Contribution Margin Income Statement

We emphasized the functional income statement in the chapters on financial accounting, so it is sometimes difficult to make the transition to the contribution margin income statement. The tendency is to equate gross margin and contribution margin. But you must remember that gross margin is the difference between revenues and cost of goods sold (fixed and variable), while contribution margin is revenues minus variable costs only. By separating fixed and variable costs, managers can determine which activity level will give a contribution margin large enough to cover fixed costs and provide the desired profit.

3. Methods of Analyzing CVP Relationships

All three methods—contribution margin, graphic, and equation—produce the same results. Students who learn the equation approach well can easily apply it to a contribution margin or graphic format. Again, the basic equation is:

Sales revenue – Variable costs – Fixed costs = Net income (Profit)

A related problem involves the variables in the equation. You have to understand the elements well enough to be able to adapt the information you are given to the equation format. For example, if you know the sales price and the number of units sold, you would state revenue as sales price times number of units sold. If a variable cost ratio is given instead of a per-unit variable cost, the ratio would have to be multiplied by the sales amount:

Sales revenue – (Variable cost ratio × Sales) – Fixed costs = Net income (Profit)

SELF-TEST

Matching

Instructions: Write the letter of each of the following terms in the space to the left of its appropriate definition.

a.	functional income statement	**j.**	regression line
b.	variable costs	**k.**	mixed costs
c.	contribution margin	**l.**	curvilinear costs
d.	relevant range	**m.**	break-even point
e.	stepped costs	**n.**	target income
f.	scattergraph, or visual fit, method	**o.**	sales mix
g.	high-low method	**p.**	CVP analysis
h.	contribution margin income statement	**q.**	profit graph
i.	fixed costs		

_____   1.   Costs that change in total in a stair-step fashion with changes in volume of activity.

_____   2.   Costs that do not vary in direct proportion to changes in activity level but instead vary at increasing or decreasing rates.

_____   3.   The difference between total revenues and total variable costs; the portion of sales revenue available to cover fixed costs and profit.

_____   4.   A method of segregating the fixed and variable components of a mixed cost by analyzing the costs at the high and low activity levels within a relevant range.

_____   5.   The range of operating level, or volume of activity, over which the relationship between costs is approximately linear.

_____   6.   Costs that contain both variable and fixed components.

_____   7.   An income statement that separates costs according to their behavior patterns; shows revenue less variable costs (contribution margin) less fixed costs.

_____   8.   Costs that vary in total proportionately with changes in level of activity within the relevant range.

_____   9.   Costs that do not vary in total with changes in activity levels, at least not within a relevant range.

_____   10.   A method of segregating the fixed and variable components of a mixed cost by plotting on a graph the total costs at several activity levels and drawing a regression line through the points.

_____   11.   An income statement that segregates costs by use; shows revenue less cost of goods sold (gross margin) less selling and administrative expenses.

_____   12.   On a scattergraph, the straight line that most closely expresses the relationship between the variables.

_____   13.   A desired profit level predetermined by management.

_____   14.   The method of determining how changes in costs and volume affect the profitability of an organization.

_____   15.   The amount of sales or the number of units sold at which total costs equal total revenues; the point at which there is no profit or loss.

_____   16.   A graph that shows how profits vary with changes in volume.

_____   17.   The relative proportion of total units sold (or total sales dollars) represented by each of a company's product lines.

True/False

Instructions: Place a check mark in the appropriate column to indicate whether each of the following statements is true or false.

	True	False
1. Total variable costs change proportionately with changes in the number of units produced.	_____	_____
2. The per-unit fixed cost decreases as production increases.	_____	_____

	True	False
3. The relevant range phenomenon is applicable only to fixed costs.		
4. An assumption of linearity is often justified over small relevant ranges.		
5. Management has much more flexibility to change production levels when costs are fixed rather than variable.		
6. When using the scattergraph method of analyzing mixed costs, total fixed costs are estimated to be that point where the fitted line crosses the vertical axis.		
7. When using the high-low method of analyzing mixed costs, the change in cost divided by the change in activity is equal to total fixed costs.		
8. A firm with a low level of variable costs has a higher contribution margin than one with a high level of variable costs.		
9. Contribution margin is equal to revenues minus fixed costs.		
10. A functional income statement divides expenses into fixed and variable categories.		
11. Break-even point is equal to total fixed costs divided by the per-unit contribution margin.		
12. Once the break-even point is reached, profits will increase by the amount of the per-unit contribution margin for each additional unit sold.		
13. An increase in the variable cost rate would decrease the per-unit contribution margin.		
14. A decrease in fixed costs reduces the number of units that must be sold to maintain the same profit level.		
15. Total fixed costs plus desired profit divided by the per-unit contribution margin is equal to the number of units needed to be sold to reach target income.		
16. An increase in variable costs increases the number of units needed to reach a target income level.		
17. A decrease in sales volume decreases total profits, assuming that other factors remain the same.		
18. On a CVP graph, total fixed costs are represented by a diagonal line.		
19. The three CVP approaches are basically very different from one another.		
20. CVP analysis assumes that all costs are linear and can be classified as fixed or variable.		
21. A company will generally maximize net income by selling the products with the highest contribution margin percentage.		
22. The issues of quality and time are not particularly relevant to CVP analysis.		

Multiple Choice

Instructions: Circle the letter that best completes each of the following statements.

1. The type of cost that changes proportionately in total with changes in the number of units produced is
   a. fixed costs.
   b. variable costs.
   c. stepped costs.
   d. mixed costs.

2. Which of the following costs is *not* likely to be a variable cost in a bicycle manufacturing firm?
   a. Cost of bike tires
   b. Cost of bike pedals
   c. Supervisor's salary
   d. Cost of bike seats

3. Per-unit fixed costs usually

   a. increase as production level increases.
   b. remain constant.
   c. decrease as production level increases.
   d. None of the above

4. Which of the following costs would probably *not* be a fixed cost?

   a. Property taxes
   b. Depreciation on warehouse
   c. Supervisor's salary
   d. Shipping cartons

5. Which of the following would probably *not* cause an increase in fixed costs?

   a. Increased automation
   b. A no-termination policy regarding employees
   c. An increase in the number of managers
   d. An increase in the number of part-time hourly employees

6. On a scattergraph, total fixed costs are estimated to be

   a. the area beneath a horizontal line that runs perpendicular to the vertical axis.
   b. that point where the average cost line crosses the horizontal axis.
   c. the slope of the average cost line.
   d. increasing as production increases.

7. When using the high-low method, the variable rate is equal to the

   a. change in cost divided by the change in activity.
   b. change in activity divided by the change in cost.
   c. change in activity minus the change in cost.
   d. change in cost minus the change in activity.

8. Which of the following statements is true?

   a. Sales revenue – Variable costs = Contribution margin
   b. Sales revenue – Fixed costs = Contribution margin
   c. Contribution margin – Variable costs = Net income
   d. Sales revenue – Contribution margin = Net income

9. Which of the following calculations relates to a contribution margin income statement?
   a. Sales – Cost of goods sold = Gross margin
   b. Sales – Variable costs – Fixed costs = Net income
   c. Gross margin – Expenses = Net income
   d. Gross margin + Cost of goods sold = Net sales

10. The break-even equation is

   a. Sales revenue = Variable costs + Fixed costs.
   b. Variable costs = Sales revenue + Fixed costs.
   c. Fixed costs = Sales revenue + Variable costs.
   d. Sales revenue = Variable costs – Fixed costs.

11. A unit that sells for $50, has a $20 variable cost, and has $2,000 of fixed costs will have a per-unit contribution margin of

   a. $50.
   b. $20.
   c. $30.
   d. $70.

12. How many units must a company sell to break even if it has fixed costs of $50,000 and a per-unit contribution margin of $20?

 a. 25,000 units
 b. 2,500 units
 c. 25 units
 d. 250 units

13. If the company in Question 12 sold 4,000 units, its profit would be

 a. $30,000.
 b. $80,000.
 c. $50,000.
 d. $20,000.

14. A decrease in total fixed costs will

 a. result in a higher break-even point.
 b. decrease net income.
 c. increase net income.
 d. increase variable costs.

15. An increase in the variable cost rate

 a. decreases the per-unit contribution margin.
 b. increases the per-unit contribution margin.
 c. has no effect on the per-unit contribution margin.
 d. increases the profits of a firm.

16. When all other factors remain constant, an increase in the selling price of a unit

 a. decreases net income.
 b. increases the per-unit contribution margin.
 c. decreases the per-unit contribution margin.
 d. has no effect on the per-unit contribution margin.

17. On the following graph, fixed costs are represented by

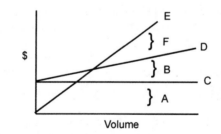

 a. Area A.
 b. Area B.
 c. Area F.
 d. Line D.

18. On the following graph, variable costs are represented by

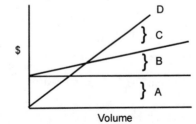

 a. Area A.
 b. Area B.
 c. Area C.
 d. Line D.

19. On the following graph, the contribution margin is represented by

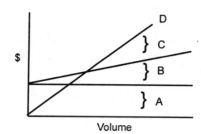

    a. Area A.
    b. Area B.
    c. Area C.
    d. None of the above

20. On the following graph, total revenues are represented by

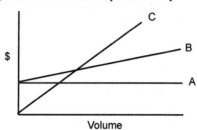

    a. Line A.
    b. Line B.
    c. Line C.
    d. None of the above

21. On the following graph, the break-even point is represented by

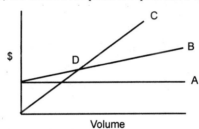

    a. Line A.
    b. Line B.
    c. Line C.
    d. Point D.

22. If a company is already profitable and has a 45 percent contribution margin ratio, how much will profits increase if sales increase $10,000?

    a. $10,000
    b. $4,500
    c. $5,500
    d. $5,000

23. Company XYZ has three products: Product A has a contribution margin ratio of 45 percent, Product B has a contribution margin ratio of 30 percent, and Product C has a contribution margin ratio of 30 percent. Company XYZ can maximize its profits by

    a. selling as much of Product A as possible.
    b. selling as much of Product B as possible.
    c. selling as much of Product C as possible.
    d. selling equal amounts of all three products.

Exercises

E11-1   Fixed and Variable Costs

Super Taste Company bottles and distributes soft drinks in the eastern part of the United States. Management estimates that at a production volume of 400,000 cases per year, total production costs are $1,460,000, and at a volume of 600,000 cases per year, total production costs are $1,940,000.

Instructions: 1. Determine total fixed and per-case variable costs for Super Taste Company.
2. Compute the total cost of bottling 750,000 cases per year.

E11-2   Fixed and Variable Costs: Scattergraph Method

Instructions: Given the following mixed costs at various levels of production, complete the following requirements.

	Units Produced	Mixed Costs
July	8	$13
August	9	15
September	12	18
October	14	19
November	11	15
December	15	20

1. Plot the information on a scattergraph and visually fit a line through the points.
2. Based on the scattergraph in No. 1, approximate the monthly fixed and variable components of mixed costs.
3. Using the data in No. 2, compute the total cost of 20 units.

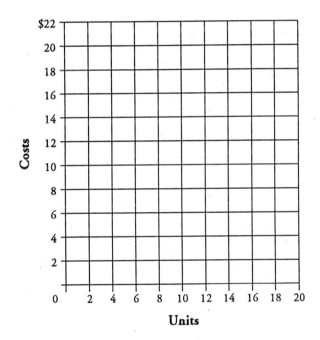

E11-3   Fixed and Variable Costs: High-Low Method

Instructions: Given the information in E11-2, use the high-low method to calculate the following:
1. Total fixed costs and per-unit variable costs.
2. Total cost of producing 20 units.

E11-4   Contribution Margin Income Statement

Fix-Up Corporation makes and sells wallpaper. Its costs and revenues for 2000 follow (assume no beginning or ending inventory).

Sales revenue (19,000 rolls)..........................	$133,000
Variable selling expenses..............................	9,500
Variable administrative expenses	7,600
Fixed selling expenses	15,000
Fixed administrative expenses......................	25,000
Direct labor..	11,400
Direct materials used	38,000
Fixed manufacturing overhead	6,000
Variable manufacturing overhead.................	13,300

Instructions: 1. Use the data above to prepare a contribution margin income statement.
2. Calculate the per-roll contribution margin.
3. Calculate the amount of profit at production and sales levels of 26,000 rolls of wallpaper.

Fix-Up Corporation

Contribution Margin Income Statement

For the Year Ended December 31, 2000

E11-5   Contribution Margin Analysis

Stagg Corporation had the following income statement for the month of November.

Sales revenue (500 units)	$100,000
Less variable costs	55,000
Contribution margin	$ 45,000
Fixed costs	31,500
Net income	$ 13,500

Instructions: Given this income statement, compute:
1. The per-unit contribution margin.
2. The break-even point in units sold.
3. The contribution margin ratio.
4. The increase in profits if another $10,000 of sales is made.

E11-6   Equation Approach for CVP Analysis

Sunset Company makes a single product that sells for $50 per unit. The contribution margin of the unit is 30 percent of the sales price, and fixed costs total $90,000.

Instructions: Find the following (each part is independent of the others):
1. The break-even point in sales dollars and unit sales.
2. Sales volume needed to make a profit of $15,000.
3. The break-even point if variable costs increase $8 per unit.
4. The break-even point if fixed costs decrease from $90,000 to $70,000.

E11-7   Graphic Approach to CVP Analysis

Instructions: Given the following graph, complete the requirements listed below:

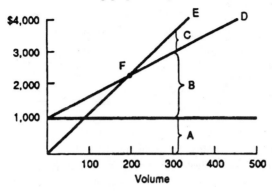

1. Specify labels A through F.
2. Determine total fixed costs.
3. Determine the break-even point in units.
4. Determine variable costs per unit.
5. Determine sales price per unit.

E11-8   Effect on Profitability of Changes in Costs, Prices, and Volumes

Rosetta Company's break-even equation is $100X = $40X + $120,000.

Instructions: Given this equation, compute the following independent requirements:
1. The company's break-even point in units sold.
2. The new break-even point in units if the sales price increases to $120.
3. The new break-even point in units if variable costs increase to $50.
4. The new break-even point in units if fixed costs decrease to $90,000.

E11-9   Sales Mix

New Marketing Corporation manufactures and sells three different types of televisions. Revenues and costs for each type of television are as follows:

	Television A		Television B		Television C	
	Amount	**%**	**Amount**	**%**	**Amount**	**%**
Sales revenue	$50,000	100	$90,000	100	$60,000	100
Variable costs...................	40,000	80	60,000	66 2/3	42,000	70
Contribution margin..........	$10,000	20	$30,000	33 1/3	$18,000	30
Sales mix	25%		45%		30%	

Instructions: Given these revenue and cost structures, complete the following:

1. Compute the break-even point in sales for the company, assuming that fixed costs total $34,800.

2. Compute the break-even point in sales for the company, assuming that fixed costs and total sales remain the same and that the sales mix is 50 percent of television A, 30 percent of television B, and 20 percent of television C.

3. Assume average sales prices per unit for television sets A, B, and C, respectively, of $250, $300, and $400. Further assume that there is unused capacity at current production levels of 40, 60, and 30 units of televisions A, B, and C, respectively. If New Marketing can sell all additional TVs it can make by discounting the selling price 15 percent, compute the total contribution margin not realized.

ANSWERS

Matching

1.	e	7.	h	13.	n
2.	l	8.	b	14.	p
3.	c	9.	i	15.	m
4.	g	10.	f	16.	q
5.	d	11.	a	17.	o
6.	k	12.	j		

True/False

1.	T	9.	F	16.	T
2.	T	10.	F	17.	T
3.	F	11.	T	18.	F
4.	T	12.	T	19.	F
5.	F	13.	T	20.	T
6.	T	14.	T	21.	T
7.	F	15.	T	22.	F
8.	T				

Multiple Choice

1.	b	9.	b	17.	a
2.	c	10.	a	18.	b
3.	c	11.	c	19.	d
4.	d	12.	b	20.	c
5.	d	13.	a	21.	d
6.	a	14.	c	22.	b
7.	a	15.	a	23.	a
8.	a	16.	b		

Exercises

E11-1   Fixed and Variable Costs

1. $\dfrac{\text{Change in cost}}{\text{Change in activity}} = \text{Per - case variable cost}$

$\dfrac{\$1,940,000 - \$1,460,000}{600,000 - 400,000} = \$2.40 \text{ per - case variable cost}$

Total costs   = Fixed costs + Variable costs

$1,940,000   = a + $2.40 (600,000 cases)

a   = $1,940,000 − $1,440,000

a   = $500,000 fixed costs

2. Total cost   = $500,000 + $2.40 (750,000 cases)

= $500,000 + $1,800,000

= $2,300,000

E11-2   Fixed and Variable Costs: Scattergraph Method

1. Scattergraph

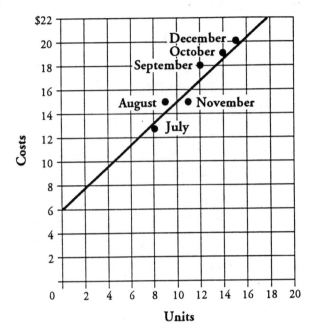

The actual line depends on how you draw it through your points. A line that crosses the cost axis between $4 and $6 would not be incorrect. The following calculations assume total fixed costs of $6.

2. Fixed cost   = $6

   Variable cost   = Slope of line

   $$= \frac{\$12 - \$8}{7 - 2} = \$0.80 \text{ per unit}$$

   Note: Any two points on the line could have been used.

3. Total cost   = Fixed cost + Variable cost (number of units)

   = $6 + $0.80(20)

   = $22

E11-3   Fixed and Variable Costs: High-Low Method

1. $\dfrac{\text{Change in total costs}}{\text{Change in units}}$ = Per - unit variable cost

   $$\frac{\$20 - \$13}{15 - 8} = \$1 \text{ per - unit variable cost}$$

   Total costs = Fixed costs + Variable costs

   At lowest point: $13 = a + $1(8)

                              a = $5 fixed costs

   At highest point: $20 = a + $1(15)

                              a = $5 fixed cost

2. Total cost   = Fixed cost + Variable cost per unit × (Number of units)
                 = $5 + $1(20)
                 = $\underline{\underline{\$25}}$

E11-4   Contribution Margin Income Statement

1. Contribution margin income statement:

Fix-Up Corporation
Contribution Margin Income Statement
For the Year Ended December 31, 2000

Sales revenue (at 19,000 rolls)		$133,000
Less variable expenses:		
Selling	$ 9,500	
Administrative......................................	7,600	
Manufacturing overhead	13,300	
Direct labor	11,400	
Direct materials	38,000	79,800
Contribution margin		$ 53,200
Less fixed expenses:		
Selling	$15,000	
Administrative......................................	25,000	
Manufacturing overhead	6,000	46,000
Net income		$ 7,200

2. Per-roll contribution margin:

$$\frac{\$53,200}{19,000} = \$2.80 \text{ per roll}$$

3. Profit at production and sales levels of 26,000 rolls of wallpaper:

$(26,000 \times \$2.80) - \$46,000 = \underline{\$26,800}$ profit

E11-5   Contribution Margin Analysis

1. $\dfrac{\$45,000}{500 \text{ units}} = \$90 \text{ per unit}$

2. $\dfrac{\text{Fixed costs}}{\text{Per - unit contribution margn}} = \dfrac{\$31,500}{\$90} = 350 \text{ units}$

3.
Revenues	100%
Variable costs	55
Contribution margin	45

4.
$10,000	additional sales
× 0.45	contribution margin ratio
$ 4,500	

E11-6   Equation Approach for CVP Analysis

1. $50 × 0.30 = $15; $50 − $15 = $35

$$\$50X = \$35X + \$90,000$$
$$\$15X = \$90,000$$
$$X = 6,000 \text{ units, or } 6,000 × \$50 = \$300,000$$

2.
$$\$50X = \$35X + \$90,000 + \$15,000$$
$$\$15X = \$105,000$$
$$X = 7,000$$

3.
$$\$50X = \$43X + \$90,000$$
$$\$7X = \$90,000$$
$$X = 12,857 \text{ units}$$

4.
$$\$50X = \$35X + \$70,000$$
$$\$15X = \$70,000$$
$$X = 4,667 \text{ units}$$

E11-7   Graphic Approach to CVP Analysis

1. Area   A = Fixed costs
   Area   B = Variable costs
   Area   C = Area of profits
   Line   D = Total cost line
   Line   E = Total revenue line
   Point   F = Break-even point

2. Total fixed costs are $1,000.

3. 200 units.

4. Variable costs per unit are $5, determined as follows:

$$\text{Total costs} = \text{Fixed costs} + (\text{Variable costs} × \text{Number of units})$$

At 200 units:
$$\$2,000 = \$1,000 + (X × 200)$$
$$\$1,000 = 200X$$
$$X = \$5$$

The variable cost per unit could be determined at any level of sales.

5. Sales price per unit is $10, determined as follows:

$$\text{Total revenues} = \text{Price per unit} × \text{Number of units}$$
$$\$2,000 \text{ sales} = X × 200$$
$$X = \$10$$

The sales price per unit could be determined at any level of sales.

E11-8   Effect on Profitability of Changes in Costs, Prices, and Volumes

1.
$$\$100X = \$40X + \$120,000$$
$$\$60X = \$120,000$$
$$X = 2,000 \text{ units}$$

2.
$$\$120X = \$40X + \$120,000$$
$$\$80X = \$120,000$$
$$X = 1,500 \text{ units}$$

3.
$$\$100X = \$50X + \$120,000$$
$$\$50X = \$120,000$$
$$X = 2,400 \text{ units}$$

4. $100X = $40X + $90,000
    $60X = $90,000
       X = 1,500 units

E11-9   Sales Mix

1.

	Television A		Television B		Television C		Total	
	Amount	%	Amount	%	Amount	%	Amount	%
Sales revenue	$50,000	100	$90,000	100	$60,000	100	$200,000	100
Variable costs	40,000	80	60,000	66 2/3	42,000	70	142,000	71
Contribution margin	$10,000	20	$30,000	33 1/3	$18,000	30	$ 58,000	29

$$\frac{\$34,800 \text{ fxed costs}}{29\% \text{ average contribution magin ratio}} = \$120,000$$

2.

	Television A		Television B		Television C		Total	
	Amount	%	Amount	%	Amount	%	Amount	%
Sales revenue	$100,000	100	$60,000	100	$40,000	100	$200,000	100
Variable costs	80,000	80	40,000	66 2/3	28,000	70	148,000	74
Contribution margin	$ 20,000	20	$20,000	33 1/3	$12,000	30	$ 52,000	26

$$\frac{\$34,800 \text{ fixed costs}}{26\% \text{ average contribution margin ratio}} = \$133,846$$

3.

	Television A	Television B	Television C
Average selling price	$250	$ 300	$ 400
Average selling price less 15%	$213 (rounded)	$ 255	$ 340
Less variable costs per unit	200	200	280
Contribution margin per unit	$ 13	$ 55	$ 60
Unused capacity	× 40	× 60	× 30
Contribution margin not realized	$520	$3,300	$1,800

Total contribution margin not realized = $5,620

Chapter 12
Standards and Performance Variances

LEARNING OBJECTIVES

After studying this chapter, you should be able to:

1. Explain why performance evaluation is such an important activity in organizations.

2. Describe the process of strategic planning in organizations.

3. Identify different kinds of organizational units in which performance evaluation occurs.

4. Explain how performance is evaluated in cost centers.

5. Explain how performance is evaluated in profit centers.

6. Explain how performance is evaluated in investment centers.

7. Explain why it is important for a company to have quality and time standards as well as financial standards.

CHAPTER REVIEW

Why Performance Evaluation Is So Important

1. Because information, products, services, and investment funds can be transferred easily in our modern economy, it is important that a business operate as efficiently and effectively as possible. Only the best companies will be able to survive in the long run.

2. Performance evaluation is important for both planning and control purposes. Forecasts and budgets of material, labor, and support needs help a business plan its operations. In addition, continuous feedback allows management to compare actual performance to expected performance in order to pinpoint and fix problem areas.

Strategic Planning

3. Strategic planning is a systematic effort to establish basic company purposes, objectives, policies, and strategies. A strategic plan also outlines plans to implement these broader objectives.

4. Four common steps in establishing a strategic plan are:

a. establish a mission statement,
b. specify broad goals or guidelines,
c. define action steps to be accomplished, and
d. establish performance measures.

Performance Evaluation in Different Types of Operating Units

5. In small businesses, one person often handles all business functions, such as sales, produc-

tion, engineering, and accounting. As businesses grow, most companies divide responsibilities on a functional (for example, sales versus production), geographical, and divisional basis. This distribution of administrative functions among several managers is called decentralization.

6. Decentralization has the following advantages:

    a. Segment managers have better information to make decisions because they are closer to the action.
    b. Segment managers can react to problems quickly.
    c. Higher-level management can spend time on broad policy and strategic issues.
    d. Segment managers have immediate and direct responsibility for the performance of their segments.
    e. Decentralization leads to more chances for advancement.
    f. Decentralization leads to more specific definition of responsibility and thus to better evaluation of performance.

7. The major problem of decentralization is the difficulty in getting managers to make decisions that are congruent with the goals of the firm as a whole. In a decentralized environment, managers are sometimes inclined to make decisions that will benefit their unit but may hurt the profitability of the entire firm.

8. The concept of assigning responsibility for controlling costs and generating revenues to individuals at various levels is called responsibility accounting.

9. Responsibility centers prepare exception reports that flow up the organization so that top management can know what is going on in all subunits.

10. There are three types of responsibility centers: (a) cost centers, where managers are respnsible for costs incurred; (b) profit centers, where managers are responsible for both costs and revenues; and (c) investment centers, where managers have responsibility for costs, revenues, and assets. Although cost centers can be found anywhere in a firm, profit and investment centers usually exist only at relatively high levels.

11. The responsibility centers of most firms compete for corporate assets. As a result, each subunit tries to perform better than the other centers. The performance of cost centers is usually measured by comparing actual costs with standard costs or flexible budget amounts. In profit centers the measure of performance is the contribution margin provided toward overall company goals. The performance of an investment center is usually measured by its return on investment (ROI) or residual income.

Evaluating Performance in Cost Centers

12. Standard costs are predetermined costs that serve as a benchmark for judging what actual costs should be. A standard cost has a quantitative component (number of units of material or number of direct labor hours) and a monetary component (cost per unit of material or cost per hour of labor). When the number of units is multiplied by the unit cost, the resulting dollar amount is the standard cost.

13. Standard costs are computed for direct materials, direct labor, and for variable and fixed manufacturing overhead.

14. Standard costs are used to develop budgets, measure performance of business units and managers, develop product costs, and reduce the cost of bookkeeping. Standard costs help managers in planning to acquire direct materials, employ direct labor, and provide sufficient manufacturing support to produce the products for sale. Standard cost information also helps management decide whether the company can handle special orders.

15. Variances are the difference between standard and actual costs of a company. By examining variances, management can determine how efficiently the company is producing its goods or providing its services.

16. The steps in operating a standard cost system after the standards have been developed are:

    a. Collecting actual costs.
    b. Comparing actual and budgeted costs to identify variances.
    c. Reporting operating results, including variances, to the responsible managers.
    d. Analyzing the causes of significant, controllable variances.
    e. Taking action to eliminate the significant variances.
    f. Journalizing actual and standard costs and recording the variances.

17. Standard costs are shown on a cost card in terms of cost per unit of product; they are included in a budget as the total expected cost for the expected volume of production (standard cost per unit times number of units).

18. The steps in establishing standard costs and identifying variances are:

a. Developing standard costs (using the experience of accountants, engineers, purchasing agents, and department managers) by multiplying the standard quantity by the standard price to arrive at a standard dollar cost.

b. Collecting actual costs.

c. Comparing actual and budgeted costs to identify variances. Variances are computed for direct materials, direct labor, and variable and fixed manufacturing overhead.

The general model below for calculating variances shows how to calculate a price (rate) variance and a quantity (usage variance). The price (rate) variance compares actual quantities of inputs with the actual and standard prices. The quantity (usage) variance compares the inputs actually used at the standard price with the inputs that should have been used at the standard price to produce the actual output.

(1)	(2)	(3)
AQ × AP	**AQ × SP**	**SQ × SP**
(Actual quantity of inputs × Actual price)	(Actual quantity of inputs × Standard price)	(Standard quantity of inputs allowed for actual output × Standard price)

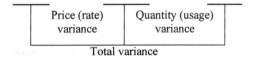

	Price (rate) variance	Quantity (usage) variance

Total variance

19. For materials and labor, there is a price standard and a quantity (usage or efficiency) standard.

a. A materials price variance can be determined at the time materials are purchased or when they are put into production. The materials price variance is computed by subtracting the actual quantity purchased or used times the standard price from the actual quantity purchased or used times the actual price:

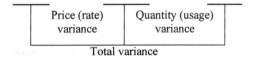

AQ × AP	**AQ × SP**
8,000 lbs. × $4.10 =	8,000 lbs. × $4.00 =
$32,800	$32,000

$800 U

b. A materials quantity variance is computed by subtracting the standard quantity times the standard price from the actual quantity used times the standard price:

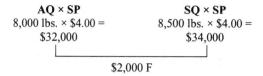

AQ × SP	**SQ × SP**
8,000 lbs. × $4.00 =	8,500 lbs. × $4.00 =
$32,000	$34,000

$2,000 F

c. The journal entry to record the materials price variance can be made when the goods are purchased or when they are placed in production. If the entry for the materials price variance is made when the goods are placed in production, the materials quantity variance is usually recorded at the same time.

To record the materials price variance when goods are purchased:

Raw Materials Inventory..............	xxx	
Materials Price Variance (U)........	xxx	
Cash (Accounts Payable)		xxx

To record the materials price variance and materials quantity variance when goods are placed in production:

Work-in-Process Inventory	xxx	
Materials Price Variance (U)........	xxx	
Materials Quantity Variance (F)		xxx
Raw Materials Inventory		xxx

d. The labor rate variance reflects the difference between actual wage rates and standard wage rates. It is computed by subtracting the actual labor hours worked times the standard wage rate from the actual labor hours worked times the actual wage rate paid:

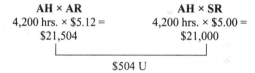

AH × AR	**AH × SR**
4,200 hrs. × $5.12 =	4,200 hrs. × $5.00 =
$21,504	$21,000

$504 U

e. The labor efficiency variance is a quantity variance that reflects the cost of using more or less actual hours than the standard. It is computed by subtracting the standard number of labor hours times the standard wage rate from the actual number of labor hours worked times the standard wage rate:

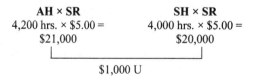

AH × SR	**SH × SR**
4,200 hrs. × $5.00 =	4,000 hrs. × $5.00 =
$21,000	$20,000

$1,000 U

f. The journal entry to record the labor efficiency and labor rate variances is made when the labor cost is known. Work-in-Process Inventory is debited with standard labor costs and Salaries Payable is credited with actual labor costs.

Work-in-Process Inventory	xxx
Labor Rate Variance (U)	xxx
Labor Efficiency Variance (U) ...	xxx
Salaries Payable	xxx

    g. The price and quantity variances for materials and labor show the following:

        (1)   The materials price variance is the extent to which actual price varies from the standard price for the quantity of materials purchased or used.

        (2)   The materials quantity variance is the extent to which actual materials used vary from the standard quantity.

        (3)   The labor rate variance is the extent to which the actual labor rate varies from the standard rate for the quantity of labor used.

        (4)   The labor efficiency variance is the extent to which the labor used varies from the standard quantity.

20. The advantages of a standard cost system are:

    a. Setting standard costs requires a careful analysis of operations.

    b. Standard costs serve as a guide for future planning.

    c. The development of standard costs is based on an understanding of cost behavior.

    d. A standard cost system is simpler to operate than a historical cost system.

    e. A standard cost system helps to identify and control problem areas.

    f. Standard costs are an integral part of responsibility accounting.

    g. A standard cost system is compatible with the principle of management by exception.

21. The disadvantages of a standard cost system are:

    a. A standard cost system is expensive and time consuming.

    b. Standard costs are of limited use for custom operations.

    c. Variances are easily misinterpreted because so many factors are involved.

    d. Standard costs must be changed to reflect changed conditions.

    e. Labor tends to view efficiency measures with mistrust.

    f. Random fluctuations are not easily distinguished from systematic fluctuations.

Evaluating Performance in Profit Centers

22. Profit centers are responsibility centers where managers are responsible for both costs and revenues. Profit centers usually exist at a higher level than cost centers.

23. Profit center performance is usually measured by a segment-margin income statement, which is used to compare the revenues and costs of the company's segments.

    a. It shows which segments are more profitable, both in absolute terms and in terms of a contribution-margin ratio, which takes into account the relative size of the segment.

    b. It provides information about the allocation of costs among segments. It distinguishes between direct and indirect costs, and between variable and fixed costs.

    c. Direct costs can be traced directly to a segment, as opposed to indirect costs, which have no obvious link to a particular segment. Managers should not be held responsible for indirect costs over which they have no control.

Evaluating Performance in Investment Centers

24. Investment centers are usually found at a higher level than cost and profit centers in most companies. The performance of an investment center is usually measured by its rate of return on investment (ROI) or residual income.

25. The ROI is defined as net income divided by average total assets:

Operating Performance	×	Asset Turnover	=	Return on Investment
$\dfrac{\text{Net income}}{\text{Net sales}}$	×	$\dfrac{\text{Net sales}}{\text{Average total assets}}$	=	$\dfrac{\text{Net income}}{\text{Average total assets}}$

These relationships show that ROI is a function of three variables: net income, net sales, and average total assets. ROI can be increased by (a) increasing net sales, (b) reducing costs, or (c) reducing the level of operating assets.

26. Residual income is the amount of net income an investment center is able to earn above a minimum rate of return on assets. It encourages management to make as much profit as possible rather than merely achieving a certain return on assets.

27. Despite the widespread use of these performance measures, they both have drawbacks:

    a. Divisions with a high ROI may not accept projects that would be good for the company as a whole if such projects lower the segment rate of return.

    b. Both ROI and residual income focus management's attention on short-run profitability.

Quality and Time Standards

28. Nonmonetary measures are also essential in properly evaluating performance. These nonmonetary standards might reflect characteristics of operations such as time and quality. Time and quality standards must be well defined, objective, and measurable.

29. Those organizations that can deliver the highest quality products to their customers at the lowest prices and in the shortest amount of time will ultimately be most successful.

COMMON ERRORS

The most common mistake made by students learning how to analyze performance is confusing the rate of return in ROI with minimum return in residual income.

Investment centers can be evaluated either by ROI or by residual income. ROI is computed by dividing net income by average total assets. The result is a calculated actual rate being earned; it is not a target or predetermined rate. With residual income, the minimum rate of return is predetermined. The amount of income needed to earn this rate is subtracted from total expected income. ROI, although it is better known and probably more widely used, has a serious drawback; it discourages investment in profitable projects whose return is less than the current ROI. With residual income, the focus is on determining how much extra or "residual" income over the minimum desired rate of return will be earned. Thus, ROI calculates the actual rate of return, while residual income uses a predetermined rate of return to compute the excess income to be earned from an investment.

SELF-TEST

Matching

Instructions: Write the letter of each of the following terms in the space to the left of its appropriate definition.

a.	variance	**l.**	responsibility center
b.	standard cost	**m.**	cost center
c.	materials price variance	**n.**	decentralized company
d.	materials quantity variance	**o.**	centralized company
e.	labor efficiency variance	**p.**	investment center
f.	labor rate variance	**q.**	return on investment
g.	historical standard	**r.**	segment margin income statement
h.	management by exception	**s.**	asset turnover ratio
i.	standard cost system	**t.**	residual income
j.	responsibility accounting	**u.**	operating performance ratio
k.	exception report	**v.**	profit center

_____ 1. The strategy that focuses attention on actual costs that vary significantly from standard costs.

_____ 2. In a standard cost system, the extent to which the actual price varies from the standard price for the quantity of materials used.

_____ 3. The difference between the predetermined standard and the actual price paid for quantity used.

_____ 4. In a standard cost system, the extent to which the labor used varies from the standard quantity.

_____ 5. In a standard cost system, the extent to which materials used vary from the standard quantity.

_____ 6. A system of product costing in which predetermined costs are used instead of actual costs.

_____ 7. A guide for judging actual performance based on average productivity of recent periods.

_____ 8. In a standard cost system, the extent to which the actual labor rate varies from the standard rate for the quantity of labor used.

_____ 9. A predetermined cost of producing a unit of output.

_____ 10. An organization in which managers at lower levels have authority to make decisions.

_____ 11. An organization in which top management makes most of the decisions for all levels of operations.

_____ 12. An organizational unit in which a manager has control over and is held accountable for costs.

_____ 13. A system of performance evaluation that holds managers responsible for costs, revenues, assets, or other elements they control.

_____ 14. A report that highlights variances from, or exceptions to, the budget.

_____ 15. The ratio of net income to net sales used in computing the return on investment.

_____ 16. An organizational unit in which a manager is responsible for costs, revenues, and assets.

_____ 17. An organizational unit in which the manager has control over, and is held accountable for, performance.

_____ 18. A measure of operating performance and efficiency in utilizing assets to generate a return for both creditors and owners; computed by dividing net income by average total assets.

_____ 19. The amount of net income an investment center is able to earn above a certain minimum rate of return on assets.

_____ 20. A statement that identifies costs directly chargeable to a segment and divides them into variable and fixed cost behavior patterns.

_____ 21. Responsibility center whose manager is held accountable for both costs and revenues.

_____ 22. The ratio of net sales to average total assets.

True/False

Instructions: Place a check mark in the appropriate column to indicate whether each of the following statements is true or false.

	True	False
1. A quantity standard is used to judge the total cost the firm should pay for the quantity purchased.	_____	_____
2. The management-by-exception strategy focuses attention on those costs that approximate the standard costs.	_____	_____
3. A materials price variance is computed by multiplying the difference between the actual and the standard price by the standard quantity.	_____	_____
4. A materials quantity variance represents the difference between the actual quantity used and the standard quantity expected to be used, multiplied by the standard price.	_____	_____
5. The labor efficiency variance is computed using the same principles used to compute the materials quantity variance.	_____	_____
6. A price variance is considered to be favorable when the actual price is higher than the standard price for goods purchased.	_____	_____
7. An efficiency variance is unfavorable when the actual usage of labor is greater than the expected usage.	_____	_____
8. The sum of the materials price variance and the materials quantity variance equals the total materials variance.	_____	_____
9. If the labor rate variance and the labor efficiency variance are computed at the same point in the production process, the sum of the two variances will equal the total labor variance.	_____	_____
10. The materials price variance is the responsibility of the production department manager when the usual materials are bought in a normal volume.	_____	_____
11. A materials quantity variance may occur because of the level of maintenance performed on a machine.	_____	_____
12. In standard costing, performance measurements are more accurate when standard input measures are used.	_____	_____
13. Standard costing is of little worth to service institutions that do not produce physical products.	_____	_____
14. Variances from standard are usually reflected in the income statement of the period in which they occur.	_____	_____
15. Statistical techniques are sometimes used to help a manager decide which variances from standard should be carefully investigated.	_____	_____
16. Once standards are developed for a standard cost system, they need not be changed even though operating conditions change.	_____	_____
17. A company in which top management makes all decisions is a decentralized firm.	_____	_____
18. Decentralization usually leads to more timely decisions than centralization.	_____	_____
19. A drawback of decentralization is that decisions made by subunit managers are sometimes short-sighted.	_____	_____
20. In a decentralized environment, managers of subunits are usually held responsible for controlling costs or generating revenues in their centers.	_____	_____
21. The manager of a cost center usually has responsibility for controlling costs and generating revenues.	_____	_____
22. Profit centers are usually found at higher levels in an organization than are investment centers.	_____	_____
23. In a profit center, segments are usually measured by return on investment.	_____	_____

	True	False
24. Indirect costs are also known as variable costs.	_____	_____
25. Indirect costs are usually controllable by segment managers.	_____	_____
26. A segment-margin income statement should contain only those costs that are controllable by the manager.	_____	_____
27. Return on investment is used to measure performance in cost centers.	_____	_____
28. Operating performance is equal to net operating income divided by net operating assets.	_____	_____
29. ROI is equal to operating performance multiplied by asset turnover.	_____	_____
30. Asset turnover refers to the rate that assets are used in a company in generating sales.	_____	_____
31. ROI can be increased by increasing the level of operating assets.	_____	_____
32. Residual income is used to measure performance in cost centers.	_____	_____
33. Residual income encourages managers to make as much profit as possible.	_____	_____
34. Goal congruence is not important to a decentralized company.	_____	_____

Multiple Choice

Instructions: Circle the letter that best completes each of the following statements.

1. Which of the following concepts is *not* generally applied in cost control in a manufacturing company?

    a. Standard costs
    b. Opportunity cost
    c. Variance analysis
    d. Management by exception

2. A standard cost system is used to control all of the following costs *except*

    a. direct materials.
    b. indirect materials.
    c. factory depreciation.
    d. indirect labor.

Use the following information to compute the variances indicated in Questions 3–8.

Standard cost per unit:
    Direct materials (2 pounds)............................ $4
    Direct labor (1 hour)   5

Actual resources used:
    Direct materials (2,100 pounds at $2.10).......   4,410
    Direct labor (990 hours at $5.20)..................   5,148
    Units of output...   1,000

3. The quantity of direct materials that should have been used is

    a. 990 pounds.
    b. 1,000 pounds.
    c. 2,000 pounds.
    d. 2,100 pounds.
    e. 2,200 pounds.

4. The number of direct labor hours that should have been used is

   a. 990 hours.
   b. 1,000 hours.
   c. 2,000 hours.
   d. 2,100 hours.
   e. 2,200 hours.

5. The materials price variance for materials actually used is

   a. $200 F.
   b. $200 U.
   c. $210 F.
   d. $210 U.

6. The materials quantity variance is

   a. $200 F.
   b. $200 U.
   c. $400 F.
   d. $400 U.

7. The labor efficiency variance is

   a. $52 F.
   b. $52 U.
   c. $50 F.
   d. $50 U.

8. The labor rate variance is

   a. $210 F.
   b. $210 U.
   c. $200 F.
   d. $198 U.

9. All the following are reasons why a variance should be investigated, *except*

   a. whether favorable or unfavorable.
   b. frequency of occurrence.
   c. impact on profitability.
   d. controllability.

10. All the following are advantages of a standard cost system, *except*

    a. it facilitates future planning.
    b. it need not change as conditions change.
    c. it facilitates the principle of management by exception.
    d. it is more useful than using actual costs when evaluating employee performance.

11. Responsibilities in companies can be divided by

    a. geographic regions.
    b. function.
    c. division.
    d. All of the above

12. Which of the following is *not* a benefit of decentralization?

    a. More timely decisions can be made.
    b. Better decisions are usually made.
    c. Top management can keep closer tabs on the activities of the entire organization.
    d. Managers and officers can be evaluated more easily.

13. Which of the following is a disadvantage of decentralization?

    a. There is less incentive for subunit managers to perform well.
    b. Subunit managers often make decisions that are not consistent with the objectives of the firm as a whole.
    c. It is more difficult to train future managers in a decentralized environment.
    d. The decision-making process is slower in a decentralized environment.

14. Which of the following is *not* a type of responsibility center?

    a. Profit center
    b. Investment center
    c. Marketing center
    d. Cost center

15. In what type of center are managers usually evaluated on the basis of the contribution margin they provide to the company?

    a. Profit center
    b. Cost center
    c. Investment center
    d. Marketing center

16. The type of center usually found at the lowest level in an organization is

    a. a profit center.
    b. a cost center.
    c. an investment center.
    d. corporate headquarters.

17. As exception reports flow up an organization, they

    a. become more specific.
    b. become more general.
    c. stay the same in terms of detail.
    d. become less useful.

18. Which of the following will increase ROI?

    a. Decreasing sales
    b. Decreasing net income
    c. Reducing the level of operating assets
    d. Increasing the level of operating assets

19. Asset turnover refers to

    a. net operating income divided by net sales.
    b. net operating income divided by average total assets.
    c. net sales divided by average total assets.
    d. net sales divided by net operating income.

20. An advantage of residual income is that

    a. it encourages managers to earn a certain return on assets.
    b. it encourages managers to make as much profit as possible.
    c. it prohibits managers from making bad investment decisions.
    d. it can be used in cost centers as well as investment centers.

21. Which of the following is true of the minimum rate of return used in the residual income approach?
    a. It is usually greater than the rate used in the ROI approach.
    b. It is usually equal to or greater than the rate used in the ROI approach.
    c. It is usually equal to or less than the rate used in the ROI approach.
    d. None of the above

Exercises

E12-1   Materials Variances

Redbud Manufacturing Company operates a standard cost system. You have been asked to review the materials purchases and usage for the month of March to determine the variances to be recorded. During March, 8,000 pounds of material were purchased at a cost of $4.50 per pound. Of that material, 6,300 pounds were used to produce 3,000 units of product. The standard price per pound is $4.40. The standard amount of material for each unit of product is 2 pounds.

Instructions: 1. Compute the materials price variance if the material is carried in inventory at the standard price.
2. Compute the materials price variance if the material is carried in inventory at the actual price and is charged to Work-in-Process Inventory at the standard price.
3. Compute the materials quantity variance.

E12-2   Labor Variances

The standard cost card for Green Machinery Company shows a standard direct labor usage of 50 hours per machine at a cost of $12 per hour. During October, the company incurred 1,800 hours of labor at a cost of $11.80 per hour to produce 35 machines.

Instructions: 1. Compute the labor rate variance for October.
2. Compute the labor efficiency variance for October.

E12-3   ROI Calculations

Meadowbrook International has three divisions: Africa, Europe, and America. Below are operating data for 2000:

	Africa	Europe	America
Net sales...............................	$100,000	$200,000	$300,000
Net operating income.................	20,000	38,000	59,000
Average total assets	60,000	110,000	185,000

Instructions: Given these data, calculate the ROI for each division.

E12-4   Segment Margin and Performance Evaluation

Maryland Corporation has two divisions: Mercer and Bethesda. Operating data for 2000 are:

	Mercer	**Bethesda**
Sales revenue	$425,000	$500,000
Variable costs	$12 per unit	$13 per unit
Fixed costs:		
Unique to department	$100,000	$180,000
Allocated from corporate headquarters	$60,000	$150,000
Sales price of product	$25	$25

Instructions: Given this information, complete the following requirements:
1. Compute the net income (loss) of each decision (ignore income taxes).
2. Compute the contribution to company profits of each division.
3. Should either division be discontinued? Why or why not?

E12-5   ROI and Residual Income

Hunt and Rees Companies operate in the same industry. In 2000, both have average total assets of $200,000 and Hunt uses a 20 percent ROI to evaluate its investment centers. Rees uses residual income with a 15 percent minimum rate of return. Both have an opportunity to invest $50,000 in a new asset that will generate a profit of $9,000.

Instructions: Given these data, complete the following requirements:
1. Compute the return on this investment.
2. Compute Rees Company's residual income on the investment.

ANSWERS

Matching

1.	h	9.	b	16.	p
2.	c	10.	n	17.	l
3.	a	11.	o	18.	q
4.	e	12.	m	19.	t
5.	d	13.	j	20.	r
6.	i	14.	k	21.	v
7.	g	15.	u	22.	s
8.	f				

True/False

1.	F	13.	F	24.	F
2.	F	14.	T	25.	F
3.	F	15.	T	26.	T
4.	T	16.	F	27.	F
5.	T	17.	F	28.	F
6.	F	18.	T	29.	T
7.	T	19.	T	30.	T
8.	T	20.	T	31.	F
9.	T	21.	F	32.	F
10.	F	22.	F	33.	T
11.	T	23.	F	34.	F
12.	T				

Multiple Choice

1.	b	8.	d	15.	a
2.	c	9.	a	16.	b
3.	c	10.	b	17.	b
4.	b	11.	d	18.	c
5.	d	12.	c	19.	c
6.	b	13.	b	20.	b
7.	c	14.	c	21.	c

Exercises

E12-1   Materials Variance

1. Materials price variance (carried at standard cost):

Actual price	$4.50
Standard price	– 4.40
Difference...................................	$0.10
Pounds purchased.......................	×8,000
Total materials price variance	$800 U

AQ × AP	**AQ × SP**
8,000 lbs. × $4.50 =	8,000 lbs. × $4.40 =
$36,000	$35,200

$800 U

2. Materials price variance (carried at actual cost):

Actual price	$4.50
Standard price	– 4.40
Difference.................................	$0.10
Material used (pounds)..............	×6,300
Total materials price variance .	$630 U

3. Materials quantity variance:

Actual usage	6,300 pounds
Standard usage (3,000 units × 2 pounds)	6,000 pounds
Difference...	300 pounds
Standard price per pound...............................	×$4.40
Total materials quantity variance	$1,320 U

Materials variances, based on amount used:

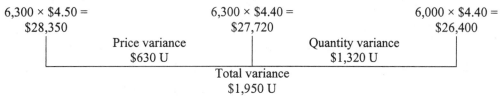

6,300 × $4.50 =	6,300 × $4.40 =	6,000 × $4.40 =
$28,350	$27,720	$26,400

Price variance $630 U   Quantity variance $1,320 U

Total variance $1,950 U

E12-2   Labor Variances

1. Labor rate variance:

Actual rate	$11.80
Standard rate	12.00
Difference...	$ 0.20
Actual hours	×1,800
Total labor rate variance.............................	$ 360 F

2. Labor efficiency variance:

Actual hours	1,800
Standard hours (35 machines × 50 hours)	–1,750
Difference...	50
Standard rate	×$12
Total labor efficiency variance.....................	$ 600 U

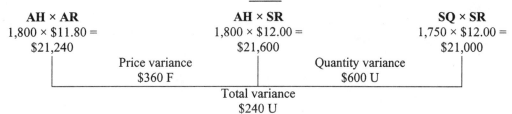

AH × AR	**AH × SR**	**SQ × SR**
1,800 × $11.80 =	1,800 × $12.00 =	1,750 × $12.00 =
$21,240	$21,600	$21,000

Price variance $360 F   Quantity variance $600 U

Total variance $240 U

E12-3   ROI Calculations

$$\text{ROI} = \text{Operating performance} \times \text{Asset turnover}$$

$$= \frac{\text{net income}}{\text{net sales}} \times \frac{\text{net sales}}{\text{average total assets}}$$

$$\text{Africa} = \frac{\$20,000}{\$100,000} \times \frac{\$100,000}{\$60,000} = 33.3\%$$

$$\text{Europe} = \frac{\$38,000}{\$200,000} \times \frac{\$200,000}{\$110,000} = 34.5\%$$

$$\text{America} = \frac{\$59,000}{\$300,000} \times \frac{\$300,000}{\$185,000} = 31.9\%$$

It appears that the division in Europe has the best performance.

E12-4   Segment Margin and Performance Evaluation

1. *Net income:*

	Mercer	Bethesda
Sales revenue	$425,000	$500,000
Variable costs	204,000	260,000
Segment margin	$221,000	$240,000
Fixed costs	160,000	330,000
Net income (loss)	$ 61,000	$ (90,000)

Note: The number of units sold is calculated by dividing total sales by the selling price.

2. *Contribution to company profits:*

	Mercer	Bethesda
Segment margin	$221,000	$240,000
Unique fixed costs	100,000	180,000
Contribution to company profits	$121,000	$ 60,000

3. Neither division should be discontinued, because each makes a positive contribution to the company's overall profits.

E12-5   ROI and Residual Income

1. $\dfrac{\text{net income}}{\text{investment}} = \dfrac{\$9,000}{\$50,000} = 18\%$

2.
Investment	$50,000
Minimum rate of return	0.15
	$ 7,500

Profit	$ 9,000
Minimum return	7,500
Residual income	$ 1,500

Chapter 13
Operating Budgets

LEARNING OBJECTIVES

After studying this chapter, you should be able to:

1. Describe different types of budgeting and identify the purposes of budgeting.
2. Describe the budgeting process and its behavioral implications.
3. Explain the master budget and its components for manufacturing firms, merchandising firms, and service firms.
4. Prepare pro-forma financial statements
5. Distinguish between static and flexible budgets.

CHAPTER REVIEW

Types and Purposes of Budgeting

1. A budget is a quantitative expression of a plan of action; it shows how a firm will acquire and use its resources over some specified period of time.

2. There are three levels of planning in a firm: (a) strategic planning, which is the making of broad policy decisions that affect a company's long-run operations; (b) capital budgeting, which is the planning for the purchase of long-term operational assets; and (c) operations budgeting, which is the setting of budget levels for sales, production, expenses, and cash for the immediate period ahead, usually one year.

3. The budgeting process has seven purposes: (a) it encourages planning; (b) it enhances communications; (c) it helps management at all levels to coordinate activities; (d) it provides authorization for investing, spending, borrowing, and producing; (e) it helps motivate employees to perform; (f) it helps resolve conflicts; and (g) it provides quantitative measures of expectations and objectives.

4. Budgeting usually evolves within a firm from (a) little or no accounting records, to (b) historical records only, and (c) complete budgeting.

The Budgeting Process

5. Most large companies have a budget committee, which includes top executives as well as those persons responsible for the items being budgeted. When managers participate in the budgeting process, they are generally more motivated to achieve the budget goals.

6. If only top management is involved in budget preparation, it is called *top-down budgeting*. When each segment manager prepares a budget for that segment's operations, it is called *bottom-up budgeting*. Most companies use a combination of the two approaches.

The Master Budget

7. The operating budget is called a master budget because it is an integrated group of detailed budgets that cover a specific time period. It usually includes a sales forecast and budgets for (a) sales, (b) production or purchases, (c) selling and administrative expenses, (d) cash, and (e) the primary financial statements.

8. It is extremely important to have an accurate sales forecast, because all budgets are based on the forecast. Because the level of sales depends on factors extraneous to a firm (such as customer tastes and economic conditions), most firms spend a considerable amount of money trying to assess future sales accurately. Common methods of forecasting include gathering opinions from executives and salespeople and using quantitative techniques and computer models.

9. Once a sales forecast has been completed as a basis for desired levels of sales and ending inventory, production or purchase levels are budgeted. The production or purchases budget (expected sales + desired ending inventory − beginning inventory) is the focal point from which most other operating budgets flow.

10. When production levels are known for a manufacturing company, direct materials and direct labor can be budgeted. These budgets are calculated as follows:

    a. Direct materials usage (number of units to be produced × direct materials per unit) and direct materials purchases budget [(desired raw materials ending inventory + raw materials needed for production − beginning raw materials inventory) × unit cost of materials].

    b. Direct labor budget (number of units to be produced × direct labor hours per unit × cost per hour).

11. Two other budgets for a manufacturing company are the manufacturing overhead and the selling and administrative expense budgets. Basically, these budgets are listings of the anticipated variable and fixed expenditures in each area.

12. Probably the most critical detailed operating budget is the cash budget, which outlines expected cash receipts and disbursements for the coming period. The cash budget points out periods when excess cash will be available and periods when short-term borrowing will be necessary. Because accuracy is critical, the cash budget is often prepared monthly.

Budgeting for Operations in a Merchandising Firm

13. Budgeting for merchandising companies is similar to budgeting for manufacturing companies except the purchases budget replaces the production, direct materials, direct labor, and manufacturing budgets used by manufacturing firms.

Budgeting for Operations in a Service Firm

14. Budgeting for service companies does not require a purchases budget because there is no manufactured or purchased inventory to account for. However, the general budgeting process is similar to the process used for other types of companies.

Pro-Forma Financial Statements

15. The final set of operating budgets are the pro-forma financial statements. These statements are based on the other budgets and are valuable because they formalize a company's estimated level of profits, assets, and liabilities. It is on the basis of these pro-forma financial statements that management assesses how well the coming year's anticipated operations fit into long-range objectives and goals.

Static versus Flexible Budgeting

16. A flexible budget projects operating costs at various levels of activity. It is more useful and versatile than a static budget, especially for performance evaluation.

17. Because they compare actual to budgeted results at a given activity level, flexible budgets allow meaningful analyses of both the cost control and production control elements of managers' responsibility.

18. The steps in preparing a flexible budget are:

    a. Determine a relevant range of production.

    b. Segregate manufacturing costs into their various cost components.

c. Using a per-unit cost for each item, prepare a budget of expected costs at various activity levels.

COMMON ERRORS

The two most common errors made by students trying to understand the material in this chapter are:

1. Including the wrong data in one of the budget schedules.

2. Incorrectly integrating the individual budgets into the pro-forma financial statements.

1. Conceptual Mistakes

The master budget consists of several schedules, each involving different categories of items and costs. With all these data, it is easy to get confused about which go where. For example, where do beginning and ending inventory numbers fit into the direct materials usage and purchases budget? Should expenses be allocated among quarters in the manufacturing overhead and the selling and administrative expense budgets? The cash budget is complex; special care should be taken in structuring this budget, including precise labeling of each item.

A conceptual or mathematical error in the first quarter will carry through the entire cash budget, and through the pro-forma financial statements as well. The only way to avoid such mistakes is to prepare a model of each schedule and refer to it constantly until the contents of the schedule become second nature. Memorizing the items will not help you to understand why a schedule is organized as it is.

2. Integrating the Individual Budgets

The pro-forma income statements will be accurate only if all the preliminary schedules are mathematically and conceptually correct. Students should ask themselves three key questions: (a) Do I understand the purpose and nature of this budget well enough to have structured it correctly? (b) Have I conceptually selected the right number for each line of the budget, including amounts carried over from previously-prepared budgets? (c) Is the budget mathematically correct? If each budget is carefully prepared, much time will be saved later in trying to correct mistakes that flow through the entire master budget.

SELF-TEST

Matching

Instructions: Write the letter of each of the following terms in the space to the left of its appropriate definition.

a. direct materials budget
b. direct labor budget
c. manufacturing overhead budget
d. capital budgeting
e. budgeting
f. selling and administrative expense budget
g. operating budget

h. cash budget
i. production budget
j. master budget
k. strategic planning
l. unit cost computation
m. flexible budget
n. pro-forma financial statements

_____ 1. A schedule of direct labor requirements for the budget period.

_____ 2. The systematic planning for capital investments.

_____ 3. An estimate of the total direct materials, direct labor, and manufacturing overhead costs required to make one unit of a product.

_____ 4. The setting of immediate goals for sales, production, expenses, and the availability of cash.

_____ 5. A schedule of production costs other than those for direct labor and direct materials.

_____ 6. A schedule of all nonproduction spending that will occur during the budget period.

_____ 7. A schedule of production requirements for the budget period.

_____ 8. A schedule of direct materials to be purchased and used in production during the budget period.

_____ 9. A schedule of expected cash receipts and disbursements during the budget period.

_____ 10. Broad, long-range planning usually conducted by top management.

_____ 11. A process of summarizing probable revenues and expenditures for a given period, which shows how a firm is expected to acquire and use its financial resources.

_____ 12. A network of many separate schedules and budgets, which together provide an overall financial plan for the coming period.

_____ 13. Financial statements prepared from components of the master budget.

_____ 14. A budget that projects revenues and costs in relation to varying activity levels.

True/False

Instructions: Place a check mark in the appropriate column to indicate whether each of the following statements is true or false.

	True	False
1. The broadest, highest-level planning in a firm is called capital planning.	_____	_____
2. A budget is a quantitative expression of a plan of action.	_____	_____
3. Budgets help motivate employees.	_____	_____
4. Top-down budgeting is always more effective than bottom-up budgeting.	_____	_____
5. Budget committees are often comprised of vice presidents of a corporation.	_____	_____
6. The group of integrated, detailed budgets is known as the master budget.	_____	_____
7. The first step in completing the master budget is the completion of the production budget.	_____	_____
8. The production budget is usually expressed in terms of units.	_____	_____
9. The production budget is equal to expected sales minus beginning inventory.	_____	_____
10. Direct materials usage must be calculated before the direct materials purchases can be determined.	_____	_____

	True	False

11. An accurate direct labor budget can help avoid such things as frequent hirings, firings, layoffs,and overtime work. .... _____ _____

12. Once a master budget is prepared, it is never changed during the year. .... _____ _____

13. Budgets prepared for a merchandise company will be identical to budgets prepared for a manufacturing company. .... _____ _____

14. A cash budget points out periods when excess cash will be available and periods when short-term borrowing will be necessary. .... _____ _____

15. The cash budget is probably one of the most important budgets prepared. .... _____ _____

16. The budgeting process is more complicated for a service company than for a manufacturing company. .... _____ _____

17. Before a pro-forma income statement can be prepared, information about unit costs, ending inventory, and cost of goods sold must be available. .... _____ _____

18. The pro-forma statement of cash flows is a composite of data from most other budgets. .... _____ _____

19. Although pro-forma income statements and balance sheets can be based on information in the other operating budgets, it is not possible to prepare a pro-forma statement of cash flows. .... _____ _____

20. A flexible budget is used in controlling manufacturing overhead costs by identifying the difference between actual incurred cost and expected cost at that production level. .... _____ _____

Multiple Choice

Instructions: Circle the letter that best completes each of the following statements.

1. Which of the following best describes activities considered a part of planning?

    a. Strategic planning
    b. Capital budgeting
    c. Operations budgeting
    d. All of the above

2. The level of planning that considers the purchase of long-term operational assets is called

    a. strategic planning.
    b. capital budgeting.
    c. operations budgeting.
    d. master budgeting.

3. The amount of money an individual has to cover variable expenses is called

    a. net take-home pay.
    b. gross salary.
    c. net disposable income.
    d. net surplus.

4. Which of the following is *not* a direct advantage of budgeting?

    a. Assistance in planning
    b. Assistance in performance evaluation
    c. Assistance in increasing sales
    d. Assistance in coordination

5. All of the following schedules are included in the master budget for a manufacturing company, *except*

   a. work-in-process inventory.
   b. direct labor.
   c. pro-forma statement of cash flows.
   d. cash budget.

6. All master budgets will be in error if

   a. the quality of raw materials varies from expectation.
   b. the efficiency of labor varies from expectation.
   c. the sales forecast is inaccurate.
   d. the borrowing rate for bank loans changes.

7. The usual master budget time period is

   a. one year.
   b. one month.
   c. six months.
   d. five years.

8. Which of the following is usually prepared last?

   a. Production budget
   b. Direct labor budget
   c. Cash budget
   d. Pro-forma statement of cash flows

9. A company's level of sales is a function of

   a. customers' tastes.
   b. economic conditions.
   c. the company's ability to provide the goods for sale.
   d. All of the above

10. Which of the following items is *not* needed in a production budget?

    a. Expected sales
    b. Desired level of work-in-process inventory
    c. Desired level of ending finished goods inventory
    d. Beginning finished goods inventory

11. Which of the following is *not* directly included in a direct materials usage and purchases budget for a manufacturing firm?

    a. Desired finished goods inventory
    b. Cost of direct materials to be purchased
    c. Desired ending raw materials inventory
    d. Beginning raw materials inventory

12. Which of the following is *not* included in a direct labor budget?

    a. Number of units to be produced
    b. Number of direct labor hours per unit
    c. Number of indirect labor hours per unit
    d. Cost per direct labor hour

13. Which of the following is *not* usually considered a manufacturing overhead item?

    a. Indirect materials
    b. Executives' salaries
    c. Depreciation on plant
    d. Indirect labor

14. Which of the following is *not* usually considered a selling or administrative expense?

    a. Delivery costs
    b. Depreciation on office building
    c. Plant utilities
    d. Advertising

15. Which of the following is *not* a section of the cash budget?

    a. Cash receipts
    b. Sales revenue
    c. Financing
    d. Cash excess or deficiency

16. The budgeting process for which type of company usually includes the largest number of budgets?

    a. Manufacturing company
    b. Service company
    c. Merchandising company
    d. All of the above have the same number of budgets.

17. Which of the following questions is usually asked by management once the master budget is finished?

    a. Is the projected net income adequate?
    b. Is the projected increase (decrease) in cash sufficient (too much)?
    c. Will there be sufficient assets and profits to purchase needed assets?
    d. All of the above

18. Which of the following budgets would *not* be included for a merchandising company?

    a. Sales budget
    b. Production budget
    c. Cash budget
    d. Selling and administrative expenses budget

19. Which of the following types of information is *not* necessary for preparing a pro-forma income statement?

    a. Unit costs
    b. Pro-forma balance sheet
    c. Ending inventory
    d. Cost of goods sold

20. Flexible budgets are used to control all of the following costs *except*

    a. direct materials.
    b. direct labor.
    c. sales commissions.
    d. manufacturing overhead.

Exercises

E13-1   Production Budgeting

Northeast Syrup Company makes two different grades of syrup for use on pancakes—an expensive pure maple syrup and a cheaper sugar syrup. The sales forecasts for these syrups for the next four months follow.

	Cases of Maple Syrup	Cases of Sugar Syrup
September 2000	1,200	2,000
October 2000	1,400	2,200
November 2000	1,300	1,800
December 2000.............	1,700	2,500

Presently (September 1, 2000), Northeast has on hand 900 cases of maple syrup and 1,500 cases of sugar syrup. Past experience has shown that the company must maintain an inventory of syrup equal to three-fourths of the next month's sales.

Instructions: Given this information, how many cases of syrup must be produced during the months of September, October, and November to meet sales and inventory demands?

E13-2   Direct Materials Usage and Purchases Budget

Oxford Company makes two products—butter and ice cream. The following materials are required to make the products.

1 Pound of Butter	1 Gallon of Ice Cream
1 gallon of milk	1 1/2 gallons of milk
	1 pound of sugar

The company anticipated that 500 pounds of butter and 600 gallons of ice cream would be made in January 2000. On December 31, 1999, the following ingredients were on hand.

Milk......................... 50 gallons

Sugar .... 400 pounds

Since milk sours quickly, management decided to keep only 30 gallons of milk on hand at all times. It also decided, however, that the inventory of sugar would be 500 pounds. Oxford pays $1.50 per gallon for milk and $0.25 per pound for sugar.

Instructions: Given this information, prepare a direct materials usage and purchases budget for January 2000.

E13-3   Direct Labor Budgeting

LaFranz Company makes three types of men's pants—blue jeans, casual slacks, and dress pants. The production budget for the next three months for each type of pants is as follows:

	Pairs of Blue Jeans	Pairs of Casual Slacks	Pairs of Dress Pants
October	600	700	1,000
November	800	500	1,100
December	900	400	900

From past experience, LaFranz knows that it takes 2 hours to make a pair of blue jeans, 2 1/2 hours to make a pair of casual slacks, and 3 hours to make a pair of dress pants. LaFranz pays its direct labor employees $6 per hour.

Instructions: Given this information, prepare a direct labor budget for each of the three months in both hours and costs.

E13-4   Cash Budgeting

Midtown Medical Clinic needs to prepare a cash budget for the month of September 2000. The following information is available.

1. The cash balance on September 1, 2000, is $200,000.

2. The actual services performed during July and August and the projected services for September are as shown below.

	July	August	September
Cash services (amounts paid by patients).............................	$ 90,000	$110,000	$120,000
Credit services (amounts billed to insurance companies)	450,000	500,000	520,000

Amounts for credit services are collected over a 2-month period, with 40 percent collected in the month of the service and 60 percent collected in the following month.

3. Estimated purchases of supplies during September will total $70,000. The supplies will be purchased on credit, with 30 percent paid in the month of purchase and the balance to be paid in the following month. During August, $100,000 of supplies were purchased.

4. Salaries paid during September will be approximately $400,000.

5. The depreciation of the clinic for September will be $80,000.

6. A short-term bank loan of $50,000 will be paid in September.

7. All other cash expenses in September will total $84,000.

Instructions: Given this information, prepare a cash budget for Midtown Medical Clinic for September.

E13-5   Computation of Unit Costs

Montana Corporation makes two products—widgets and gidgets. Over the past several years, the company has maintained accurate records of its costs and resource requirements and has determined that the following are required to make its products:

Widgets	**Production Requirements**	
Material X......................................	200	pounds
Material Y......................................	300	pounds
Direct labor....................................	12	hours
Variable manufacturing overhead.....	12	hours
Gidgets	**Production Requirements**	
Material Y......................................	80	pounds
Material Z......................................	250	pounds
Direct labor....................................	10	hours
Variable manufacturing overhead.....	10	hours

Montana knows it must pay $1 per pound for material X, $2 per pound for material Y, $3 per pound for material Z, and $8 per hour worked by direct labor employees.

Instructions: If Montana applies variable manufacturing overhead at the rate of $3 per direct labor hour, compute the unit costs of widgets and gidgets.

E13-6   Flexible Budgeting

Smith Company has developed the following static budget for the month, which represents projected manufacturing costs at 100 percent production capacity.

Manufacturing Cost	Unit Cost	Total Cost
Direct labor	$0.75	$18,750
Direct materials	1.25	31,250
Variable manufacturing overhead	1.80	45,000
Total	$3.80	$95,000

Instructions: From the information above, develop a flexible budget for production levels of 80 percent and 90 percent capacity.

ANSWERS

Matching

1.	b	6.	f	11.	e	
2.	d	7.	i	12.	j	
3.	l	8.	a	13.	n	
4.	g	9.	h	14.	m	
5.	c	10.	k			

True/False

1.	F	8.	T	15.	T
2.	T	9.	F	16.	F
3.	T	10.	T	17.	T
4.	F	11.	T	18.	T
5.	T	12.	F	19.	F
6.	T	13.	F	20.	T
7.	F	14.	T		

Multiple Choice

1.	d	8.	d	15.	b
2.	b	9.	d	16.	a
3.	c	10.	b	17.	d
4.	c	11.	a	18.	b
5.	a	12.	c	19.	b
6.	c	13.	b	20.	c
7.	a	14.	c		

Exercises

E13-1   Production Budgeting

	Cases of Syrup					
	September		October		November	
	Maple	**Sugar**	**Maple**	**Sugar**	**Maple**	**Sugar**
Expected sales..................................	1,200	2,000	1,400	2,200	1,300	1,800
Add desired ending inventory...........	1,050	1,650	975	1,350	1,275	1,875
Total needed	2,250	3,650	2,375	3,550	2,575	3,675
Less beginning inventory.................	900	1,500	1,050	1,650	975	1,350
Budgeted production.........................	1,350	2,150	1,325	1,900	1,600	2,325

	September		October		November	
	Maple	**Sugar**	**Maple**	**Sugar**	**Maple**	**Sugar**
Next month's sales	1,400	2,200	1,300	1,800	1,700	2,500
	×0.75	×0.75	×0.75	×0.75	×0.75	×0.75
Desired ending inventory.................	1,050	1,650	975	1,350	1,275	1,875

E13-2   Direct Materials Usage and Purchases Budget

Direct materials usage:

Direct Materials	Butter	Ice Cream	Total Usage	Unit Cost of Materials	Cost of Materials Used
Milk	500 gallons	900 gallons	1,400 gallons	$1.50	$2,100
Sugar..................	—	600 pounds	600 pounds	0.25	150
					$2,250

Direct materials purchase requirements:

	Milk		Sugar		Total
Desired ending inventory......................	30	gallons	500	pounds	
Units needed for production	1,400	gallons	600	pounds	
Total needed	1,430	gallons	1,100	pounds	
Less beginning inventory	50	gallons	400	pounds	
Direct materials to be purchased	1,380	gallons	700	pounds	
Unit cost	$ 1.50	per gallon	$0.25	per pound	
Total cost	$2,070		$ 175		$2,245

E13-3   Direct Labor Budgeting

October	Production (Pairs)	Direct Labor Hours per Pair	Total Hours	Cost per Hour	Total Direct Labor Cost
Blue jeans	600	2	1,200	$6	$ 7,200
Casual slacks	700	2 1/2	1,750	6	10,500
Dress pants	1,000	3	3,000	6	18,000
Totals			5,950		$35,700

November	Production (Pairs)	Direct Labor Hours per Pair	Total Hours	Cost per Hour	Total Direct Labor Cost
Blue jeans	800	2	1,600	$6	$ 9,600
Casual slacks	500	2 1/2	1,250	6	7,500
Dress pants	1,100	3	3,300	6	19,800
Totals			6,150		$36,900

December	Production (Pairs)	Direct Labor Hours per Pair	Total Hours	Cost per Hour	Total Direct Labor Cost
Blue jeans	900	2	1,800	$6	$10,800
Casual slacks...............	400	2 1/2	1,000	6	6,000
Dress pants..................	900	3	2,700	6	16,200
Totals			5,500		$33,000

E13-4   Cash Budgeting

Beginning cash balance, September 1, 2000................		$200,000
Cash receipts:		
September cash services	$120,000	
Collection of September credit services[1]	208,000	
Collection of August credit services[2]	300,000	
Total cash receipts		628,000
Total cash available		$828,000
Less disbursements:		
Purchase of supplies[3]	$ 21,000	
August accounts payable[4]	70,000	
Salaries	400,000	
Repayment of loan	50,000	
Other cash needs	84,000	
Total cash needed		625,000
Projected cash balance, September 30, 2000..............		$203,000

[1]$520,000	[2]$500,000	[3]$70,000	[4]$100,000
×0.40	×0.60	×0.30	×0.70
$208,000	$300,000	$21,000	$ 70,000

E13-5   Computation of Unit Costs

Widgets

Input	Input Cost	Units		Amount
Material X................................	$1 per pound	200	pounds	$200
Material Y................................	$2 per pound	300	pounds	600
Material Z...............................	$3 per pound	—		—
Direct labor............................	$8 per hour	12	hours	96
Variable overhead....................	$3 per hour	12	hours	36
Total.......................................				$932

Gidgets

Input	Input Cost	Units		Amount
Material X................................	$1 per pound	—		—
Material Y................................	$2 per pound	80	pounds	$ 160
Material Z...............................	$3 per pound	250	pounds	750
Direct labor............................	$8 per hour	10	hours	80
Variable overhead....................	$3 per hour	10	hours	30
Total.......................................				$1,020

E13-6   Flexible Budgeting

Manufacturing Cost	80%	90%
Direct labor......................................	$15,000	$16,875
Direct materials................................	25,000	28,125
Variable manufacturing overhead.....	36,000	40,500
Total...	$76,000	$85,500

Chapter 14
Nonroutine Decisions and Relevant Information

LEARNING OBJECTIVES

After studying this chapter, you should be able to:

1. Explain the difference between routine and nonroutine decisions.

2. Understand the concept of differential costs and revenues and be able to identify those costs and revenues that are relevant to making nonroutine decisions.

3. Identify several examples of nonroutine decisions and be able to analyze and select the best alternative for each example.

CHAPTER REVIEW

Routine and Nonroutine Decisions

1. Routine decisions involve ongoing current operations and are made daily, weekly, or monthly. Nonroutine decisions are generally made less frequently and are more strategic in nature (e.g., dropping a product line, accepting a special order, or entering a new market).

2. In order to make intelligent decisions, managers need to know the costs and probable consequences of various alternatives.

   a. In making a decision, a manager must weigh the quantitative factors against the qualitative ones and determine their relative importance.

   b. In generating information for decision making, a difficult task is to determine which costs are relevant. Cost concepts that especially apply to nonroutine decisions include differential costs, sunk costs, and opportunity costs.

Differential Costs and Revenues

3. Differential costs and revenues are current or future costs and revenues that are different for each of the alternatives being considered. If they are the same for the alternatives, they can be ignored in making the decision.

4. Sunk costs are past costs that cannot be changed by future actions, so they are of no future value.

5. In order to judge which of two or more alternatives costs less, a decision maker may use the

total-cost approach or the differential-cost approach.

   a. In the total-cost approach, both common and differential costs are identified and assigned to the alternatives. The alternative with the lowest total cost would be selected, assuming that qualitative factors are not significant.

   b. In the differential-cost approach, each alternative is assigned only the differential costs, and the alternative with the lowest total differential costs would be selected.

   c. The relative attractiveness of alternatives is the same for both the total-cost and the differential-cost approaches. The differential-cost approach is appropriate for most situations, but the total-cost approach is desirable when managers need assurance that all costs have been considered in making a decision.

6. Once the quantitative analysis of alternatives has been completed, qualitative factors must be analyzed to determine whether they lead to the same conclusion. If they do not, a manager must decide which choice will be most beneficial to the company.

Examples of Short-Term, Nonroutine Decisions

7. Nonroutine decisions may involve revenues, expenses, and/or investments. Typical short-term, nonroutine decisions that generally involve revenues and expenses but not significant investment are:

   a. Special orders, including whether to make or buy a component or whether to purchase services or provide them internally.

   b. Whether to add or drop a product or a line of products (i.e., exiting or entering markets).

   c. How to use existing critical resources to the best profit advantage.

   d. Whether to continue processing a product or to sell it as is.

   e. What prices to set for products.

Special Orders

8. The relevant costs in making a decision about whether to make a component or buy it are the costs that can be avoided (or will change) if the alternative is selected. Any cost that will be incurred whether a part is purchased or manufactured is not a differential cost and is not relevant to the decision.

9. Often, one of the relevant costs of a make-or-buy decision is the opportunity cost of using the facilities in another manner. The revenue foregone (e.g., rent) by making a component is an opportunity cost.

10. Special-order pricing generally applies when a firm has unused capacity that can be utilized to fill the special order. The firm will increase its profits on special orders as long as the price charged is greater than the incremental costs of manufacturing the product. This is the contribution approach to setting a price. It assumes that the special price will not trigger complaints from other customers, and that other qualitative factors are positive.

Exiting or Entering a Market

11. In deciding to exit or enter a market, the effects on profits, quality, and speed of delivery should be considered.

12. A product or segment should not be dropped unless it does not make a positive contribution toward covering indirect fixed costs, or an alternative product or segment will contribute more toward covering the indirect fixed costs.

   a. Variable costs are usually avoidable, since they vary directly with volume.

   b. Indirect fixed costs are unavoidable, since they will be incurred whether or not the product or segment is dropped.

Selecting the Best Use of a Scarce Resource

13. When a firm that produces more than one product is operating at or near capacity, management must decide how much of each product to make and sell to maximize net income.

   a. The decision is based on the principle that a firm will maximize net income by selling the product that contributes most toward covering the fixed costs in relation to the critical resource factor.

   b. A critical resource is one that determines operating capacity by its availability. If machine hours are the critical resource, those products should be produced and sold for which the revenues exceed the variable costs by the highest margin per machine hour.

Deciding at What Stage to Sell a Product

14. When products evolve out of a joint manufacturing process, management must answer the question: Should a product be sold at the point of separation from the joint process or should it

be processed further at additional cost with the expectation of selling it at a higher price?

    a. A manager compares the additional costs incurred for further processing with the additional revenues from selling at a higher price. If the additional revenues are greater than the additional costs, then the net income is increased, and the additional processing is worthwhile—unless qualitative factors suggest otherwise.

    b. The costs the firm incurs before the point of separation—the joint product costs—are incurred whether the separate products are sold at the point of separation or are processed further. Thus, they are not relevant to the choice between the two alternatives.

15. In deciding whether to sell products at the point of separation or after further processing, a manager must consider the qualitative factors as well as the financial factors.

Setting Selling Prices

16. The price normally charged for a product must be high enough to cover total costs and still provide a reasonable return on the owners' investment. Therefore, all costs are relevant to the pricing decision—variable costs as well as a fair share of fixed costs. If total costs are compiled by function (materials, labor, overhead), a markup is added to cover selling and administrative costs and a reasonable return on investment. If total costs are compiled on the basis of behavioral characteristics (contribution approach), a markup is added to cover all fixed costs and provide a reasonable return on investment.

COMMON ERRORS

Once you clearly understand the concept of differential costs and can distinguish them from sunk costs, applying the differential-cost concept to nonroutine

decisions does not present any major problems. But until this happens, the two most common errors are:

    1. Treating certain sunk costs as differential costs.

    2. Overlooking unrecorded opportunity costs that are actually relevant differential costs.

1. Treating Sunk Costs as Differential Costs

Costs that are common to all the alternative courses of action being considered are not differential costs and therefore can be ignored in the quantitative analysis. An example would be sunk costs that have already been incurred, such as the book value of a machine that must be written off as a loss or recovered in future depreciation. Costs common to the alternatives also would include those that will continue, such as that portion of the president's salary allocated to a department or a product. Another example of a sunk cost that would be common to the alternatives of selling a product or processing it further is the joint cost of producing several products up to the time they are separated, since these joint costs will have been incurred regardless of whether or not individual products are processed further.

2. Overlooking Unrecorded Opportunity Costs

Since opportunity costs are not recorded in conventional accounting records, they are easy to overlook in the decision-making process. An opportunity cost is defined as the benefit lost if the next best alternative is not selected. If a company has been making a component, for example, one of the costs of using its own facilities is the lost rental income from the facility. Likewise, the lost interest income from having funds tied up in inventory is a cost of carrying the inventory. So, one of the differential costs is the measurable value of an alternative use of resources. Ignoring opportunity costs can often lead to a wrong decision.

SELF-TEST

Matching

Instructions: Write the letter of each of the following terms in the space to the left of its appropriate definition.

a. joint product costs
b. critical resource factor
c. differential costs
d. qualitative considerations

e. total cost
f. opportunity cost
g. sunk costs
h. nonroutine decisions

_____ 1. The element in the manufacturing process that determines capacity by its availability.

_____ 2. Costs that are not the same among the alternatives being considered by management.

_____ 3. Costs that have been incurred and cannot be changed by current or future decisions.

_____ 4. The amount of money that could be earned by putting financial resources to their best alternative use compared with the one being considered or used.

_____ 5. All the costs of a product or an alternative decision.

_____ 6. Those factors affecting a decision that are not subject to quantitative measure.

_____ 7. All costs incurred before products are separated for independent processing.

_____ 8. Decisions made less frequently and that usually have a more significant strategic impact on operations than routine decisions.

True/False

Instructions: Place a check mark in the appropriate column to indicate whether each of the following statements is true or false.

	True	False
1. Nonroutine decisions may involve both revenues and expenses.	_____	_____
2. Qualitative factors are always more important than quantitative factors in making nonroutine decisions.	_____	_____
3. Outsourcing may reduce costs and improve quality of needed services.	_____	_____
4. If costs are the same for two alternatives, they can be ignored in making a nonroutine decision.	_____	_____
5. Sunk costs are relevant to nonroutine decisions because they have already been incurred.	_____	_____
6. Fixed costs are never differential costs and therefore are not relevant to nonroutine decisions.	_____	_____
7. In judging which of two alternatives is less costly, a manager can usually make a correct decision based on which alternative has the lower total cost.	_____	_____
8. The total-cost approach to choosing among alternatives is often more time consuming because it involves both differential costs and costs that are the same.	_____	_____
9. The differential-cost approach produces the same total cost as the total-cost approach.	_____	_____
10. The differential-cost approach leads to selecting the same alternative as the total-cost approach.	_____	_____
11. Since historical cost information collected for external financial reporting is usually quite accurate, it is more useful than budgeted information in the decision-making process.	_____	_____
12. In deciding whether to make or buy a component, only costs that are common to both alternatives are relevant.	_____	_____

	True	False

13. In a make-or-buy decision, any cost that will be incurred whether the part is purchased or manufactured is not a differential cost and is not relevant to the discussion. .... _____ _____

14. If idle facilities do not have any practical alternative use, the opportunity cost is zero and can be ignored in a make-or-buy decision. .... _____ _____

15. Opportunity costs represent actual transactions and therefore are recorded in the General Ledger accounts. .... _____ _____

16. In considering whether to drop or add a product line, the direct fixed costs are always avoidable and therefore are always relevant to the decision. .... _____ _____

17. A product should be dropped if it does not make a positive contribution toward covering indirect fixed costs, assuming that there is no alternative product to consider and that there are no qualitative factors to the contrary. .... _____ _____

18. A product that develops from a joint production process should be processed further if the additional revenues are larger than the additional costs. .... _____ _____

19. If a firm is operating at capacity and is producing two or more products using scarce resources, the decision concerning which product to produce and sell is based on the contribution margin generated by each unit of the critical resource. ..... _____ _____

20. For normal pricing of products, managers should only consider differential costs similar to the pricing of special orders. .... _____ _____

Multiple Choice

Instructions: Circle the letter that best completes each of the following statements.

1. Which of the following decisions would likely *not* be considered a nonroutine decision?
   a. Dropping a product line
   b. Setting the price on a special order
   c. Preparing the work schedule for next week's production
   d. Deciding to outsource all legal work for the company

2. In deciding which of two trucks should be purchased to replace an old truck, which costs should management consider relevant?
   a. The historical costs associated with the old truck
   b. Future costs that will be classified as fixed costs
   c. Future costs that will be classified as variable costs
   d. Future costs that will be different for the two trucks

3. Which type of cost is important in the decision-making process but is *not* recorded in conventional accounting records?
   a. Sunk cost
   b. Differential cost
   c. Opportunity cost
   d. Direct cost

4. In making nonroutine decisions, which of the following guidelines is most appropriate?
   a. Always choose the alternative that reduces total costs.
   b. Always choose the alternative that is most attractive from a qualitative standpoint.
   c. Always choose the alternative that is most attractive from a profit, quality, and speed of delivery standpoint.
   d. Always choose the alternative that creates the fewest behavioral (people) problems.

5. Le Blanc Manufacturing Company is operating at less than full capacity. The production manager is trying to decide whether to make a part that he usually buys. The accounting department has compiled the following estimated total-cost figures if the part is manufactured.

	Unit Cost	Total Cost of 5,000 Units
Direct material..................................	$ 4.00	$ 20,000
Direct labor	7.50	37,500
Variable manufacturing overhead ...	3.00	15,000
Direct fixed costs.............................	1.50	7,500
Indirect fixed costs	6.00	30,000
Total	$22.00	$110,000

The company has been buying this part in quantities of 5,000 units for $17.50 per unit. If the idle facilities have an alternative use, the relevant revenue from the alternative use is called a(an)

a. differential cost.
b. sunk cost.
c. standard cost.
d. opportunity cost.

6. Based on the data in Question 5, the unit costs that Le Blanc Manufacturing Company should consider in deciding whether to make the part would total

a. $4.00.
b. $11.50.
c. $14.50.
d. $16.00.
e. $22.00.

7. Based on the data in Question 5, if Le Blanc Company uses total-cost analysis in deciding whether to make the part, the unit cost of buying the part would be

a. $14.00.
b. $17.50.
c. $23.50.
d. $25.00.

8. The Rockford Company received an order from a foreign customer for 1,000 lamps at a price of $45 each. What will be the effect on profit if the order is accepted (assuming no effect on domestic orders, no disadvantageous qualitative factors, and no increase in fixed manufacturing overhead as a result of this order), assuming the following data (per unit)?

Direct materials	$12
Direct labor	16
Variable manufacturing overhead	9
Variable selling and administrative expenses.....	3
Total manufacturing overhead	125% of direct labor hours

a. Profit increase of $5,000
b. Profit decrease of $3,000
c. Profit increase of $8,000
d. Profit decrease of $22,000

9. The management of Feitz Company was studying the profitability of the company's three primary products and was concerned that Product C showed a loss in the previous year. A summary statement of earnings and other data are as follows:

	Product			
	A	**B**	**C**	**Total**
Sales revenue..	$100,000	$180,000	$126,000	$406,000
Cost of goods sold.......................................	48,000	70,000	112,000	230,000
Gross margin..	$ 52,000	$110,000	$ 14,000	$176,000
Operating expenses	20,000	30,000	30,000	80,000
Income (loss) before taxes..........................	$ 32,000	$ 80,000	($ 16,000)	$ 96,000
Units sold	10,000	12,000	18,000	
Sales price per unit......................................	$10	$15	$7	
Variable cost of goods sold per unit.............	$2.50	$3.00	$5.00	
Variable operating expenses per unit	$1.50	$2.00	$1.50	

The relevant costs to consider in deciding whether Feitz Company should drop Product C are called

a. sunk costs.
b. direct costs.
c. indirect costs.
d. fixed costs.

10. Based on the data in Question 9, if Product C is discontinued, the effect on earnings before income taxes will be a

a. $9,000 decrease.
b. $14,000 decrease.
c. $9,000 increase.
d. $14,000 increase.

11. Transcontinental Manufacturing Company produces baskets and door mats. The company can sell as many baskets and mats as it can produce, but production is limited by the availability of machine hours. The revenue, cost, and machine-hour data for the baskets and mats are as follows:

	Baskets	**Mats**
Selling price	$15	$9
Variable costs...............................	$10	$5
Machine hours per unit.................	1	0.6

What is the per unit contribution margin for baskets?

a. $4
b. $5
c. $9
d. $10

12. Based on the data in Question 11, how much would the contribution margin be in total dollars if 1,200 machine hours were available for production and the entire machining time was used to produce mats?

a. $5,000
b. $6,000
c. $7,000
d. $8,000

13. Based on the data in Question 11, how much larger will earnings be if the company produces mats instead of baskets and 1,200 machine hours are available for production?

a. $1,000
b. $2,000
c. $4,000
d. $6,000

14. Cheshire Company manufactures Products R, S, and T from a joint process. Joint product costs were $120,000. Additional information regarding units produced, sales values, and additional costs is as follows:

Product	Units Produced	Sales Value at Separation	Sales Value after Further Processing	Additional Processing Costs
R	9,000	$60,000	$75,000	$12,000
S	6,000	56,000	65,000	8,000
T	3,000	24,000	27,000	5,000

Assuming that joint product costs are allocated on the basis of relative sales values at the point of separation, the total cost allocated to Product S would be

a. $40,000.
b. $48,000.
c. $56,000.
d. $60,000.

15. Based on the data in Question 14, the net profits of Cheshire Company will be maximized if which product or products are processed further after the separation?

a. Product R
b. Product S
c. Products R and T
d. Products R and S

16. Based on the data in Question 14, the additional profit realized by processing Product R further would be:

a. $1,000.
b. $3,000.
c. $4,000.
d. $15,000.

17. Arnett Manufacturing Company is trying to price a new lamp. One manager suggests the price should be based on total costs, but the accountant thinks the price should be a markup based on contribution margin. The following information has been assembled by the accounting department:

Direct materials	$12
Direct labor	16
Variable manufacturing overhead	9
Variable selling and administrative expenses.....	3
Total manufacturing overhead	125% of direct labor cost

If the selling price is set at $80 and price is based on a markup of contribution margin, what is the markup as a percentage of selling price?

a. 25 percent
b. 30 percent
c. 40 percent
d. 50 percent

18. Based on the data in Question 17, if the selling price is again set at $80 and price is based on a markup of total manufacturing costs, what is the markup as a percentage of selling price?

a. 25 percent
b. 30 percent
c. 40 percent
d. 50 percent

Exercises

E14-1   Make-or-Buy Decision

South Town Company uses 8,000 units of a certain part annually in its assembly process. The costs of making and buying the part are:

Cost to make

Direct materials......................................	$ 8	
Direct labor...	14	
Variable manufacturing overhead.............	7	
Fixed manufacturing overhead	6	
Total cost to make......................................		$35
Cost to buy..		$31

If South Town buys the part rather than making it, the released facilities could be rented for $16,000 per year. Of the fixed manufacturing overhead, $4 will not be incurred if the part is purchased.

Instructions: Should South Town make or buy the part, assuming that there are no qualitative factors to consider?

E14-2   Purchasing Services or Providing Them Internally

The Kwon Company currently operates a small lunch room for its executives. The yearly costs associated with this service are:

Wages of part-time employees	$18,750
Food and beverages	55,000
Other variable costs	12,500
Portion of allocated fixed costs.....................	15,000

Quick Lunch, Inc. will provide lunch for the twenty-five executives for a flat fee of $8,000 per month. The lunch room could be used for storage, which would save Kwon Company $1,000 per month rental expense.

Instructions: Should Kwon outsource its lunch service to Quick Lunch, Inc.?

E14-3   Dropping a Product Line

Proctor Company sells tennis shoes and tennis rackets. The company is thinking about dropping tennis rackets because of losses. The following report was compiled by the accounting department:

	Shoes	Rackets	Total
Sales revenue	$375,000	$40,000	$415,000
Variable costs	200,000	28,000	228,000
Contribution margin	$175,000	$12,000	$187,000
Direct fixed costs	100,000	10,000	110,000
Segment margin	$ 75,000	$ 2,000	$ 77,000
Indirect fixed costs	25,000	5,000	30,000
Net income	$ 50,000	$ (3,000)	$ 47,000

Instructions: Assuming that the decision to drop tennis rackets as a line will not affect the sale of tennis shoes, should the racket line be dropped?

E14-4 Using Critical Resources

State Manufacturing Company produces two products, both of which require the use of a special process. Only 120 hours of processing time are available each month. Information about selling prices, costs, and processing time for each product is as follows:

	Product	
	A	**B**
Selling price..............................	$20	$28
Variable cost............................	$12	$18
Processing time per unit	3 hrs.	4 hrs.

Instructions: Given the processing-time constraint, which product should be made?

E14-5   Maximizing Profits

Baby Toy Company produces three unique toys: Spacey, Fishey, and Racey. Production is limited by the skilled labor necessary to produce these special toys. Cost and production data on these toys are as follows:

	Spacey	Fishey	Racey
Per unit contribution margin......................	$7	$4	$6
Toys produced per hour.............................	40	80	50
Expected sales per month (units)................	10,000	100,000	25,000

Instructions: The company is limited to 2,000 direct labor hours per month. How many units of each product should be produced to maximize profits?

E14-6   Selling a Product or Processing It Further

A refinery that produces fuel oil has 400,000 gallons of fuel oil in its tanks, but is operating at less than full capacity. The manager is trying to decide whether or not to refine the fuel oil further and sell it as gasoline.

Selling prices per gallon:
  Fuel oil................... $0.40
  Gasoline................. $0.75

Processing costs to convert 400,000 gallons of fuel oil to a normal yield (90 percent) of 360,000 gallons of gasoline total $105,000.

Instructions: Based on the above data, should the manager decide to convert the fuel oil to gasoline?

E14-7   Setting Prices

Burke Manufacturing Company makes and sells for $22 per unit a single product that has been sold only in the United States. At present the company has a substantial excess plant capacity. Current production costs for 10,000 units are as follows: direct materials, $90,000; direct labor, $40,000; variable manufacturing overhead, $40,000; and fixed manufacturing overhead, $20,000. The sales department has just received an order for 5,000 units from a French company.

Instructions: Assuming that none of the fixed costs will change if the order is accepted, what is the lowest price the company can accept and not reduce its profit?

ANSWERS

Matching

1.	b	4.	f	7.	a
2.	c	5.	e	8.	h
3.	g	6.	d		

True/False

1.	T	8.	T	15.	F
2.	F	9.	F	16.	F
3.	T	10.	T	17.	T
4.	T	11.	F	18.	T
5.	F	12.	F	19.	T
6.	F	13.	T	20.	F
7.	T	14.	T		

Multiple Choice

1.	c	7.	c	13.	b
2.	d	8.	a	14.	c
3.	c	9.	b	15.	d
4.	c	10.	a	16.	b
5.	d	11.	b	17.	d
6.	d	12.	d	18.	a

Exercises

E14-1   Make-or-Buy Decision

Cost to Make		Cost to Buy	
Direct materials..	$ 8	Purchase price..	$31
Direct labor	14		
Variable overhead...	7		
Fixed overhead	4		
Rental value of facilities ($16,000/8,000)...			(2)
Total cost to make..................................	$33	Total cost to buy	$29

South Town should buy the part.

E14-2   Purchasing Services or Providing Them Internally

From a financial point of view, Kwon Company should outsource its lunch service, provided the quality of the lunches is satisfactory, as shown below.

Cost of Outsourcing		Differential Costs of Keeping Small Lunch Room	
Quick Lunch, Inc., yearly fee	$96,000	Wages of part-time employees	$18,750
Less rent saved by Kwon Company..........	(12,000)	Food and beverages	55,000
Net cost of outsourcing............................	$84,000	Other variable costs	12,500
			$86,250

Note: The fixed costs will be incurred under either alternative so they are not differential costs.

E14-3   Dropping a Product Line

Tennis rackets should not be dropped unless an alternative product line can be added that will make a greater contribution to profit than the $2,000 now made by tennis rackets:

Contribution margin	$12,000
Less direct fixed costs	10,000
Addition to profit from sale of tennis rackets	$ 2,000

E14-4   Using Critical Resources

	Product	
	A	**B**
Contribution margin:		
A: $20 – $12	$8.00	
B: $28 – $18		$10.00
Contribution margin per hour of processing time:		
A: $8 ÷ 3 hours	2.67	
B: $10 ÷ 4 hours		2.50
Total contribution if all processing time is devoted to:		
A: 120 hours ÷ 3 hours	40 units	
Contribution per unit	×$8	
Total contribution	$320	
B: 120 hours ÷ 4 hours		30 units
Contribution per unit		×$10
Total contribution		$300

Product A should be processed and sold first to the extent of sales demand.

E14-5   Maximizing Profits

	Hours	× Units per Hour	= Expected Sales
Fishey	1,250	80	100,000
Racey	500	50	25,000
Spacey	250	40	10,000
	2,000		135,000

Contribution per direct labor hour should be maximized up to the available market demand.

E14-6   Selling a Product or Processing It Further

Additional sales revenue for 360,000 gallons of gasoline at $0.35 ($0.75 – $0.40)	$126,000
Further processing costs	105,000
Total	$ 21,000
Lost revenue on 40,000 gallons of fuel oil (40,000 × $0.40)	16,000
Additional profit from converting to gasoline	$ 5,000

The fuel oil should be converted to gasoline.

E14-7   Setting Prices

Avoidable costs:

Direct materials	$90,000/10,000 units =	$ 9
Direct labor	$40,000/10,000 units =	4
Variable manufacturing overhead	$40,000/10,000 units =	4
Lowest price		$17

Chapter 15
Strategic and Capital Investment Decisions

LEARNING OBJECTIVES

After studying this chapter, you should be able to:

1. Understand the importance of capital budgeting and the concepts underlying strategic and capital investment decisions.

2. Describe and use two nondiscounted capital budgeting techniques: the payback method and the unadjusted rate of return method.

3. Describe and use two discounted capital budgeting techniques: the net present value method and the internal rate of return method.

4. Explain how to use capital budgeting techniques in ranking capital investment projects.

5. Understand the need for evaluating qualitative factors in strategic and capital investment decisions.

CHAPTER REVIEW

Conceptual Basis of Capital Budgeting

1. The process of establishing plans that outline an organization's strategies for achieving its long-term objectives is called strategic planning. One aspect of strategic planning is capital budgeting, a systematic method of making decisions concerning long-term investments in operational assets.

2. A capital budget determines which operational assets will be acquired, their cost, and when they will be purchased.

3. Capital, as used in business, is the total amount of money and other resources that individuals and companies use to earn profits.

4. The success of an investment depends on the amount of future net cash inflows (or future cash savings) an investment will produce in relation to its cost (cash outlays).

5. Capital budgeting is critical to long-run profitability because decisions to invest in assets such as land, buildings, and equipment involve large outlays of capital, extend over several years, and are not easily terminated.

6. Capital budgeting helps decision makers answer two types of questions: the screening function of capital budgeting helps decide whether an investment is acceptable, and the ranking function helps decide which of several acceptable investments should be chosen.

7. The time value of money refers to the fact that a dollar today is worth more than a dollar tomorrow.

8. Discounting is used to compare amounts of money at different points in time. It takes into account interest, which represents the cost of money.

9. Cash outflows include the initial cash paid for an investment and any other expected future cash outlays associated with a project, including maintenance expenses, increased manufacturing overhead costs, and working capital required by the project. Periodic depreciation charges are not considered cash outflows, since they are not cash expenses.

10. Cash inflows include all current and expected future revenues or savings directly associated with an investment.

Nondiscounted Capital Budgeting Techniques

11. The four most common capital budgeting techniques are (a) the payback method, (b) the unadjusted rate of return method, (c) the net present value method, and (d) the internal rate of return method.

12. The net present value method and the internal rate of return method take the time value of money into consideration and are theoretically more correct than the payback method and the unadjusted rate of return method, which ignore the time value of money.

13. The payback method is widely used in business because it is simple to apply and provides a preliminary screen for investment opportunities. It determines the length of time required by the net cash inflows of an investment to equal the original investment outlay.

14. One strength of the payback method is that it can be used to determine whether an investment fits within an acceptable time frame. Its major weaknesses are that it does not measure the profitability of investments or take into account the time value of money.

15. The unadjusted rate of return provides a measure of the profitability of an investment by dividing the future increases in annual net income by the initial cost of the investment. If the resulting rate of return is greater than the company's standard, the investment is acceptable quantitatively.

16. Unlike the payback method, the unadjusted rate of return method attempts to measure the prof-

itability of an investment. Its primary weakness is that it does not consider the time value of money.

Discounted Capital Budgeting Techniques

17. The most theoretically correct discount rate to use in calculating an investment's net present value is the company's cost of capital. The cost of capital is basically a weighted average of the cost of a firm's debt and equity capital.

18. The net present value method appropriately takes into consideration the time value of money by discounting future cash inflows and outflows to their present values. By comparing these net cash flows, this method arrives at a net present value figure. If the net present value is zero or positive, the investment is acceptable from a quantitative standpoint. The discount rate used in computing the net present value is the minimum rate of return a company will accept. Least-cost decisions are an exception and are based on the smallest negative net present value.

19. The internal rate of return method derives the "true" rate of return an investment yields. This rate is then compared with the company's hurdle rate (the minimum rate of return that a company is willing to accept). If an investment's internal rate of return is greater than or equal to the hurdle rate, the investment is acceptable quantitatively.

20. The payback reciprocal method may be used to approximate an investment's internal rate of return.

Capital Rationing

21. Often, a firm must choose from among acceptable investments because of limited financial resources. Capital rationing is the process of allocating resources among ranked acceptable investments.

22. When the internal rate of return method is used to rank investments, the investment giving the highest rate of return is ranked first.

23. When the net present value method is used to rank investment opportunities, a profitability index is used. The profitability index is the present value of an investment's net cash inflows divided by the initial cost. The higher the profitability index, the more profitable the investment.

24. Under certain conditions, the internal rate of return and the net present value methods may give different rankings. When this happens, the profitability index should be used to select the most profitable alternative.

Qualitative Factors in Strategic and Capital Investment Decisions

25. In making capital budgeting decisions, the effect of a decision on the quality and the time with which products can be delivered to customers must be considered.

26. Qualitative factors are important in analyzing any investment opportunity. These factors are often so important that they override quantitative factors.

COMMON ERRORS

The two most common problems students have in understanding capital budgeting are:

1. Remembering the formulas for the four capital budgeting techniques.

2. Knowing which present value table to use in computing the net present values.

1. The Four Capital Budgeting Formulas

The formulas are summarized as follows:

a. *Payback method:*

$$\frac{\text{Investment cost}}{\text{Annual net cash inflows}} = \text{Payback period}$$

b. *Unadjusted rate of return method:*

$$\frac{\text{Increase in future average annual net income}}{\text{Initial investment cost}} = \text{Unadjusted rate of return}$$

c. *Net present value method:*

Cash inflows × discount factors
Less cash outflows × discount factor
= Net present value of net cash flows

d. *Internal rate of return method:*

$$\frac{\text{Investment cost}}{\text{Annual net cash inflows}} = \text{Present value factor}$$

Present value factor in PV table for given period = Internal rate of return

2. Selecting the Appropriate PV Table

Present value tables are available for both lump-sum amounts and annuities (see text pages 737-738). Annuities involve equal payments over equal periods of time. Table I in the text provides the present value factors for a lump-sum amount of $1 for various periods at various interest rates. Use this table whenever a lump-sum cash inflow or outflow is involved. Table II shows present value factors for an annuity of $1 for various periods at various interest rates; use it when a series of equal cash flows are involved—for example, when a purchase is made on a time-payment contract calling for equal payments over the next several years.

SELF-TEST

Matching

Instructions: Write the letter of each of the following terms in the space to the left of its appropriate definition.

a.	discounted cash flow methods	**i.**	hurdle rate
b.	internal rate of return	**j.**	capital rationing
c.	least-cost decision	**k.**	interpolation
d.	net present value method	**l.**	cost of capital
e.	profitability index	**m.**	net present value
f.	cash outflows	**n.**	cash inflows
g.	unadjusted rate of return method	**o.**	payback method
h.	internal rate of return method	**p.**	payback reciprocal method

_____ 1. Any current or expected revenues or savings directly associated with an investment.

_____ 2. Capital budgeting techniques that take into account the time value of money by comparing discounted cash flows.

_____ 3. A capital budgeting technique in which the "true" discount rate produces a net present value of zero for an investment.

_____ 4. A capital budgeting technique in which the reciprocal of the payback period is used in computing an investment's approximate internal rate of return.

_____ 5. A decision to undertake the project with the smallest negative net present value.

_____ 6. A method of determining a present or future value that is not given in the present or future value tables in order to calculate the exact internal rate of return.

_____ 7. The "true" discount rate that will produce a net present value of zero when applied to the cash flows of an investment.

_____ 8. The initial cost and other expected outlays associated with an investment.

_____ 9. A capital budgeting technique in which the amount of time it takes the net cash inflows of a project to repay the initial cost is determined.

_____ 10. The minimum rate of return an investment must provide in order to be acceptable.

_____ 11. The difference between the present values of expected cash inflows and outflows of an investment.

_____ 12. The weighted-average cost of a firm's debt and equity capital; the rate of return a company must earn to satisfy the demands of owners and creditors.

_____ 13. A capital budgeting technique in which a rate of return is calculated by dividing an investment's future average annual income by the initial investment costs.

_____ 14. A capital budgeting technique in which the discounted expected cash inflows and outflows of an investment are compared.

_____ 15. The present value of cash inflows divided by the cost of an investment.

_____ 16. The process of allocating limited resources among ranked acceptable investments.

True/False

Instructions: Place a check mark in the appropriate column to indicate whether each of the following statements is true or false.

	True	False
1. Return on investment is highest when an investment produces the most benefits at the least cost.	_____	_____
2. While qualitative factors should be considered in making capital budgeting decisions, they should never override quantitative factors.	_____	_____
3. Inflation and interest are not important considerations in making capital budgeting decisions.	_____	_____

	True	False

4. The screening function of capital budgeting helps management decide which of several acceptable investments is most profitable. .... _____ _____

5. Depreciation expenses often are not considered in making investment decisions, since they are not cash expenses. .... _____ _____

6. The four most common capital budgeting techniques are the payback method, the payback reciprocal method, the net present value method, and the internal rate of return method. .... _____ _____

7. The net present value method and the internal rate of return method take into account the time value of money. .... _____ _____

8. The payback method does not take into account the time value of money. For this reason, it should never be used as a capital budgeting tool. .... _____ _____

9. The unadjusted rate of return is another name for the return on investment. .... _____ _____

10. An investment with a zero or positive net present value is acceptable from a quantitative standpoint. .... _____ _____

11. The internal rate of return derives an investment's "true" rate of return. If the internal rate of return is greater than or equal to zero, the investment is acceptable. .... _____ _____

12. Under certain circumstances, the payback reciprocal method may be used to approximate an investment's internal rate of return. .... _____ _____

13. A company's cost of capital is basically a weighted-average cost of its debt capital and its equity capital. .... _____ _____

14. Capital budgeting is the process of selecting those investment projects that offer the highest returns. .... _____ _____

15. The net present value method and the internal rate of return method always give the same results when used to screen investment opportunities. .... _____ _____

16. The net present value method and the internal rate of return method always give the same results when used to rank investment opportunities. .... _____ _____

17. The profitability index shows how profitable a company has been over the past several years. .... _____ _____

18. The profitability index will always select the most profitable investment alternative relative to cost. .... _____ _____

19. Capital rationing is the systematic planning for the financing of long-term investments. .... _____ _____

Multiple Choice

Instructions: Circle the letter that best completes each of the following statements.

1. Which of the following is a situation in which capital budgeting would *not* be useful?
   a. Determining what credit terms will apply to credit sales to customers
   b. Deciding whether to lease or to buy a new tractor
   c. Deciding whether to buy a large or a small car for the sales manager
   d. Deciding whether to overhaul or to replace a company's delivery truck

2. Which of the following capital budgeting techniques takes into account the time value of money?
   a. Payback method
   b. Unadjusted rate of return method
   c. Net present value method
   d. Payback reciprocal method

3. Which of the following is *not* considered to be a cash inflow when performing capital budgeting?

   a. Decreased electricity costs because of a more energy-efficient machine
   b. The future disposal value of a newly purchased machine
   c. Increased sales revenue because more units are produced using a new machine
   d. The savings because a new machine has a lower annual depreciation expense than the old machine it replaced

4. Which of the following is *not* a reason for using capital budgeting?

   a. Large amounts of money are often spent to purchase long-term investments.
   b. Long-term investment decisions are often difficult to reverse.
   c. Long-term investments will affect a company's profitability for several years.
   d. Credit managers insist that a company earn a certain rate of interest on money loaned.

5. If a machine costs $5,000 and will generate annual net cash inflows of $1,000 for the next 8 years, what is the payback period?

   a. 8 years
   b. 5 years
   c. 6 years
   d. 3 years

6. What is the payback reciprocal for the machine in Question 5?

   a. 125 percent
   b. 15 percent
   c. 20 percent
   d. 33 percent

7. If a delivery truck costs $10,000 and will generate increased annual net income of $2,000 per year for the next 6 years, what is the truck's unadjusted rate of return?

   a. 20 percent
   b. 12 percent
   c. 5 percent
   d. 33 percent

8. Which of the following does *not* apply to the net present value method?

   a. All cash flows are discounted to their present values.
   b. A discount rate must be chosen to discount cash flows to their present values.
   c. Depreciation must be added to the net cash outflows.
   d. Acceptable investment projects have either zero or positive net present values.

9. Which of the following is most likely to be a least-cost decision?

   a. Deciding which truck to purchase
   b. Deciding which type of antipollution equipment to install
   c. Deciding which of several machines will minimize costs
   d. Deciding whether or not to produce a new product

10. Which of the following does *not* apply to the internal rate of return method?

   a. It takes into account the time value of money.
   b. When cash flows are uneven, it often involves trial-and-error calculations.
   c. It determines the "true" discount rate that an investment yields.
   d. It requires a discount rate to discount future cash flows to their net present values.

11. Another name for the hurdle rate is

    a. cost of capital.
    b. unadjusted rate of return.
    c. internal rate of return.
    d. return on investment.

12. Which of the following is *not* an important factor to consider in making capital investment decisions?

    a. Costs
    b. Quality
    c. Time (speed of delivery to customers)
    d. All are important factors to consider.

13. Which of the following is a qualitative factor that should be considered by a firm deciding whether or not to open a new steel factory?

    a. The price of iron
    b. The required antipollution equipment
    c. The cost to the company of transporting workers to the factory
    d. The effects the factory will have on the environment

14. A machine costing $7,500 will save a company $2,000 annually in operating costs for the next 5 years. The company uses a discount rate of 12 percent. What is the machine's net present value? (Use the present value tables on pages 487-490 of the text.)

    a. $2,500
    b. $(290)
    c. $0
    d. $290

15. A delivery truck costs $12,000 and will save the company $4,000 annually for the next 4 years. What is the truck's internal rate of return? (Use the present value tables on pages 487-490 of the text.)

    a. Between 11 and 12 percent
    b. Between 12 and 13 percent
    c. Between 13 and 14 percent
    d. Between 14 and 15 percent

16. Which of the following is compared with an investment's internal rate of return to determine whether or not the investment is acceptable?

    a. Hurdle rate
    b. Discount rate
    c. Unadjusted rate of return
    d. Interest rate

17. All of the following are uncertainties in making capital budgeting decisions, *except* the

    a. useful life of the project.
    b. disposal value of the project.
    c. initial investment cost.
    d. amount of future cash flows.

18. Capital rationing is concerned primarily with

    a. sensitivity analysis.
    b. least-cost decisions.
    c. ranking.
    d. screening.

19. A company is trying to decide which of the following four investment projects is most profitable.

Investment Project	Cost	Net Present Value
A	$ 100	$ 200
B	10,000	3,000
C	6,000	4,000
D	1,000	800

Which project should the company select?

a. Project A
b. Project B
c. Project C
d. Project D

20. Which capital budgeting method is best for ranking purposes?

a. Payback period
b. Internal rate of return
c. Unadjusted rate of return
d. Net present value method

Exercises

E15-1   Payback Periods

Baxter Company is deciding which of the following three investments to make. Because of its extremely tight cash position, the company cannot invest in any project with a payback period longer than 3 years.

Investment A costs $12,000 and has net cash inflows of $4,000 per year for 6 years.
Investment B costs $5,000 and has net cash inflows of $1,500 per year for 8 years.
Investment C costs $8,000 and has net cash inflows of $3,000 per year for 3 years.

Instructions: Which of the following investments should be considered?

E15-2   Unadjusted Rates of Return

IFT Company is considering the following three investments.

> Investment A costs $10,000 and will increase net income by $1,000 per year for 12 years.
> Investment B costs $500 and will increase net income by $100 per year for 8 years.
> Investment C costs $6,000 and will increase net income by $750 per year for 10 years.

Instructions: Compute the unadjusted rate of return each project will yield.

E15-3   Present Values

Your lawyer advises you that you have inherited a large sum of money. You may choose whether to receive $200,000 now or $20,000 at the end of each year for the next 30 years.

Instructions: Which option would you choose if you could earn 10 percent per year on your investments? Which option would you choose if you could earn 8 percent per year? (Use the present value tables on pages 487-490 of the text.)

E15-4   Investment Decision

You have the opportunity to purchase a machine for $100,000. Your neighbor wants to lease the machine from you for $20,000 per year for the next 8 years. At the end of 8 years, the machine will have a $2,000 scrap value. Your discount rate is 12 percent.

Instructions: Should you purchase the machine?

E15-5   Internal Rate of Return

Last Chance Company has the opportunity to invest $100,000 in a machine that will save it $17,000 per year for the next 10 years. After 10 years, the machine will be worthless.

Instructions: What is the machine's internal rate of return? Should the company invest in the machine if its cost of capital is 12 percent?

ANSWERS

Matching

1.	n	7.	b	12.	l
2.	a	8.	f	13.	g
3.	h	9.	o	14.	d
4.	p	10.	i	15.	e
5.	c	11.	m	16.	j
6.	k				

True/False

1.	T	8.	F	14.	F
2.	F	9.	F	15.	T
3.	F	10.	T	16.	F
4.	F	11.	F	17.	F
5.	T	12.	T	18.	T
6.	F	13.	T	19.	F
7.	T				

Multiple Choice

1.	a	8.	c	15.	b
2.	c	9.	b	16.	a
3.	d	10.	d	17.	c
4.	d	11.	a	18.	c
5.	b	12.	d	19.	a
6.	c	13.	d	20.	d
7.	a	14.	b		

Exercises

E15-1   Payback Periods

The payback periods for the investments are:

$$\text{Investment A} = \frac{\$12,000}{\$4,000} = 3 \text{ years}$$

$$\text{Investment B} = \frac{\$5,000}{\$1,500} = 3.3 \text{ years}$$

$$\text{Investment C} = \frac{\$8,000}{\$3,000} = 2.7 \text{ years}$$

Investments A and C should be considered.

E15-2   Unadjusted Rates of Return

The unadjusted rates of return for the three investments are:

$$\text{Investment A} = \frac{\$1,000}{\$10,000} = 10\%$$

$$\text{Investment B} = \frac{\$100}{\$500} = 20\%$$

$$\text{Investment C} = \frac{\$750}{\$6,000} = 12.5\%$$

E15-3   Present Values

At 10 percent interest, the present value of 30 payments of $20,000 each is $188,538. Since this amount is less than $200,000, it is preferable to take the $200,000 now.

At 8 percent interest, the present value of 30 payments of $20,000 is $225,156. Since this amount is greater than $200,000, it is preferable to receive the 30 annual payments of $20,000 each.

E15-4   Investment Decision

Present value of 8 annual payments of $20,000...........	$ 99,352.00
Present value of $2,000 after 8 years	807.80
Total...	$100,159.80
Initial cost	100,000.00
Net present value	$ 159.80

The investment is acceptable from a quantitative standpoint.

E15-5   Internal Rate of Return

The investment's internal rate of return is approximately 11 percent. It should not be accepted if the firm's cost of capital is 12 percent.

WORKING PAPERS

Survey of Accounting

Stice, Stice, Albrecht, Skousen

P2-1 Balance Sheet Classifications and Relationships

P2-2 Preparation of a Classified Balance Sheet

1.

2.

P2-3 Balance Sheet Preparation with a Missing Element

1.

2.–3.

P2-4 Income Statement Preparation

P2-5 Income Statement Preparation

P2-6   Expanded Accounting Equation

P2-7 Income Statement Preparation

1.

P2-8 Statement of Cash Flows

1.

2.

P2-9 Statement of Cash Flows

P2-10 Unifying Concepts: Net Income and Financial Ratio Analysis

1.

2.–4.

P2-11 Unifying Concepts: Net Income and Statement of Retained Earnings

1.

2.

P2-11 Concluded

3.

4.

P2-12 Financial Ratios

P2-13 Comprehensive Financial Statement Preparation

1.

P2-13 Continued

2.

P2-13 Concluded

3.–7.

P2-14 Elements of Comparative Financial Statements

P3-1 Journal Entries and Trial Balance

1.

P3-1 Continued

2.

Cash	Accounts Receivable	Inventory
Office Building	Accounts Payable	Mortgage Payable
Notes Payable	Capital Stock	Retained Earnings
Sales Revenue	Cost of Goods Sold	Salaries Expense
Utilities Expense	Interest Expense	

P3-1 Concluded

2. Continued

3.

P3-2 Journalizing and Posting

1.

JOURNAL   PAGE

	DATE	DESCRIPTION	POST REF.	DEBIT	CREDIT	
1						1
2						2
3						3
4						4
5						5
6						6
7						7
8						8
9						9
10						10
11						11
12						12
13						13
14						14
15						15
16						16
17						17
18						18
19						19
20						20
21						21
22						22
23						23
24						24
25						25
26						26
27						27
28						28
29						29
30						30
31						31
32						32

P3-2 Concluded

2.

Cash	Accounts Receivable	Inventory

Supplies	Accounts Payable	Capital Stock

Sales Revenue	Cost of Goods Sold	Insurance Expense

Utilities Expense	Wage Expense

3.

_____

_____

_____

_____

_____

_____

_____

P3-3 Journal Entries from Ledger Analysis

1.

P3-4 Journalizing and Posting Transactions

1.

JOURNAL   PAGE _____

	DATE		DESCRIPTION	POST REF.	DEBIT	CREDIT	
1							1
2							2
3							3
4							4
5							5
6							6
7							7
8							8
9							9
10							10
11							11
12							12
13							13
14							14
15							15
16							16
17							17
18							18
19							19
20							20
21							21
22							22
23							23
24							24
25							25
26							26
27							27
28							28
29							29
30							30
31							31
32							32

P3-4 Concluded

2.

Cash	Accounts Receivable	Equipment

Inventory	Accounts Payable	Cost of Goods Sold

Rent Expense	Utilities Expense	Salary Expense

Property Tax Expense	Sales Revenue

P3-5 Unifying Concepts: Compound Journal Entries, Posting, Trial Balance

1.

JOURNAL   PAGE _____

	DATE		DESCRIPTION	POST REF.	DEBIT	CREDIT	
1							1
2							2
3							3
4							4
5							5
6							6
7							7
8							8
9							9
10							10
11							11
12							12
13							13
14							14
15							15
16							16
17							17
18							18
19							19
20							20
21							21
22							22
23							23
24							24
25							25
26							26
27							27
28							28
29							29
30							30
31							31
32							32

P3-5 Continued

2.

Cash	Accounts Receivable	Inventory

Land	Building	Equipment

Office Equipment	Truck	Notes Payable

Capital Stock	Sales Revenue	Cost of Goods Sold

Interest Expense

P3-5 Concluded

3.

P3-6 Unifying Concepts: T-Accounts, Trial Balance, and Income Statement

1.

ASSETS

Cash	Accounts Receivable	Notes Receivable

Inventory	Supplies	Land

Building	Equipment

LIABILITIES

Accounts Payable	Notes Payable	Mortgage Payable

OWNERS' EQUITY

Capital Stock

P3-6 Continued

1. Continued   RETAINED EARNINGS

Sales Revenue	Rent Revenue	Interest Revenue

Cost of Goods Sold	Wages Expense	Utilities Expense

Interest Expense

P3-6 Continued

2.

P3-6 Concluded

3.

P3-7 Correcting a Trial Balance

P3-8 Unifying Concepts: First Steps in the Accounting Cycle

1.

JOURNAL   PAGE

	DATE	DESCRIPTION	POST REF.	DEBIT	CREDIT	
1						1
2						2
3						3
4						4
5						5
6						6
7						7
8						8
9						9
10						10
11						11
12						12
13						13
14						14
15						15
16						16
17						17
18						18
19						19
20						20
21						21
22						22
23						23
24						24
25						25
26						26
27						27
28						28
29						29
30						30
31						31
32						32

P3-8 Continued

1. Continued

JOURNAL   PAGE

	DATE		DESCRIPTION	POST REF.	DEBIT	CREDIT	
1							1
2							2
3							3
4							4
5							5
6							6
7							7
8							8
9							9
10							10
11							11
12							12
13							13
14							14
15							15
16							16
17							17
18							18
19							19
20							20
21							21
22							22
23							23
24							24
25							25
26							26
27							27
28							28
29							29
30							30
30							30
31							31

P3-8 Continued

2.

	Cash			Short-Term Investments	

	Accounts Receivable			Inventory	

	Land			Buildings	

	Equipment			Notes Payable	

	Accounts Payable			Salaries and Wages Payable	

P3-8 Continued

2. Continued

Mortgage Payable	Capital Stock

Retained Earnings	Dividends

Sales Revenue	Miscellaneous Revenue

Cost of Goods Sold	Property Tax Expense

Advertising and Selling Expense	Utilities Expense

Salaries and Wages Expense	Interest Expense

Income Tax Expense	

P3-8 Continued

3.

P3-8 Continued

4.

P3-8 Continued

4. Continued

P3-8 Concluded

5.

P3-9 Adjusting Entries

JOURNAL

PAGE

	DATE	DESCRIPTION	POST REF.	DEBIT	CREDIT	
1						1
2						2
3						3
4						4
5						5
6						6
7						7
8						8
9						9
10						10
11						11
12						12
13						13
14						14
15						15
16						16
17						17
18						18
19						19
20						20
21						21
22						22
23						23
24						24
25						25
26						26
27						27
28						28
29						29
30						30
31						31
32						32

P3-10 Account Classifications and Debit-Credit Relationships

Account Title	(1) B/S or I/S	(2) A, L, OE, R, E	(3) Real or Nominal	(4) Closed or Open	(5) Debit/ Credit

P3-11 Unifying Concepts: Analysis of Accounts

1. _____
_____
_____
_____
_____
_____
_____
_____
_____
_____
_____
_____
_____
_____
_____
_____
_____
_____

2. _____
_____
_____
_____
_____
_____
_____
_____
_____
_____
_____
_____
_____
_____
_____
_____
_____

P3-11 Concluded

3.

4.

P4-1 Sales Transactions

Company R—Seller

JOURNAL   PAGE _____

	DATE		DESCRIPTION	POST REF.	DEBIT	CREDIT	
1							1
2							2
3							3
4							4
5							5
6							6
7							7
8							8
9							9
10							10
11							11
12							12
13							13
14							14
15							15
16							16
17							17
18							18
19							19
20							20
21							21
22							22
23							23
24							24
25							25
26							26
27							27
28							28
29							29
30							30
31							31
32							32

P4-2 Analysis of Allowance for Bad Debts

1.

JOURNAL

PAGE

	DATE	DESCRIPTION	POST REF.	DEBIT	CREDIT	
1						1
2						2
3						3
4						4
5						5
6						6
7						7
8						8
9						9
10						10
11						11
12						12
13						13
14						14

P4-2 Concluded

2.

JOURNAL

PAGE

	DATE		DESCRIPTION	POST REF.	DEBIT	CREDIT	
1							1
2							2
3							3
4							4
5							5
6							6
7							7
8							8
9							9
10							10
11							11
12							12
13							13
14							14
15							15
16							16
17							17
18							18
19							19
20							20
21							21
22							22
23							23
24							24
25							25
26							26
27							27
28							28
29							29
30							30
31							31
32							32

P4-3   Accounting for Accounts Receivables

1.

P4-3 Concluded

2.

P4-4 Analysis of Receivables

1.–2.

P4-4 Concluded

3.

JOURNAL

PAGE _____

	DATE		DESCRIPTION	POST REF.	DEBIT	CREDIT	
1							1
2							2
3							3
4							4
5							5
6							6
7							7
8							8
9							9
10							10
11							11
12							12
13							13
14							14

P4-5 Computing and Recording Bad Debt Expense

1.

JOURNAL

PAGE _____

	DATE		DESCRIPTION	POST REF.	DEBIT	CREDIT	
1							1
2							2
3							3
4							4
5							5
6							6
7							7
8							8
9							9
10							10
11							11
12							12

P4-5 Concluded

2.

JOURNAL   PAGE

	DATE		DESCRIPTION	POST REF.	DEBIT	CREDIT	
1							1
2							2
3							3
4							4
5							5
6							6
7							7
8							8
9							9
10							10
11							11
12							12
13							13
14							14

3.

JOURNAL   PAGE

	DATE		DESCRIPTION	POST REF.	DEBIT	CREDIT	
1							1
2							2
3							3
4							4
5							5
6							6
7							7
8							8
9							9
10							10
11							11
12							12
13							13
14							14

P4-6 Unifying Concepts: Aging of Accounts Receivable and Uncollectible Accounts

JOURNAL

PAGE

	DATE		DESCRIPTION	POST REF.	DEBIT	CREDIT	
1							1
2							2
3							3
4							4
5							5
6							6
7							7
8							8
9							9
10							10
11							11
12							12
13							13
14							14
15							15
16							16
17							17
18							18
19							19
20							20
21							21
22							22
23							23
24							24
25							25
26							26
27							27
28							28
29							29
30							30
31							31
32							32

P4-7 Estimating Uncollectible Accounts

1.–3.

JOURNAL

	DATE		DESCRIPTION	POST REF.	DEBIT	CREDIT	
1							1
2							2
3							3
4							4
5							5
6							6
7							7
8							8
9							9
10							10
11							11
12							12
13							13
14							14
15							15
16							16
17							17
18							18
19							19
20							20
21							21
22							22
23							23
24							24
25							25
26							26
27							27
28							28
29							29
30							30
31							31
32							32

P4-7 Concluded

4.

JOURNAL

	DATE		DESCRIPTION	POST REF.	DEBIT	CREDIT	
1							1
2							2
3							3
4							4
5							5
6							6
7							7
8							8
9							9
10							10
11							11
12							12
13							13
14							14
15							15
16							16
17							17
18							18
19							19
20							20
21							21
22							22

5.

P5-1 Perpetual and Periodic Journal Entries

1.

JOURNAL   PAGE

	DATE		DESCRIPTION	POST REF.	DEBIT	CREDIT	
1							1
2							2
3							3
4							4
5							5
6							6
7							7
8							8
9							9
10							10
11							11
12							12
13							13
14							14

2.

JOURNAL   PAGE

	DATE		DESCRIPTION	POST REF.	DEBIT	CREDIT	
1							1
2							2
3							3
4							4
5							5
6							6
7							7
8							8
9							9
10							10
11							11
12							12
13							13
14							14

P5-1 Continued

2. Continued

JOURNAL

PAGE

	DATE	DESCRIPTION	POST REF.	DEBIT	CREDIT	
1						1
2						2
3						3
4						4
5						5
6						6
7						7
8						8
9						9
10						10
11						11
12						12
13						13
14						14

JOURNAL

PAGE

	DATE	DESCRIPTION	POST REF.	DEBIT	CREDIT	
1						1
2						2
3						3
4						4
5						5
6						6
7						7
8						8
9						9
10						10
11						11
12						12
13						13
14						14

P5-1 Continued

2. Continued

JOURNAL   PAGE _____

	DATE		DESCRIPTION	POST REF.	DEBIT	CREDIT	
1							1
2							2
3							3
4							4
5							5
6							6
7							7
8							8
9							9
10							10
11							11
12							12
13							13
14							14

JOURNAL   PAGE _____

	DATE		DESCRIPTION	POST REF.	DEBIT	CREDIT	
1							1
2							2
3							3
4							4
5							5
6							6
7							7
8							8
9							9
10							10
11							11
12							12
13							13
14							14

P5-1 Continued

3.

P5-1 Concluded

3. Continued

P5-2 Income Statement Calculations

P5-3 Income Statement Calculations

	Company A	Company B	Company C	Company D

P5-4 Inventory Cost Flow Alternatives

1.

a. FIFO

	UNITS	TOTAL COST

P5-4 Continued

b. LIFO

	UNITS	TOTAL COST

P5-4 Concluded

c. Average cost

	UNITS	TOTAL COST

2.

P5-5 Periodic Inventory Cost Flow Method

1a.

_____

_____

_____

_____

_____

_____

_____

_____

_____

_____

_____

b.

_____

_____

_____

_____

_____

_____

_____

_____

_____

_____

_____

c.

_____

_____

_____

_____

_____

_____

_____

P5-6 Payroll Accounting

1.

JOURNAL

	DATE		DESCRIPTION	POST REF.	DEBIT	CREDIT	
1							1
2							2
3							3
4							4
5							5
6							6
7							7

2.

	DATE		DESCRIPTION	POST REF.	DEBIT	CREDIT	
1							1
2							2
3							3
4							4
5							5
6							6
7							7

3.

	DATE		DESCRIPTION	POST REF.	DEBIT	CREDIT	
1							1
2							2
3							3
4							4
5							5
6							6
7							7

P5-7 Unifying Concepts: The Income Statement

P5-7 Concluded

P5-8 Income Statement Analysis

	2000	1999	1998
Gross sales revenue	$42,000	(9)	$25,800
Sales discounts	-0-	100	100
Sales returns	-0-	200	700
Net sales revenue	42,000	(10)	(1)
Beginning inventory	(15)	8,000	(2)
Purchases	24,800	(11)	15,000
Purchase discounts	700	300	500
Freight-in	(16)	-0-	500
Cost of goods available for sale	29,000	25,000	(3)
Ending inventory	3,800	(12)	(4)
Cost of goods sold	(17)	(13)	(5)
Gross margin (40%)	(18)	14,000	(6)
Selling expenses	4,000	(14)	(7)
General and administrative expenses	(19)	3,200	3,000
Income before income taxes	9,000	8,000	4,000
Income taxes	4,500	4,000	(8)
Net income	(20)	4,000	2,000

P5-9 Calculating and Interpreting Inventory Ratios

1. _____

_____

_____

_____

_____

_____

_____

2. _____

_____

_____

_____

_____

_____

_____

_____

P5-10   Common-Size Income Statements

1.
_____

_____

_____

_____

_____

_____

_____

_____

_____

_____

_____

_____

P5-10   Concluded

2.
_____

_____

_____

_____

_____

_____

_____

_____

_____

_____

_____

P5-11 Ratio Analysis

1. _____

_____

_____

_____

_____

2. _____

_____

_____

_____

_____

3. _____

_____

_____

_____

_____

_____

_____

_____

_____

_____

P5-12 Liquidity Ratios

4.

		Formula	2000	1999
1.	A/P Turnover			
2.	Number of days' sales in A/P			
3.	A/R Turnover			
	Number of days' sales in A/R			
4.	Inventory Turnover			
	Number of days' sales in inventory			

5. _____
_____
_____
_____
_____
_____
_____
_____
_____
_____
_____
_____
_____
_____
_____
_____

P6-1 Present and Future Value Computations

P6-2 Present and Future Value Computations

P6-3 Accounting for Notes Payable

1.–3.

JOURNAL

PAGE _____

	DATE		DESCRIPTION	POST REF.	DEBIT	CREDIT	
1							1
2							2
3							3
4							4
5							5
6							6
7							7
8							8
9							9
10							10
11							11
12							12
13							13
14							14
15							15
16							16
17							17
18							18
19							19
20							20
21							21
22							22
23							23
24							24
25							25
26							26
27							27
28							28
29							29
30							30
31							31
32							32

P6-4 Accounting for a Mortgage

1.–2.

JOURNAL   PAGE _____

	DATE		DESCRIPTION	POST REF.	DEBIT	CREDIT	
1							1
2							2
3							3
4							4
5							5
6							6
7							7
8							8
9							9
10							10
11							11
12							12
13							13
14							14
15							15
16							16
17							17
18							18
19							19

3.

P6-5 Lease Accounting

1.–2.

JOURNAL

PAGE _____

	DATE		DESCRIPTION	POST REF.	DEBIT	CREDIT	
1							1
2							2
3							3
4							4
5							5
6							6
7							7
8							8
9							9
10							10
11							11
12							12
13							13
14							14
15							15
16							16
17							17
18							18
19							19
20							20
21							21
22							22
23							23
24							24
25							25
26							26
27							27
28							28
29							29
30							30
31							31
32							32

P6-5 Concluded

3.

P6-6 Reporting Liabilities on the Balance Sheet

P6-7 Accounting for Bonds

1.

_____

_____

_____

_____

_____

_____

_____

_____

_____

_____

_____

_____

_____

_____

_____

_____

_____

_____

_____

_____

_____

_____

_____

2.

JOURNAL   PAGE

	DATE	DESCRIPTION	POST REF.	DEBIT	CREDIT	
1						1
2						2
3						3
4						4
5						5

P6-7 Concluded

3.–4.

JOURNAL   PAGE _____

	DATE		DESCRIPTION	POST REF.	DEBIT	CREDIT	
1							1
2							2
3							3
4							4
5							5
6							6
7							7
8							8
9							9
10							10
11							11
12							12
13							13
14							14
15							15
16							16
17							17
18							18
19							19

P6-8 Reporting Liabilities on the Balance Sheet

P6-9 Stock Transactions and Analysis

JOURNAL

	DATE		DESCRIPTION	POST REF.	DEBIT	CREDIT	
1	1.	(a)					1
2							2
3							3
4							4
5							5
6							6
7							7

(b) _____

	DATE		DESCRIPTION	POST REF.	DEBIT	CREDIT	
1	2.	(a)					1
2							2
3							3
4							4
5							5
6							6
7							7

(b) _____

	DATE		DESCRIPTION	POST REF.	DEBIT	CREDIT	
1	3.	(a)					1
2							2
3							3
4							4
5							5
6							6
7							7

(b) _____

P6-9 Concluded

JOURNAL

	DATE		DESCRIPTION	POST REF.	DEBIT	CREDIT	
1	4.	(a)					1
2							2
3							3
4							4
5							5
6							6
7							7
8							8
9							9
10							10
11							11
12							12
13							13

(b) _____

_____

	DATE		DESCRIPTION	POST REF.	DEBIT	CREDIT	
1	5.	(a)					1
2							2
3							3
4							4
5							5
6							6
7							7
8							8
9							9
10							10
11							11
12							12
13							13

(b) _____

P6-10 Stock Transactions and the Stockholders' Equity Section

1.

JOURNAL   PAGE

	DATE		DESCRIPTION	POST REF.	DEBIT	CREDIT	
1							1
2							2
3							3
4							4
5							5
6							6
7							7
8							8
9							9
10							10
11							11
12							12
13							13
14							14
15							15
16							16
17							17
18							18
19							19
20							20
21							21
22							22
23							23
24							24
25							25
26							26
27							27
28							28
29							29
30							30
31							31
32							32

P6-10 Continued

2.

P6-10 Concluded

Preferred Stock		Common Stock

Paid-In Capital in Excess of Par, Preferred Stock		Paid-In Capital in Excess of Par, Common Stock

Treasury Stock		Paid-in Capital, Treasury Stock

Retained Earnings

P6-11 Recording Stockholders' Equity Transactions

JOURNAL

PAGE

	DATE		DESCRIPTION	POST REF.	DEBIT	CREDIT	
1							1
2							2
3							3
4							4
5							5
6							6
7							7
8							8
9							9
10							10
11							11
12							12
13							13
14							14
15							15
16							16
17							17
18							18
19							19
20							20
21							21
22							22
23							23
24							24
25							25
26							26
27							27
28							28
29							29
30							30
31							31
32							32

P6-12 Stock Transactions and the Stockholders' Equity Section

1.

JOURNAL   PAGE

	DATE		DESCRIPTION	POST REF.	DEBIT	CREDIT	
1							1
2							2
3							3
4							4
5							5
6							6
7							7
8							8
9							9
10							10
11							11
12							12
13							13
14							14
15							15
16							16
17							17
18							18
19							19
20							20
21							21
22							22
23							23
24							24
25							25
26							26
27							27
28							28
29							29
30							30
31							31
32							32

P6-12 Continued

JOURNAL

PAGE

	DATE		DESCRIPTION	POST REF.	DEBIT	CREDIT	
1							1
2							2
3							3
4							4
5							5
6							6
7							7
8							8
9							9
10							10
11							11
12							12
13							13
14							14
15							15
16							16
17							17
18							18
19							19
20							20
21							21
22							22
23							23
24							24
25							25
26							26
27							27
28							28
29							29
30							30
31							31
32							32

P6-12 Continued

2.

P6-12 Concluded

Preferred Stock		Common Stock	

Paid-In Capital in Excess of Par, Preferred Stock		Treasury Stock	

Paid-in Capital, Treasury Stock		Dividends, Preferred Stock	

Retained Earnings		Dividends, Common Stock	

P6-13 Dividend Calculations

P6-14 Stockholders' Equity Calculations

1.

JOURNAL   PAGE

	DATE		DESCRIPTION	POST REF.	DEBIT	CREDIT	
1							1
2							2
3							3
4							4
5							5
6							6
7							7
8							8
9							9
10							10
11							11
12							12
13							13
14							14
15							15

2.

P6-15 Unifying Concepts: Stock Transactions and the Stockholders' Equity Section

1. _____

_____

_____

JOURNAL   PAGE

	DATE		DESCRIPTION	POST REF.	DEBIT	CREDIT	
1							1
2							2
3							3
4							4
5							5
6							6
7							7
8							8
9							9
10							10
11							11
12							12
13							13
14							14
15							15
16							16
17							17
18							18
19							19
20							20
21							21
22							22
23							23
24							24
25							25
26							26
27							27
28							28

P6-15 Continued

JOURNAL

	DATE		DESCRIPTION	POST REF.	DEBIT	CREDIT	
1							1
2							2
3							3
4							4
5							5
6							6
7							7
8							8
9							9
10							10
11							11
12							12
13							13
14							14
15							15
16							16
17							17
18							18
19							19
20							20
21							21
22							22
23							23
24							24
25							25
26							26
27							27
28							28
29							29
30							30
31							31
32							32

P6-15 Continued

2.

P6-15 Concluded

Calculations:

Preferred Stock

Common Stock	**Common Stock, No Par**

Paid-In Capital in Excess of Par, Preferred Stock	**Paid-In Capital in Excess of Par, Common Stock**

Treasury Stock	**Paid-In Capital, Treasury Stock**

Retained Earnings	**Treasury Stock, Common, No Par**

P6-16 Unifying Concepts: Stockholders' Equity

1.

JOURNAL

PAGE

	DATE		DESCRIPTION	POST REF.	DEBIT	CREDIT	
1							1
2							2
3							3
4							4
5							5
6							6
7							7
8							8
9							9
10							10
11							11
12							12
13							13
14							14
15							15
16							16
17							17
18							18
19							19
20							20
21							21
22							22
23							23
24							24
25							25
26							26
27							27
28							28
29							29
30							30
31							31
32							32

P16-16 Continued

P16-16 Concluded

Calculations:

Preferred Stock	

Common Stock	

Paid-In Capital in Excess of Par, Preferred Stock	

Paid-In Capital in Excess of Par, Common Stock	

Treasury Stock	

Paid-In Capital, Treasury Stock	

Retained Earnings	

P6-17 Ratios

P7-1 Acquisition, Depreciation, and Disposal of Assets

JOURNAL

PAGE _____

	DATE		DESCRIPTION	POST REF.	DEBIT	CREDIT	
1							1
2							2
3							3
4							4
5							5
6							6
7							7
8							8
9							9
10							10
11							11
12							12
13							13
14							14
15							15
16							16
17							17
18							18
19							19
20							20
21							21
22							22
23							23
24							24
25							25
26							26
27							27
28							28
29							29
30							30
31							31
32							32

P7-2 Purchasing Property, Plant, and Equipment

1. _____

_____

_____

_____

2. _____

_____

_____

_____

_____

_____

_____

_____

P7-3 Acquisition of an Asset

1. _____

_____

_____

_____

_____

_____

_____

_____

2. _____

_____

_____

3. _____

_____

_____

_____

_____

P7-4 Depreciation Calculations

1.

_____
_____
_____
_____
_____
_____
_____
_____

2.

_____
_____

3.

JOURNAL

PAGE _____

	DATE		DESCRIPTION	POST REF.	DEBIT	CREDIT	
1							1
2							2
3							3
4							4
5							5

P7-5 Purchase of Multiple Assets for a Lump Sum

JOURNAL   PAGE

	DATE		DESCRIPTION	POST REF.	DEBIT	CREDIT	
1							1
2							2
3							3
4							4
5							5
6							6
7							7
8							8
9							9
10							10
11							11
12							12
13							13
14							14
15							15
16							16
17							17
18							18
19							19
20							20
21							21
22							22
23							23
24							24

P7-6 Basket Purchase and Partial-Year Depreciation

1.

	DATE		DESCRIPTION	POST REF.	DEBIT	CREDIT	
1							1
2							2
3							3
4							4
5							5
6							6
7							7
8							8
9							9
10							10

JOURNAL   PAGE

2.

P7-7 Acquisition, Depreciation, and Sale of an Asset

1.

JOURNAL PAGE

	DATE	DESCRIPTION	POST REF.	DEBIT	CREDIT	
1						1
2						2
3						3
4						4
5						5
6						6
7						7
8						8

2.

3.

JOURNAL PAGE

	DATE	DESCRIPTION	POST REF.	DEBIT	CREDIT	
1						1
2						2
3						3
4						4
5						5
6						6
7						7
8						8
9						9
10						10
11						11
12						12
13						13
14						14

P7-8 Acquisition, Depreciation, and Sale of an Asset

1.

JOURNAL

PAGE _____

	DATE		DESCRIPTION	POST REF.	DEBIT	CREDIT	
1							1
2							2
3							3
4							4
5							5
6							6
7							7
8							8
9							9
10							10
11							11
12							12
13							13
14							14
15							15
16							16
17							17
18							18
19							19
20							20
21							21
22							22
23							23
24							24

2.–3.

_____

_____

_____

_____

_____

_____

_____

P7-9 Accounting for Natural Resources

	JOURNAL				PAGE	

	DATE		DESCRIPTION	POST REF.	DEBIT	CREDIT	
1							1
2							2
3							3
4							4
5							5
6							6
7							7
8							8
9							9
10							10
11							11
12							12
13							13
14							14

P7-10 Accounting for Intangible Assets (Goodwill)

JOURNAL

	DATE		DESCRIPTION	POST REF.	DEBIT	CREDIT	
1							1
2							2
3							3
4							4
5							5
6							6
7							7
8							8
9							9
10							10
11							11
12							12
13							13
14							14
15							15
16							16
17							17
18							18
19							19
20							20
21							21
22							22
23							23
24							24
25							25
26							26
27							27
28							28
29							29
30							30
31							31
32							32

P7-11 Investment in Securities—Recording and Analysis

JOURNAL   PAGE

	DATE	DESCRIPTION	POST REF.	DEBIT	CREDIT	
1						1
2						2
3						3
4						4
5						5
6						6
7						7
8						8
9						9
10						10
11						11
12						12
13						13
14						14
15						15
16						16
17						17
18						18
19						19
20						20
21						21
22						22
23						23
24						24
25						25
26						26
27						27
28						28
29						29
30						30
31						31
32						32

P7-11 Concluded

JOURNAL

PAGE

	DATE		DESCRIPTION	POST REF.	DEBIT	CREDIT	
1							1
2							2
3							3
4							4
5							5
6							6

Cash

Investment in Trading Securities—Corporation A

Investment in Trading Securities—Corporation B

Bond Interest Receivable

Investment in Available-for-Sale Securities— Corporation C

Bond Interest Revenue

Dividend Revenue

Realized Loss on Sale of Trading Securities

Realized Gain on Sale of Trading Securities

1. _____

2. _____

3. _____

P7-12 Investments in Trading Securities

JOURNAL PAGE

	DATE	DESCRIPTION	POST REF.	DEBIT	CREDIT	
1						1
2						2
3						3
4						4
5						5
6						6
7						7
8						8
9						9
10						10
11						11
12						12
13						13
14						14
15						15
16						16
17						17
18						18
19						19
20						20
21						21
22						22
23						23
24						24
25						25
26						26
27						27
28						28
29						29
30						30
31						31
32						32

P7-13 Recording Investment Transactions

Cash

Investment in Trading Securities,
Corporation A Stock

Dividend Revenue

Investment in Trading Securities,
Corporation B Bonds

Bond Interest Revenue

Investment in Available-for-Sale Securities,
Corporation C Stock

Bond Interest Receivable

Realized Loss on Sale of Trading Securities

P7-13 Concluded

Unrealized Gain on Trading Securities—Income

Unrealized Increase/Decrease in Value of Available-for-Sale Securities—Equity

Market Adjustment—Trading Securities

Market Adjustment—Available-for-Sale Securities

1. _____
2. _____
3. _____
4. _____

P7-14 Investments in Available-for-Sale Securities

1. _____

_____

_____

_____

_____

_____

_____

_____

_____

P7-14 Concluded

JOURNAL   PAGE

	DATE		DESCRIPTION	POST REF.	DEBIT	CREDIT	
1							1
2							2
3							3
4							4
5							5
6							6
7							7
8							8
9							9
10							10
11							11
12							12

2. _____

_____

_____

3. ## JOURNAL   PAGE

	DATE		DESCRIPTION	POST REF.	DEBIT	CREDIT	
1							1
2							2
3							3
4							4

4. _____

_____

_____

_____

_____

_____

P7-15 Investment Portfolio

1.

		JOURNAL			PAGE
DATE		DESCRIPTION	POST REF.	DEBIT	CREDIT
1					
2					
3					
4					
5					
6					
7					
8					
9					
10					
11					
12					
13					
14					

2.

P8-1 Transaction Analysis

1.–4.

5.

P8-2 Analysis of the Cash Account

1.

JOURNAL

PAGE

	DATE		DESCRIPTION	POST REF.	DEBIT	CREDIT	
1							1
2							2
3							3
4							4
5							5
6							6
7							7
8							8
9							9
10							10
11							11
12							12
13							13
14							14
15							15
16							16
17							17
18							18
19							19
20							20
21							21
22							22
23							23
24							24
25							25
26							26
27							27
28							28
29							29
30							30
31							31
32							32

P8-2 Concluded

2.

P8-3   Analyzing Cash Flows

1.–4.

JOURNAL

	DATE		DESCRIPTION	POST REF.	DEBIT	CREDIT	
1							1
2							2
3							3
4							4
5							5
6							6
7							7
8							8
9							9
10							10
11							11
12							12
13							13
14							14
15							15
16							16
17							17
18							18
19							19
20							20
21							21

5.

P8-4 Cash Flow from Operations (Indirect Method)

1.

2.

P8-5 Cash Flow from Operations (Direct Method)

1.

2.

P8-6 Cash Flow from Operations (Indirect and Direct Methods)

1.

P8-6 Concluded

2.

_____
_____
_____
_____

_____

| | ACCRUAL BASIS | ADJUSTMENTS | | CASH BASIS |
		DEBITS	CREDITS	

_____
_____
_____
_____
_____
_____

3.

_____
_____
_____
_____
_____
_____

P8-7 Computation of Net Income from Cash Flow from Operations (Direct Method)

	ACCRUAL BASIS	ADJUSTMENTS		CASH BASIS
		DEBITS	CREDITS	

P8-8 Income Statement from Cash Flow Data

P8-9 Statement of Cash Flows (Indirect Method)

P8-10 Statement of Cash Flows (Direct Method)

1.

	ACCRUAL BASIS	ADJUSTMENTS		CASH BASIS
		DEBITS	CREDITS	

2.

P8-10 Concluded

3.

P8-11 Statement of Cash Flows (Indirect Method)

1.

P8-11 Concluded

2.

_____
_____
_____
_____
_____
_____
_____
_____
_____
_____
_____
_____
_____
_____
_____
_____
_____
_____
_____
_____
_____
_____
_____
_____
_____
_____
_____
_____
_____
_____
_____
_____
_____
_____
_____
_____
_____
_____
_____
_____

P8-12 Unifying Concepts: Analysis of Operating, Investing, and Financing Activities

1.

P8-12 Concluded

2.

P10-1 Job-Order Costing—Journal Entries

JOURNAL

	DATE	DESCRIPTION	POST REF.	DEBIT	CREDIT	
1						1
2						2
3						3
4						4
5						5
6						6
7						7
8						8
9						9
10						10
11						11
12						12
13						13
14						14
15						15
16						16
17						17
18						18
19						19
20						20
21						21
22						22
23						23
24						24
25						25
26						26
27						27
28						28
29						29
30						30
31						31
32						32

P10-1   Concluded

JOURNAL

PAGE

	DATE		DESCRIPTION	POST REF.	DEBIT	CREDIT	
1							1
2							2
3							3
4							4
5							5
6							6
7							7
8							8
9							9
10							10
11							11
12							12
13							13
14							14
15							15
16							16
17							17
18							18
19							19
20							20
21							21
22							22
23							23
24							24
25							25
26							26
27							27
28							28
29							29
30							30
31							31
32							32

P10-2 Accounting for Manufacturing Transactions—Journal Entries

1.

JOURNAL   PAGE _____

	DATE		DESCRIPTION	POST REF.	DEBIT	CREDIT	
1							1
2							2
3							3
4							4
5							5
6							6
7							7
8							8
9							9
10							10
11							11
12							12
13							13
14							14
15							15
16							16
17							17
18							18
19							19
20							20
21							21
22							22
23							23
24							24
25							25
26							26
27							27
28							28
29							29
30							30
31							31
32							32

P10-2 Concluded

2.

Cash		Accounts Receivable	

Raw Materials Inventory		Work-in-Process Inventory	

Finished Goods Inventory		Accumulated Depreciation— Manufacturing Equipment	

Manufacturing Overhead		Accounts Payable	

Wages Payable		Property Taxes Payable	

Commissions Payable		Sales	

Cost of Goods Sold		Sales Commission Expense	

Administrative Expenses	

P10-3 Manufacturing Cost Flows

1. _____

_____
_____
_____
_____
_____
_____
_____
_____
_____
_____
_____
_____
_____
_____
_____
_____
_____
_____
_____
_____
_____
_____
_____

2.

JOURNAL

PAGE _____

	DATE		DESCRIPTION	POST REF.	DEBIT	CREDIT	
1							1
2							2
3							3
4							4
5							5
6							6
7							7
8							8
9							9
10							10

P10-4 Manufacturing Costs—Job-Order Costing

P10-4 Concluded

P10-5 Job-Order Cost Flows Using T-Accounts

1. _____

_____

_____

_____

_____

_____

_____

_____

_____

_____

_____

_____

_____

2.

Raw Materials Inventory	Cash (or Accounts Payable)

Work-in-Process Inventory	Manufacturing Overhead

Finished Goods Inventory	Advertising Expense

P10-5 Concluded

Rent and Utilities Expense—Administrative

Accum. Depr.—Machinery and Equipment

Sales and Administrative Salaries

3.

		JOURNAL			PAGE

	DATE	DESCRIPTION	POST REF.	DEBIT	CREDIT	
1						1
2						2
3						3
4						4
5						5

P10-6 Applying Manufacturing Overhead

P10-6 Concluded

P10-7 Applying Manufacturing Overhead

P10-7   Concluded

P10-8 Unifying Concepts: Job-Order Costing and Cost of Goods Manufactured Schedule

1.

JOURNAL

PAGE

	DATE		DESCRIPTION	POST REF.	DEBIT	CREDIT	
1							1
2							2
3							3
4							4
5							5
6							6
7							7
8							8
9							9
10							10
11							11
12							12
13							13
14							14
15							15
16							16
17							17
18							18
19							19
20							20
21							21
22							22
23							23
24							24
25							25
26							26
27							27
28							28
29							29
30							30
31							31
32							32

P10-8 Continued

JOURNAL

PAGE _____

	DATE	DESCRIPTION	POST REF.	DEBIT	CREDIT	
1						1
2						2
3						3
4						4
5						5
6						6
7						7
8						8
9						9
10						10
11						11
12						12
13						13
14						14
15						15
16						16
17						17
18						18
19						19
20						20
21						21
22						22
23						23
24						24
25						25
26						26
27						27
28						28
29						29
30						30
31						31
32						32

P10-8 Continued

2.

P10-8   Concluded

3.

P10-9 Unifying Concepts: Job-Order Costing and Manufacturing Overhead Costs

1.

JOURNAL   PAGE _____

	DATE		DESCRIPTION	POST REF.	DEBIT	CREDIT	
1							1
2							2
3							3
4							4
5							5
6							6
7							7
8							8
9							9
10							10
11							11
12							12
13							13
14							14
15							15
16							16
17							17
18							18
19							19
20							20
21							21
22							22
23							23
24							24
25							25
26							26
27							27
28							28
29							29
30							30
31							31
32							32

P10-9 Continued

JOURNAL

	DATE	DESCRIPTION	POST REF.	DEBIT	CREDIT	
1						1
2						2
3						3
4						4
5						5
6						6
7						7
8						8
9						9
10						10
11						11
12						12
13						13
14						14
15						15
16						16
17						17
18						18
19						19
20						20
21						21
22						22
23						23
24						24
25						25
26						26
27						27
28						28
29						29
30						30
31						31
32						32

P10-9 Concluded

2.

P10-10 Analysis of Job-Order Cost Flows

1.

P10-10 Continued

2.

P10-10 Concluded

3.

4.

P10-11 Unifying Concepts: Job Order Costing

1. _____

JOURNAL   PAGE

	DATE		DESCRIPTION	POST REF.	DEBIT	CREDIT	
1							1
2							2
3							3
4							4
5							5
6							6
7							7
8							8
9							9
10							10
11							11
12							12
13							13
14							14
15							15
16							16
17							17
18							18
19							19
20							20
21							21
22							22
23							23
24							24
25							25
26							26
27							27
28							28
29							29
30							30
31							31

P10-11 Continued

P10-11 Continued

2.

JOURNAL   PAGE _____

	DATE		DESCRIPTION	POST REF.	DEBIT	CREDIT	
1							1
2							2
3							3
4							4
5							5
6							6
7							7
8							8
9							9
10							10
11							11
12							12
13							13
14							14
15							15
16							16
17							17
18							18
19							19
20							20
21							21
22							22
23							23
24							24
25							25
26							26
27							27
28							28
29							29
30							30
31							31
32							32

P10-11 Continued

3.–5.

P10-11 Concluded

6.

Raw Materials Inventory		Finished Goods Inventory	

Work-in-Process Inventory	

P10-12 Computing Overhead Rates and Client Billing in a Service Firm

P10-13 Service Costing—Journal Entries

JOURNAL

PAGE _____

	DATE	DESCRIPTION	POST REF.	DEBIT	CREDIT	
1						1
2						2
3						3
4						4
5						5
6						6
7						7
8						8
9						9
10						10
11						11
12						12
13						13
14						14
15						15
16						16
17						17
18						18
19						19
20						20
21						21
22						22
23						23
24						24
25						25
26						26
27						27
28						28
29						29
30						30
31						31
32						32

P10-14 Service Costing—Journal Entries

1.

JOURNAL

PAGE

	DATE		DESCRIPTION	POST REF.	DEBIT	CREDIT	
1							1
2							2
3							3
4							4
5							5
6							6
7							7
8							8
9							9
10							10
11							11
12							12
13							13
14							14
15							15
16							16
17							17
18							18
19							19
20							20
21							21
22							22
23							23
24							24
25							25
26							26

P10-14   Concluded

2.

_____

_____

_____

_____

_____

_____

_____

_____

_____

_____

_____

_____

_____

_____

P10-15 Service Cost Flows

1.

JOURNAL

	DATE		DESCRIPTION	POST REF.	DEBIT	CREDIT	
1							1
2							2
3							3
4							4
5							5
6							6
7							7
8							8
9							9
10							10
11							11
12							12
13							13
14							14
15							15
16							16
17							17
18							18
19							19
20							20
21							21
22							22
23							23
24							24
25							25
26							26
27							27
28							28
29							29
30							30
31							31
32							32

P10-15 Concluded

JOURNAL

	DATE	DESCRIPTION	POST REF.	DEBIT	CREDIT	
1						1
2						2
3						3
4						4
5						5
6						6
7						7
8						8
9						9
10						10
11						11
12						12
13						13
14						14
15						15

2.–3.

P11-1 Graphing Revenues and Costs

1.

_____

_____

_____

_____

_____

_____

2. _____

_____

_____

_____

_____

P11-2 High-Low and Scattergraph Methods of Analysis

1.

P11-2 Concluded

2.

3. _____
_____
_____
_____
_____
_____
_____
_____
_____
_____
_____
_____
_____
_____

P11-3 Contribution Margin Income Statement

1.

2.

3.

P11-4 Contribution Margin Income Statement

1. _____

_____

_____

2. _____

_____

_____

_____

_____

_____

_____

_____

_____

_____

_____

P11-5 Functional and Contribution Margin Income Statement

1.

P11-5 Concluded

2. _____

3. _____

P11-6 Contribution Margin and Functional Income Statements

1.

P11-6   Concluded

3. _____

_____

_____

_____

_____

_____

_____

_____

4. _____

_____

_____

_____

_____

_____

_____

_____

5. _____

_____

_____

_____

_____

_____

_____

6. _____

_____

_____

_____

_____

_____

_____

_____

_____

P11-7 Unifying Concepts: High-Low Method, Contribution Margins, and Analysis

1.

2.

	Star Life	Weekly News

P11-7 Concluded

3. _____

	Star Life	Weekly News

4. _____

P11-8 Contribution Margin Analysis

P11-8 Concluded

P11-9 Contribution Margin Analysis

P11-9 Concluded

P11-10 Break-Even Analysis

P11-11 CVP Graphic Analysis

P11-12 Contribution Margin Analysis—Changes in Variables

P11-12 Continued

P11-12 Concluded

P11-13 Income Statement and Break-Even Analysis

1. _____

_____

2. _____

3. _____

P11-14 CVP Analysis—Changes in Variables

P11-14 Concluded

P11-15 CVP Analysis—Return on Sales

P11-16 Unifying Concepts: CVP Analysis and Changes in Variables

P11-16 Concluded

P11-17 Sales Mix and Contribution Margin Not Realized

P11-17 Concluded

P12-1 Unifying Concepts: The Income Statement

1. _____

	Budget	Actual	Variance

2. _____

	Budget	Actual	Variance

P12-2 Materials and Labor Variances

1.

P12-2 Concluded

2.

JOURNAL   PAGE _____

	DATE		DESCRIPTION	POST REF.	DEBIT	CREDIT	
1							1
2							2
3							3
4							4
5							5
6							6
7							7
8							8
9							9
10							10
11							11
12							12
13							13
14							14
15							15
16							16
17							17
18							18
19							19
20							20
21							21
22							22
23							23
24							24
25							25
26							26
27							27
28							28
29							29
30							30
31							31
32							32

P12-3 Materials and Labor Variances

P12-4 Materials and Labor Variances

P12-4 Concluded

P12-5 Materials and Labor Variances

1. _____

_____

_____

_____

_____

_____

_____

_____

_____

_____

_____

_____

_____

_____

_____

_____

_____

_____

_____

_____

_____

_____

_____

_____

_____

_____

_____

_____

_____

_____

_____

_____

_____

_____

_____

_____

_____

_____

P12-5 Concluded

2.

JOURNAL

PAGE

	DATE	DESCRIPTION	POST REF.	DEBIT	CREDIT	
1						1
2						2
3						3
4						4
5						5
6						6
7						7
8						8
9						9
10						10
11						11
12						12
13						13
14						14
15						15

3.

JOURNAL

PAGE

	DATE	DESCRIPTION	POST REF.	DEBIT	CREDIT	
1						1
2						2
3						3
4						4
5						5
6						6
7						7
8						8
9						9
10						10
11						11
12						12

P12-6 Materials and Labor Variances

P12-6 Concluded

P12-7 Materials and Labor Variance Analysis

P12-7 Concluded

P12-8 Determining How Variances Are Computed

P12-9 Evaluation of Profit Centers—Segment Margin

	Store Total	Grocery Dept.	Fresh Produce Dept.	Dry Goods Dept.

P12-10 Evaluation of Profit Centers—Segment Margin

1. _____

_____

_____

	Total	Computer Consulting	Construction

2.–3.

_____

P12-11 ROI and Contribution—Margin Analysis

1.–2.

	Fax Machine	Calculator	Computer	Total

3.–5.

P12-12 ROI

P12-13 ROI

P12-14 ROI and Residual Income

	Without Investment		New Investment		Total	

P12-15 ROI and Residual Income

	San Francisco	Los Angeles	Phoenix

P12-16 ROI and Residual Income

P12-16 Continued

P12-16 Concluded

P12-17 Measuring Performance: Residual Income and ROI

1.–2.

	Current					Proposed Investment				

3.

P12-18 ROI and Residual Income

1. _____

	Without Investment	New Investment	Total

2.

	Without Investment	New Investment	Total

P13-1 Personal Budgeting

1. _____

_____

_____

2. _____

_____

_____

3. _____

_____

_____

P13-2 Personal Budgeting

1.

2.

3.

P13-3 Production Budgeting

P13-4 Production and Direct Materials Budget

P13-5 Computation of Unit Costs

P13-6   Unifying Concepts: Production and Direct Materials Budgets and Cost of Goods Sold Computations

P13-6 Concluded

**P13-7 Unifying Concepts: Sales, Cash Collections, Production, Direct Materials,
and Direct Labor Budgets**

1.

	April	May	June

2.

	April	May	June

3.

	April	May	June

P13-7 Continued

P13-7 Concluded

	April	May	June

5.

	April	May	June

P13-8   Unifying Concepts: Sales, Cash Collections, and Purchases Budgets

1.

	April	May	June

2.

	April	May	June

3.

	April	May	June

P13-9 Cash Budgeting (Manufacturing Company)

1.

P13-10 Cash Budgeting (Merchandising Company)

P13-10 Concluded

P13-11 Cash Budgeting

P13-12 Budgeting for a Service Company

1.

Computations:

P13-12 Concluded

2.–3.

P13-13 Unifying Concepts: The Pro-Forma Income Statement, Balance Sheet, and Statement of Cash Flows

1. _____

P13-13   Continued

2. _____

P13-13 Concluded

3.

P13-14 The Pro-Forma Income Statement and Balance Sheet

1. _____

_____

_____

P13-14 Continued

P13-14 Concluded

2.

P13-15 The Pro-Forma Statement of Cash Flows

Name _____

P13-16 Static Versus Flexible Budgeting (Service Firm)

1. _____

_____

_____

_____

2. _____

_____

_____

	22,000	26,000	30,000	34,000

3. _____

_____

_____

_____

P13-17 Static Versus Flexible Budgeting (Service Firm)

1.

2.

P14-1 Special-Order Pricing

P14-2 Make-or-Buy Decisions

Name _____

P14-2 Concluded

P14-3 Choosing Between Two Machines

1.

	Buy	Make with Machine A	Make with Machine B

2.

P14-4 Purchasing Services from Outside

P14-4 Concluded

P14-5 Unifying Concepts: Make-or-Buy Decisions (Differential Costs, Sunk Costs, Opportunity Costs)

P14-6 Dropping a Product Line

P14-7　Adding and Dropping Product Lines

1.

	A	B	C	D	Total

2.

3.

P14-8 Shutting Down or Continuing Operations

P14-9 Determining Production with a Critical Resource Limitation

P14-10 Determining Production with a Critical Resource Limitation

1.

	X-121	Y-707

2.

P14-11 Contribution Margin per Unit of a Critical Resource

	Super Dunk	Pete Tulip	Zonk

P14-12 Unifying Concepts: Production and Advertising

P14-12 Concluded

P14-13 Processing Past the Point of Separation

P14-14 Normal Selling Price

P15-1 Net Present Value Method

P15-2 Net Present Value Method—Uneven Cash Flows

Item	Year	Amount	Factor	Present Value

P15-3 Internal Rate of Return

1. _____

_____

_____

_____

_____

_____

_____

_____

_____

_____

_____

		Rate of Return	Present Value Factor	
			High Factor and True Rate	High and Low Factors

2. _____

_____

_____

_____

_____

_____

_____

_____

_____

_____

_____

_____

P15-4 Internal Rate of Return and Hurdle Rate

P15-5 Payback, Net Present Value, and Internal Rate of Return Methods

P15-6 Using the Payback Reciprocal Method to Approximate the Internal Rate of Return

P15-7 Payback Reciprocal Method

P15-8 Choosing Among Alternatives

P15-9 Lease-or-Buy Decision

P15-10 Rent-or-Purchase Decision

P15-11 Sell-or-Rent Decision

P15-12 Unifying Concepts: Net Present Value and Internal Rate of Return Methods

1.

Cash Flow	Amount	Discount Factor	Present Value

2.

P15-13 Net Present Value Best Used to Rank Alternatives

P15-14 Screening and Ranking Alternatives

P15-15 Unifying Concepts: Comparing the Internal Rate of Return and the Net Present Value Methods

P15-16 Unifying Concepts: Payback, Internal Rate of Return, and Payback Reciprocal Methods

_____
_____
_____
_____
_____
_____
_____
_____
_____
_____
_____
_____
_____
_____
_____
_____
_____
_____
_____
_____
_____
_____
_____
_____
_____
_____
_____
_____
_____
_____
_____
_____
_____
_____
_____

P15-17 Unifying Concepts: Capital Rationing Using the Payback and Net Present Value Methods

Name _____

P15-17 Concluded